MINDS
BEHIND THE
MUSIC

MINDS
BEHIND THE
MUSIC

WYMER
PUBLISHING
Bedford, England

First published in Great Britain in 2021
by Wymer Publishing
www.wymerpublishing.co.uk
Tel: 01234 326691
Wymer Publishing is a trading name of Wymer (UK) Ltd

Print edition (with plate section): **ISBN: 978-1-912782-87-1**

Edited by Jerry Bloom

Typeset by Andy Bishop / 1016 Sarpsborg

eBook formatting by Coinlea

A catalogue record for this book is available from the British Library.

Cover design: Phil Gardiner / 1016 Sarpsborg
Cover photos courtesy of the author / artists.

MUSIC STARS UNITE TO SAVE THE PLANET

Contents

Freddie Made Me Do It

Why did I start this project? Trust me, over the past few months I've often considered this question. Music managers, pop agents, sarcastic rock stars and the endless chasing have more than once seemed like a nightmarish battle of wills. But if we can't stand up for what we believe in then why bother getting out of bed in the morning?

It all started after I'd finished making a documentary about overpopulation. I popped on the old musical machine, hit the random button and the Queen song, "Is This The World We Created?" came on. It's a truly beautiful song delivered brilliantly by Freddie. The words struck me like no other. We claim to be the most advanced species on planet Earth, and yet if we were to judge on the levels of destruction, we'd be the worst. There and then I decided I had to do something. In my past life I was a marketing man. Yeah I know, line up to take aim. My head spun, I must be able to use some of my rubbish skills to help out our planet and all the suffering we create!

And then it struck me! I had absolutely no idea what to do. Needless to say I was in a bit of a mood that afternoon. And so off to bed I went. I woke up with the whole idea in my head. Music stars have a massive amount of influence in the world. I mean, why else would people wear hoodies and a certain brand of training shoes? It's a selfie and selfless world we often live in. If I could possibly get through to a few musicians and get them to give me interviews then maybe people would read a book. If I went for rock, pop and folk stars I'd be getting a wide range of people interested. Even if they bought the book and went straight to the chapter with their music hero in, it would be worthwhile. The questions would have to be interesting of course and so why not ask them stupid questions? Like do you believe in aliens? Obviously I was perfectly capable of coming up with stupid questions. Boy was I surprised with the answers.

And so, that morning I put together an email and opened up the web browser. I already knew a few music stars and I tried them first. Within an hour I had responses. Within a week I had dozens of stars all saying yes Phil! Blimey. I have to say it, the response from the music world has been amazing and I want to thank each and every one of them for putting in the effort. Apart from those who didn't of course. I just deleted them from my play lists. You know who you are. Of course, you can always get in touch now and we'll consider you for the follow up book.

9

Humans Are Stupid

So what's the big deal? Why did I suddenly decide to turn my world upside down and talk to the loonies from the music industry?

Mankind has predicted, prophesied and foretold the end times. From the Bible to Rasputin and from Nostradamus to modern science — all have seen the stupidity of humanity and its path of self-destruction.

Today we are closer than ever before to our ultimate demise. With weapons of mass destruction proliferating the growing powers of the world we have new and terrifying ways of wiping ourselves out. With modern genetic science we play God and change nature with consequences we cannot even imagine. With ever more polluting and poisoning industries and commodities we push the Earth to the brink. With overpopulation we rape and pillage the planet like never before. And now with science creating biological weapons and the masses huddled together in filthy, live animal marketplaces, in countries like China we are opening up a Pandora's box of epidemiological horror stories. As we now know all too well.

Viruses are almost intelligent. They learn, share information and mutate. They are but one of the many threats to mankind.

Humanity is being plunged into the dark abyss of our own making and it was all predicted many years ago by those who saw the truth.

The Black Death was also known as the Pestilence, the Great Bubonic Plague, the Great Plague or the Plague. It was the most devastating pandemic recorded in human history and resulted in the deaths of an estimated 75 to 200 million people in Eurasia, peaking in Europe from 1347 to 1351. The bacterium Yersinia pestis, which results in several forms of plague, is believed to have been the cause.

The Black Death was the first major European outbreak of plague and the second plague pandemic. It had profound effects on the course of European history.

It is believed to have originated in Asia, from where it travelled along the Silk Road, reaching Crimea by 1343. From there, it was most likely carried by fleas living on the black rats that travelled on merchant ships, spreading throughout the Mediterranean and reaching the rest of Europe via the Italian Peninsula.

It is estimated to have killed 30% to 60% of Europe's population and reduced the world population from an estimated 475 million to 350 million in the 14th century. It took 200 years for Europe's population to recover to its previous level and some regions only recovered by the 19th century. Outbreaks of the plague continue to emerge. But as we know only too well, life-threatening viruses continue to emerge and cause mass panic and change the course of human history.

Ever since the end of the Black Death in 1350 the human population has been growing continuously at an alarming rate and there is no sign of it stopping anytime soon.

The biggest increase has been in most recent times. From the 1950s onward and due largely to medical advancement and the increase in agricultural productivity, the rate of increase has been significant. This in itself should tell us something. That this is a modern problem created recently and we have no precedent, no history to work upon. We don't know exactly what is going to happen. We don't know if a super virus will come along again as it did in 1918 and kill millions of people. We don't know if we will eat ourselves into mass extinction. We don't know if the destruction of natural species such as bees will seal our fate. We don't know if an asteroid will wipe us out or even artificial intelligence. We do know that overpopulation, no matter which way you look at it, is not good. We do know that we are running out of fossil fuels, food supplies, methods of producing more and more power and space.

What does the future hold for a planet that is swarming in two-legged locusts hell bent on devouring every possible resource the Earth has to offer?

In 2016 the British government held a theoretical exercise. It was called operation Cygnus and it was intended to discover just how well prepared the country was for a pandemic. The exercise showed that the pandemic would cause the country's health system to collapse from a lack of resources, with the Chief Medical Officer at the time stating that a lack of medical ventilators was a serious problem. In 2020 it all came true and the British were still not prepared. If a wealthy nation with knowledge created from such exercises is still not ready for one of nature's most powerful weapons then what about the rest of the world? The fact is that there are too many humans on the planet to create a system ready enough to cope.

The United Nations has expressed concerns over the large population growths in places such as the Saharan Africa. The present population of planet earth is heading fast towards eight billion. Many scientists have produced computer models on just how many humans the planet can cope with under existing conditions. These range from 4 to 16 billion. This means human overpopulation may have already peaked. It does not take into account how governments of the globe would cope with a virus that spreads faster and wider than ever before.

Whichever model we use, the fact remains that any logical, scientific approach to population reveals a lot of problems and most scientists are highly concerned. By 2040 it is expected there will be around 10 billion people. Such numbers are impossible for the human mind to deal with, let alone the planet itself.

It is generally accepted that our beautiful planet will simply not be able to cope with future generations at such huge scales.

Rising levels of atmospheric carbon dioxide, global warming, pollution and the poisoning of our oceans with chemicals and plastics are all being made worse by the rising populations.

In addition to this our hunger for more and more is tearing apart the environment. The supplies of fresh water and food is simply not keeping up with demand and millions of people are dying of starvation. In poorer countries standard hygiene is something people in rich countries have the benefit of. Market places where filthy, live animals are traded spread contagion's. Viruses love to mix and merge. They love to learn from each other, from the DNA of their hosts and they strive with the power of evolution to survive and grow. They are, in many ways, like humanity. And like humans they very often kill their host, just as we are killing our planet. Add into the mix military and commercial genetic testing of weapons and drugs using AI technology and you have a perfect storm. But there are more threats to our future than viruses.

Our overuse of fossil fuels means that we simply cannot regenerate sufficient quantities to keep up with demand and so we will simply run out.

Places such as Great Britain with a population of 70 million simply cannot grow enough food or produce enough power to keep the people alive and so it has to import on massive scales. Imagine what would happen if there were a total lock down of the world in a pandemic situation or world war? Millions of people would starve. Millions of people would turn on their government and each other. Anarchy on the streets of Britain and all because of our own stupidity. A stupidity driven by the drive to survive. To breed and breed.

The Second World War was a prime example of this when the island nation had to import food and fight hard to keep open supply routes. Rationing continued for over a decade after the end of the war. Thousands died of starvation.

Matters are made even worse by mankind when we consider our political and philosophical ways. Over the course of the last two hundred years we have developed a system called the throwaway society. We over consume, make cheap throwaway products that harm the environment and we are veracious. This, in line with overpopulation, makes the future seem very dark without a radical new rethink on the way we all live.

And yet, even though we know all of this and have done so for sometime, there is little or no action to stop overpopulation.

But these concerns are not new. In the second century the total inhabitants of planet earth are estimated to have been around a 190 million or 3 percent of today's.

One of the residents of the city of Carthage was a man named Terullian. He wrote: "What most frequently meets our view is our teeming population. Our numbers are burdensome to the world, which can hardly support us... In very deed, pestilence, and famine, and wars, and earthquakes have to be regarded as a remedy for nations, as the means of pruning the luxuriance of the human race."

In other words, nature will seek to rebalance things.

Our own nature helps to keep our population down as well. Diseases from our dirt, infant mortality, poor conditions and wars have all managed to keep the rates low. The population of the planet had remained below 25 million right up until the industrial revolution.

At the turn of the 19th century that figure had increased to a billion and intellectuals began predicting that humanity would outgrow the earth's resources. And yet, businessmen decided that huge population growth was perfect for them because it brought them wealth. Bigger marketplaces, bigger work forces, bigger armies. Better methods of control and manipulation were required and introduced.

It is predicted now that population growth will continue unabated into the next century.

Adrian Raftery, a University of Washington professor of statistics and sociology said: "The consensus over the past 20 years or so was that world population, which is currently around 7 billion, would go up to 9 billion and level off or probably decline. We found there's a 70 percent probability the world population will not stabilise this century. Population, which had sort of fallen off the world's agenda, remains a very important issue." [1]

A recent UN projection suggests the population will grow to as many as 15 billion by 2100.

Over a third of Nobel prize-winning scientists were questioned about their thoughts and they said that human overpopulation and environmental degradation are the two greatest threats facing humankind.

According to over 15,000 scientists and 184 countries the rapid human overpopulation of the planet was the primary driver behind many ecological and even societal threats.

According to the United Nations the population is increasing by 75 million every year. According to the CIA's figures it's at 145 people every minute.

Almost all of this growth will take place in the lesser developed world. These underdeveloped countries are home to around 5.5 billion people already. This is expected to increase to around 8 billion by 2050. The remainder of the planet or the developed part of the world, is expected to remain pretty much as it is now. But, there is one place that will not, the United States of America. That is expected to increase by a massive 44%.

There are various factors contributing to the growth rate and it isn't, amazingly, the birth rate. In fact in the 1950s women had an average of 5 children, nowadays it's half that rate. What has changed is that we are living longer and child mortality rates are much lower.

One thing these kinds of figures reveals is this: because deaths in the developed regions is expected to outstrip births, the population growth is actually going to come from immigration. This is one of those unspoken reasons that countries such as Germany allow so many migrants in, because their own populations are declining and getting older. Without migration, the populations of most developed countries would actually fall.

In 1800 only 3% of the world's population lived in cities. Today that figure exceeds 50%. Meaning that most of the people on planet earth live in cities. Huddled together en masse. When the virus outbreaks come, these become the epicentres of global pandemics.

And here is a startling figure: in 1950 there were only 83 cities of a population of over one million. Now there are nearly five hundred. At these rates urban populations will double every 38 years. Three out of five people alive will be living in a city.

Most of this increase is in Asia and Africa where one billion people currently live in shanty towns. Everybody in the field agree that these places are breeding grounds for major problems such as poverty, unemployment, drug addiction, crime, disease and much more.

But cities are not staying at one million inhabitants. In fact we now have a classification of megacity where the population is over ten million. These include Seoul, Karachi, Mexico City, Mumbai, Sau Paulo, London, New York and Greater Tokyo which has a population of over 35 million. That's more than the entire population of Canada.

By 2025 we will have hyper cities or cities with 20 million plus. Places such as Lagos in Nigeria which only had 300,000 people in 1950 and now has over 20 million. That is a massive increase and it's happening all over the world. In China their cities are home to over 800 million people.

What we need is to control this. What really happens from an historical perspective is that we develop new ways of dealing with it. Technology is always boosted by two things, war and population increase. In the past we went through three major technology revolutions. The tool-making revolution, the agricultural revolution and the industrial. All three helped mankind overcome the overpopulation crisis by producing more food and goods. It also increased the power of the rich elite and has been doing so for a long time.

Today we are undergoing a scientific revolution where genetics, chemicals and computer science are all being used to change the way we eat and live. All of this will boost the growth rates, not help them decline. A ready supply of food and goods, immunisations, medicines, better sanitation and environmental conditions all helped population grow and birth rates outstrip death rates.

One thing that reduced the birth rates in the developed countries was birth control. Even though many still cling to outdated religious intolerance of birth control, it actually reduced the birth rates. Only the poor countries of the world, unable to afford mass birth control did not see a decline. Religions such as the Catholic Church need to have a serious re-appraisal of their beliefs in the matter if they truly do care for humanity and planet earth.

So overpopulation of Planet Earth is a fact and it's only going to get worse. All of this has been agreed upon by scientists across the world. So what problems are going to arise because of it?

Firstly it will cause health issues. As we have seen the populations of the planet are increasingly moving closer and closer to each other in mega and hyper cities. This increases the chance of spreading infectious diseases and epidemics. Virologists are already warning of Virus X, saying that we are due for a major catastrophe along the lines of bird flu or worse. In addition to this the overuse of antibiotics has made them virtually useless.

In 2020 we saw the outbreak of Covid-19. It spread from China across the entire planet and killed as it spread. The whole world went into lockdown and a major financial catastrophe was started as countries scrambled to save their economies from collapse. These viruses mutate at alarming rates. It's almost as if they have their own collective intelligence. Soon a coronavirus or similar will mutate that we can't stop.

Health issues are made even worse by the conditions the masses live in with dirty and unhygienic surroundings. Filth builds faster in areas of overpopulation. It accumulates at a faster and faster rate, causing more disease. The way that some nations treat their animals doesn't help. Bringing live animals to the marketplace brings disease.

Because of the close proximity of people, when disease does break out it is spread more easily on public transport and places such as hotels, parks and airports.

We are not the first humans to have witnessed a pandemic and we will not be the last. There have been many who have predicted such things, from Rasputin to Nostradamus and even the Bible.

In Luke chapter 21, Jesus spoke about the signs that would precede the end of the world. Jesus said that one of those signs would be pestilences, "And there will be great earthquakes in various places, and famines and pestilences; and there will be fearful sights and great signs from heaven." The meaning of a pestilence, according to the Hebrew and Greek definitions, is a plague or disease.

In Matthew 24 Jesus said, "For nation will rise against nation, and kingdom against kingdom, and in various places there will be famines and earthquakes. But all these things are merely the beginning of birth pangs." In several versions of the Bible the word "pestilences" appears between famines and earthquakes.

He explained that just as a woman's contractions or labour pains get more frequent and severe as a baby is nearing birth, so these events or signs will also become more frequent and severe as the world nears the second coming of Jesus, or end of mankind.

Very similar predictions or prophecies have been spoken of by mystics and seers throughout the ages, from Mother Shipton and Nostradamus to Rasputin. These people saw one thing and it wasn't the future. They saw patterns.

Whatever we believe in, the fact remains that humanity repeats cycles over and over again and observation of actions and reactions both within humanity and from nature itself gives clear signs that something will always come along to take down our civilisations.

The problem today is this — there are now many more people in the world and we are further away from nature. We live on the just in time principle through our goods and foods. So when a supermarket can no longer get bread or milk then thousands starve because there are no stocks. In 2020 mass panic buying saw the world run out of food, hand sanitisers and believe it or not, toilet rolls.

Another major problem looming on the horizon is unemployment. This is already at huge levels in many parts of the overpopulated world but it is set to get even bigger with the introduction of artificial intelligence which is predicted to take up to or more than half of the world's jobs. Nobody has a solution to this problem and yet they proceed at an alarming rate.

Unemployment spreads poverty like a plague. Most of the overpopulated world is simply not wealthy enough to cope with the problems. Unrest rises, lawlessness and wars erupt and spread. Mass migrations occur and pass the unrest, disease and poverty around. The rich say not in my backyard and push back. The masses are fed propaganda and become protectionist and nationalistic. This is happening right now in many parts of the world.

And because the most overpopulated places in the world are the poorest, the education systems are also poor. Poorly educated people make bad decisions about life and often live miserable lives. And their uneducated ways means diseases can spread to the rest of us.

Lack of education causes problems for the rest of us because the environment is affected by those who do not understand sustainability. The bigger the population the bigger the need to rape and pillage the planet, the bigger the waste and filth and disease and the cycle gets worse.

Running out of ground water and land for crops, in addition to deforestation and higher pollution, are all happening right now at alarming rates.

There simply is not enough fresh water for drinking in addition to sewage treatment and so filth spreads. Richer countries such as Saudi Arabia use technology to reclaim water from waste and sea water. But poorer countries cannot. But hey, let's spend more money on arms instead of helping out our fellow man.

Overpopulation means increased air and water pollution, contamination of the soil we need for crops, billions of tons of plastic entering the water system, desertification and deforestation and so much more. All of this causes wildfires, global warming, animal, plant and insect extinctions, pandemics and so much more.

Biodiversity on planet earth is reducing at the same time as the human population is increasing. There is a direct correlation.

Sir David King, former chief scientific adviser to the UK government, told a parliamentary inquiry: "It is self-evident that the massive growth in the human population through the 20th century has had more impact on biodiversity than any other single factor."[2]

The intensive farming required to feed so many people actually results in the evolution and spread of antibiotic resistant diseases, water and air pollution and new viruses that affect us. We then have to find new methods of fighting these problems and cause even more problems.

As every day passes the chances of there emerging a major killer virus get higher. And it is the poor, living in overcrowded areas that will suffer the most. If they don't die of the disease, they will die of starvation, thirst and poor diets.

Indeed, the countries with the fastest growth rates are those with the lowest life expectancy.

Poverty, crime, drugs, disease, pollution, infant mortality, conflict, lawlessness and more are just a few of the results of humanities insanity of overpopulating the planet. What is the point of continuing with human birth rates if all we are doing in the majority of the world is causing suffering?

As human overpopulation drives resources and basic necessities, such as food and water, to become scarcer, there will be increased competitiveness for these resources which leads to elevated crime rates due to drug cartels and theft by people in order to survive.

According to the Centre for Biological Diversity, "The largest single threat to the ecology and biodiversity of the planet in the decades to come will be global climate disruption due to the build-up of human-generated greenhouse gases in the atmosphere... we not only need smaller footprints, but fewer feet." [3]

Every national academy of science of every major country in the world agrees. Every professional scientific society in every field related to the field of climate endorses it.

98 percent of all scientists that are most active in publishing in the field of climate science agree with it. The consensus is unequivocal: human activities are causing climate change. The effects of climate change are profound and far-reaching. Learning the hard way that we can't separate the economy from the ecological systems that support it, climate change, perhaps the greatest challenge and threat humanity has ever faced, has been left largely unchecked by world leaders to continue unabated threatening the basis of civilisation itself.

Human overpopulation is a major driving force behind the loss of ecosystems, such as rainforests, coral reefs, wetlands and Arctic ice. Rainforests once covered 14% of the Earth's land surface, now they cover a bare 6% and experts estimate that the last remaining rainforests could be consumed in less than 40 years and certainly by the end of the century at the current rate of deforestation.

Due mainly to warming temperatures, acidifying oceans and pollution, close to 30% of the ocean's reefs have already vanished since 1980, including half of the reefs in the Caribbean and 90% of the Philippines' coral reefs and scientists forecast that Australia's Great Barrier Reef may be dead by the year 2050 and all coral reefs could be gone by the end of the century.

Furthermore, the area of permanent ice cover is now declining at a rate of 11.5% per decade. If this trend continues, summers in the Arctic could become ice-free in the next 30 years. Wetlands are increasingly under threat in the United States, but also all over the world. In the U.S., less than half of original wetlands remain with 53% being lost, which is about 104 million acres. In Europe, between 60% and 70% of wetlands have been completely destroyed. As human populations continue to grow, so will our footprint on the interconnected, ecological infrastructures of life.

Human beings are currently causing the greatest mass extinction of species since the extinction of the dinosaurs 65 million years ago at rates 1000 to 10,000 times faster than normal. The 2012 update of the Red List of Threatened Species shows that of the 63,837 species examined worldwide nearly a third of the total are at threat of extinction.

If present trends continue, scientists warn that within a few decades, at least half of all plant and animal species on Earth will be extinct, as a result of climate change, habitat loss, pollution, acidifying oceans, invasive species, over-exploitation of natural resources, overfishing, poaching and human overpopulation.

We are now losing 30,000 species per year, or three species per hour, which is faster than new species can evolve.

If this trend continues then humanity itself is at risk.

Hunger and malnutrition kill nearly 6 million children a year, and more people are malnourished in sub-Saharan Africa this decade than in the 1990s. In sub-Saharan Africa, the number of malnourished people grew to 203.5 million people.

And yet China, the world's most populous country, suffers from an "obesity surge". Around 200 million people are thought to be overweight or 22.8% of the population, and 60 million are obese. One in three people in the UK are now overweight and similar stories can be found in the US and Europe.

Overpopulation has without doubt adversely impacted the environment of Earth starting at least as early as the 20th century. According to the Global Footprint Network, "today humanity uses the equivalent of 1.5 planets to provide the resources we use and absorb or waste". [4]

The fact is, in the United States alone, humans consume 30% more of the world's resources than is sustainable. Year in, year out, mankind is eating his own marrow.

In fact, it is not just the good old US of A that is over harvesting the planet, 85 other countries in the world are doing the same. And because they don't have enough in their own countries for the desires of their people, they rape and pillage others. African nations which do not over harvest but desire all the trappings of the west, sell their natural resources on the cheap to America, China, Russia and Europe.

Hundreds of men die each year digging little shiny rocks out of the ground for rich slobs in the so-called civilised world to dangle from their ear lobes.

Like retards we actually have no idea what we are doing and most don't care. Even with statistics we are like blind lemmings, still willing to jump off the cliff.

The truth however is scary. Mankind produces waste at such scales that it is almost impossible to comprehend. Every day we throw out enough waste to fill 12 of the world's largest container ships. That's nearly 4,500 container ships in just one year. It equates to about 1,500 million tons of waste every year. And it's not just the waste we throw out. For every bag of waste you throw in the trash can, there have in fact already been 70 bags of waste just in the manufacturing of your goods. Every one bag equals 70 bags of waste!

But that is the tip of the iceberg because those statistics were just for the United Kingdom. A small island nation. The world statistics are actually unbelievable.

Every year the world dumps a massive 6 billion tons of waste. If all this waste was put on trucks they would stretch around the world 64 times.

By 2100 these figures will treble. And these figures are in no way accurate. They are well under the real, unreported truth.

Apart from the packaging waste generated from luxury items and their manufacture, the most startling waste crime in the world today is that of food. When we consider the starving of the world it is tantamount to mass murder.

While so many obese people eat enough food every day for an entire family, starvation affects nearly 1 billion people in the world and it is not because we don't have enough food, it is because we waste so much. Global food supplies far outweighs global demand. There is enough to feed everybody. But we don't share because we are greedy. If not murder, then it is manslaughter, because we know about the problem and do nothing. In a throwaway world where waste does not matter to us, it seems we are more than happy to throwaway humans too.

Nearly 1 billion people in the world attempt to live on less than $2 per day. The figure has in fact improved over the past thirty years as Western consumer capitalist systems have been adopted.

98% of those in hunger live in developing countries. 553 million in the Asian and Pacific regions, 47 million in Latin America and the Caribbean and 227 million in Africa.

In India there are nearly 200 million people undernourished.

Every year nearly 10 million people die of hunger. That's more than AIDs, TB and malaria combined. Because of the patriarchal societies these people live in, 60% of those that die are women. And because of that 3.1 million children die every year of malnutrition.

And yet, even with these statistics the rest of the world carries on throwing away half their food.

Our throwaway society affects much more than just humans. Apart from the fact that we destroy our wildlife on a massive scale and poison the bees, we actually grow and kill more animals than we need to, and because we waste so much, the fact is that we as a species are causing suffering of innocent animals on a massive scale.

The production of meat is actually very inefficient. It takes 75 times more energy to produce meat than corn, leaving a massive energy footprint affecting the environment. It also takes up a lot of space. We need an area 7 times the size of Europe to produce food for the cattle that feeds the people of Europe.

If we ate crops instead of meat it would actually change the world. To feed crops to 20 people we need one hectare of land. The same land would feed enough livestock to eventually feed 1 or 2 people. Here's the frightening statistic:

by 2050 there will be less than 0.1 hectare of land per person on this planet. Not enough on current feeding methods to feed us all. If we don't change our ways soon, we will be facing major catastrophe.

As for the burning of fossil fuels, the statistics are simple. To produce 1 calorie of protein from corn or soybean it takes 2 or 3 calories of fossil fuel. For the same amount of beef we need 54 calories of fuel. Meat therefore takes more land and energy, costing us and the environment more than the planet can afford. In addition to this, while 1 billion people starve, half of the world's crops are fed to animals so that we can enjoy our burgers.

And yet, even after we have gone to the amazing lengths to rear animals and slaughter them, we throw half of them away uneaten. It is a crime against nature and common sense. It will be the end of us.

Our waste creates more trouble for us in other ways.

We throwaway our consumer goods without a care in the world and then we suffer the consequences of rodents and insects which harbour gastrointestinal parasites, worms, yellow fever and a host of other plagues waiting to come and teach us a lesson. When we burn those huge piles of waste we release millions of tons of toxins into the environment, which we then breath in and wonder why we get cancer. Toxic chemicals from our waste seep into the groundwater, soil and river systems. We then drink it, use it for meat production and water our crops.

In the air and in the water our waste screws the eco-system. This is not just a thing we read about; this is the environment we raise our children in. When we treat our waste we actually create greenhouse gas emissions such as methane. This then contributes to global warming and soon we are complaining that our fields are flooded or there's no rain for the crops. Either way we look at waste, we are seriously screwing ourselves.

We also like to dump our waste in areas predominately lived in by our starving brothers and sisters. We have even given it a cute little name, Nimby. It means "not in my back yard" and we really do mean it. After all, we have the money and brains to be able to shit on our fellow humans don't we.

The funny thing about this dumping of waste on our poor neighbours is that we are actually making things even worse because the energy footprint created to move billions of tons of waste every year comes back and slaps us in the face when global warming decides to flood our green and pleasant land.

And it is not just a sad and sorry state we are creating for the world. We are creating sad people too. What do you think happens to a person's mind when he or she cannot attain the perfect lifestyle with the luxuries of the celebs? Suicide rates are huge in the west where we apparently have all this wealth.

It is sad. It is also very sad that we identify ourselves with these new consumer products. Are you a PC or Mac person? You a Coke or Pepsi man? We actually state these things with pride because of the power of propaganda. We state it because we wish to be associated with the image that brand has created. To drink Coke is to be all-American isn't it? To be a Mac user is to be wealthy, cool and artistic isn't it? These are building blocks of our own identity.

These are images we wish to portray to the world as images of our own identity. It has always been this way. It is nothing new. But it is used by clever marketing techniques to get us to consume. To buy more and more junk that we then send down to the landfill site to destroy the planet just a little more.

Mankind is now so brainwashed and so overwhelmed with information that he no longer realises how far he has come away from the natural habitat he lived in for millennia. He can no longer see the difference between information, entertainment and blatant propaganda. The money behind the media of the world comes from consumerism.

It thrives upon it and is paid by it. News does not come free; it has to be paid for. Entertainment is not sent from the gods; it needs a wage packet. Subtle advertising, product placement, celebrity endorsements and more all subconsciously convince us to get more plastic shit.

Shopping is a social experience, a day out in wonderland. Online shopping is easy and addictive. With plastic card in hand we venture into the safety of the store and emerge like hunters with our prey in shiny plastic bags emblazoned with social status symbols. And then, we throw them all away in the trash.

We are not all evil and many of us recognise the need to do something urgent. The problem is that mankind is greedy and that overrides the need to protect the planet for the future or feed his brothers and sisters.

What is happening and which is encouraging is the fact that waste is such a big business now. This means that disposal of waste is actually turning into recycling of waste or even re-use. It is known as resource recovery, because it has been recognised that waste is in fact a resource. Many scientists around the globe are searching out ways of using waste for it's next specific purpose, rather than how to hide it away for a future generation to worry about.

Recyclable materials are extracted and recycled. Non-recyclable waste is burned and the energy extracted for electricity production. Various methods are used including gasification and anaerobic digestion. They call it waste to energy.

There is hope on the horizon in other ways too. Meat has successfully been grown in the lab. Fake meat that tastes like the real thing. No animals suffering. Less pollution and energy footprint and more land to grow crops.

A fashionable surge in the world of retro goods has created a new industry of recycling old stuff. Antiques and nick-nacks are cleaned up and suddenly become cool. Plastic goods from the eighties are now the latest must have.

Recycling, solar and wind energy, sustainable farming and more are all becoming more and more popular.

Around the world the capitalists are recognising the need to be in on the ground with these cutting-edge technologies. Not to save the world, but to turn a profit.

And if that is what it takes, then so be it. Our job as consumers is to consume less and apply pressure upon those in power by selectively buying those products that are environmentally sustainable. If the small man speaks en masse then the big man will listen. Use your voice and stand up in defence of our planet for the sake of your children.

And our voice needs to be raised, to say some things that may feel wrong. That allowing humanity to continue to grow at this rate is bad for the planet and us. That there is little point in giving birth to children that will know nothing but suffering. H. G. Wells, the great science fiction writer, was asked by the United Nations to research population and its problems. He was a brave man who made the observation that population needed to be controlled. He was hated for what he said and yet he was correct in his statements.

When rabbits were introduced into Australia by the British it caused a huge problem. There were no predators to keep the rabbit population down and they bred, well, like rabbits. They devastated crops and spread disease among the existing species. They are an analogy for what humanity is doing to the planet. We have no predators but each other. We breed and breed. We spread out of control and destroy other species at an alarming rate.

Our answer to the rabbit problem was genocide. We introduced a highly infectious and deadly disease into the rabbit population called myxomatosis. One day, in a dystopian future, mankind, nature or indeed, artificial intelligence will make a decision about the overpopulation of the earth by humanity and it may not be one we will all like. Is it not therefore better to control the levels of births as opposed to increasing the level of deaths?

Not all decisions in life are easy and we are living through a period when the most difficult of questions has to be asked. Is it not time to force control for the sake of ourselves and all life on planet earth?

One day virus x will come out of nowhere and it will be of our own making. Whether we create it in a laboratory or it arises because of our evil ways towards those innocent animals we so easily call livestock. They are not stock, they are living, sentient beings with emotions. The coronavirus pandemic of 2020 is a massive wake up call for us all. It came out of nowhere and spread across the globe rapidly and left human bodies piled up as it went.

Viruses are living organisms that strive to survive. It is not in their interest to kill everyone. Indeed, it is almost intelligent and some scientists believe there is a collective intelligence at a sub-atomic level. They keep the fit alive to spread further afield and kill the sick and elderly. Killing everybody would be self-defeating to the virus itself. But, these organisms love to adapt and change and when they come into contact with other viruses such as those that do have extremely high death rates, then they adapt and change into a rapidly spreading super killer.

The Covid-19 pandemic is a wake-up call for humanity. This virulent and deadly virus is now unleashed. It will merge and morph. It will adapt and change. And one day it may meet up with a deadly ally such as Ebola and then we are all screwed.

What Covid-19 does show us is this, we, even now in the 21st century are extremely weak and vulnerable on many levels. Without antibodies we have no immune system capable of fighting the virus and the weak die. Because vaccines take years to create then we have nothing to fight it with. And while we are scrambling around attempting to make vaccines, the virus is adapting and changing just like influenza does every year. It is a constant battle to stay one step ahead.

On another level it revealed how weak our financial systems really are. Panic sets off more panic and pretty soon billions have been lost over night, inflation rates soar and the poorest of the world suffer on a massive scale. Prices rise, millions lose their jobs, loans are unpaid, banks run out of money and deep depression sets in. More and more people start to fall into the poverty trap and suicides increase. We are a crazy species out of control running rapidly towards our own self-destruction.

War, overpopulation, weapons of mass destruction, poverty, global warming and ultimately disease are all building daily to bring natural balance back into the world and eradicate the greatest threat the Earth has ever seen — humanity.

In the Bible there is a book called Revelation. It talks about end times. This book was written in a different age when people believed in deities. But the message was very clear and it is a lesson we must all learn.

In the book there are four horsemen of the apocalypse. Each horseman has a seal with a message for mankind before the second coming of Jesus, when all humans will be taken away.

Together, these legendary horsemen are prophesied "to kill with sword or warfare, with hunger or famine, with death, pestilence and disease, and by the beasts of the earth." Twenty five percent of mankind will be slain. Or nearly 2 billion people.

These scribes of 2,000 years ago understood one thing, the nature of man. They knew we would repeat our mistakes again and again. It is in-built. The apocalypse or the end of mankind will be caused by mankind.

So what can you do? I bet most of you have a social media presence. Use it. Spread the word. Throw away less, buy organic, eat less meat, pressure your government, join together and be strong. Read and learn more about what you can do. Knowledge is power. Mother Earth needs you.

And now of course, after all that depressing stuff, you want to hear from the music stars don't you. Let's dive straight in, but please remember these questions were devised to both entertain and get inside the mind of your favourite banjo player. They all had the same questions and no it doesn't become boring and tedious, because let's face it, you're all gonna go straight for the names you recognise and ignore the rest.

Have fun!

PS. If you're a star yourself and want to be in the next one let me know. I may have been discharged from the mental asylum by the time this book comes out.

1: World population to keep:
https://www.washington.edu/news/2014/09/18/world-population-to-keep-growing-this-century-hit-11-billion-by-2100/growing this century, hit 11 billion by 2100 | UW News (washington.edu)

2: Submission 54 - Jane O'Sullivan – Migrant Intakhttps:
www.pc.gov.au/__data/assets/pdf_file/0007/190609/sub054-migrant-intake.pdfe into Australia - Public inquiry (pc.gov.au)

3: Human Population Growth and Climate Change (biologic https://www.biologicaldiversity.org/programs/population_and_sustainability/climate/aldiversity.org)

4: Population and environment:
https://www.science.org.au/curious/earth-environment/population-environmental challenge - Curious (science.org.au)

© James Eckersley

Francis Rossi
Status Quo

Now seriously, you need me to do a bio of Francis Rossi? Erm, you know that really big rock band that has been around since Noah floated his Ark? Yeah, that Status Quo. Well, Francis Rossi is that bloke stood up front singing. I really shouldn't have to write anymore and besides Francis said quite enough during our interview.

If you could be any other musician past or present, which one would it be and why?

I don't have that thing, I don't have a favourite anything, so I find that weird whenever people ask that question.

If anybody then maybe Jeff Lynne. But I don't want to be anybody else. No I don't because it's fucking difficult enough being me, to being someone else.

It looks good on the outside whomever it is, but I know, Jeff for instance, had some things go wrong in his life, from his management and so on and so on.

Oh you get people saying, "I wouldn't mind being you". Ah, you've got no fucking idea, the internal dialogue alone would do you. Let alone being that bloke up on the stage that most people can't stick because they're Status Quo.

It's the truth, I do speak the truth.

If you had to name one song from any genre that really speaks to you, which one would it be and why?

You see, you narrow it down to one, and immediately came to mind was "Lonely Boy", because the song reminded me of my first son, who I'm sure was disappointed when his brother came along, because he didn't understand that.

I love the structure of the song and I love the whole way it was done - the story. And I love Andrew Gold. I love the idea. That is what we call a 145 sequence and you move the base note around so that it suddenly sounds WOW.

But the record? Probably a track by Johnny and the Hurricanes, "When I Was Young", because I never wanted to play lead guitar and it was all, da, da, da, da da da, da, da da, "Red River Rock", which was a country song, and they did it instrumentally.

And one more, either "Walk Right Back", or "Kathie's Clown".

They all had profound effects, with the Everly Brothers stuff with "Lonely Boy" and Johnny and the Hurricanes. But probably in sequence Johnny and the Hurricanes, Everly Brothers obviously and then "Lonely Boy."

I can't go for one because, what a sad fucking life he's had, that he only likes one record or one song, you know, poor sod, no.

Are you a Mulder or Scully? Do you believe aliens have visited planet earth and if so what do you think they think about mankind?

Well if they did, they would think we were a bunch of fucking schmucks surely.

Well yeah, because of that equation, the amount of stars, planets around it, you really think this is the only one?

What was the happiest day of your life and why?

Fuck, the thing is, favourite song, favourite person, I got a picture on the wall in this music room of mine, and I got my children, we were at the Status Quo premier of the movie, which was fucking shite, and they are all there, and I was doing something the other day with a journalist who was asking who was my favourite child. I realised each one of them are my favourite, because each one is quite unique and I love them all, but they're all my favourites, and I've recently been trying to tell them that.

Happiest day of my life (pause). I haven't the fucking foggiest, because you're trying to think of what was the moment that was the best and I'm not sure.

At the time that's like seeing my first son born which was WOW and then fuck me then came the second one and that was marvellous too.

You know what I mean? So I'm not good with those questions.

If "God" (whatever you idea is on that) were stood before you now, what one question would you ask him/her and why?

Urm, there was a great one with Eddie Izzard once, he (the interviewer) said to him, if he was God for a day. First I'd get rid of that fucking pooing thing, you know having next to hell down there, that was a fucking mistake alright.

He said make the system so you eat and (there's) no way discard it, you imagine the planet would be a better place.

What was the question again?

Probably how and why, you see it's very difficult when one starts to think and really think. Whether it's the Big Bang theory, the entire fucking universe thing, which is eternity itself perhaps.

We are just energy, I think possibly we are, life's energy, which is why I'm sure we all feel we can't die. Only in this carcass, but your life source can't die. I always remember that when I was a kid thinking that doesn't make sense, then it would make sense that we go back to the big One, all part thing, so there wouldn't be a God per say to talk to, see?

As an expressive artist in the music industry, how does the state of the planet make you feel?

I've probably got a very strange opinion on this because I'm sure, well I can see and know that we have not made things better really, however there was very little chance you could inhabit it without soiling it in some way. I also believe in the cyclical thing.

I was watching a TV program and the guy looks out across somewhere in the Northeast of America and he said, you know it was a beautiful lagoon 200 million years ago and you go, oh fuck, yeah you forget things have evolved and are cyclical.

We know that deserts were sea beds once, look at it.

So I do believe some of it is cyclical and we have probably accelerated it somewhat. I'm sure we've caused some damage but I'm sure some of it is cyclical. And we couldn't have had an existence here without having some mark and going back to the joke about shite, well what was supposed to happen to that then? Seven and a half billion people, maybe more, and a lot of them shite big time, particularly in the West, which is more overindulgent.

Do you think as a person of some influence that there is a duty on us to help influence humanity for the better?

As long as we know what is for the better, and as I said to you, we always adopt the moral high ground on whatever it is, and say we can't have this and then say, no actually we were wrong. Drink, cigarettes and shit in food. Assuming I think I know, therefore I will adopt the moral high ground and tell you what to fucking do and then go, oh no I was wrong.

Somebody said, "do you know what the secret of life is?" I said, "no it's a fucking secret".

I know of people who think one has a duty and that it's immoral if you don't. Again it's adopting the moral high ground and they might as well adopt a new religion and tell them what the fuck to do. Perhaps that's where religion went wrong.

What one cause would you say you feel most associated with and why? Whether it's equality, poverty, politics, the environment or other?

I don't think so, other than, if you like the idea that, "do unto others", you know? A level playing field and so on. It bothers me with most causes and charities, the CEOs on three and a half to four hundred thousand a year, and the proliferation of charities.

I think we can be exploited. I'm sure some people are fabulous but not all people are genuine, so causes bother me.

If you were stood before the leaders of the world, what would you say to them?

(Laughs) begins in C and ends in S.

I'm sure that surely there's one or two go into power thinking, genuinely thinking, I can do something here.

The whole thing with democracy is fabulous, but surely you know nothings going to happen.

This country, we swing Left we swing Right, we swing Left we swing Right. Soon as we get in any election, we're gonna be democratic here of course, we all have a vote and then what's a name gets in and the fella that's just lost says,

27

"well we put up a great fight, and we want to thank you all for voting, but what we need now is to get these people out and get a good government in". He's been in two point five minutes and you are democratically backing him up I take it.

It becomes about the Saturday game you know? You just back your team whatever they do.

So I think politics ends up that way and we become very partisan and our team won regardless. Where to me you really want a coalition government.

And finally my last question is in fact one written by Freddie Mercury:
If there's a God in the sky, looking down what can he think of what we've done to the world that He created?
I would say, what we all believe, we've messed up.

What would God think? He'd probably think you've messed up somewhat. But there are some truly beautiful things going on in the world and people who truly care and so on.

But they have to care about things that shouldn't be happening. Yeah god would probably think we've messed up, wouldn't he?

Note: Francis said an awful lot more, but to be honest I don't think either of us could afford the legal bills.

Bobby Rydell

Quite simply, Bobby Rydell is a legend. In the 1960s he was one of the infamous teen idols. It all started in 1950 when he won a TV talent show and became a regular on the show. By 1960 he was touring with The Everly Brothers, Marv Johnson. The Champs and The Crickets.

His first million-selling hit was "We Got Love" and his second was "Wild One." His success continued with hit after hit and he even appeared on the cinema screens as Hugo Peabody in the movie Bye Bye Birdie with Dick Van Dyke. Bobby had a total of 34 top 100 hits, making him one of the top five artists of the era. He appeared on numerous TV shows, including the Red Skelton Show, Jack Benny, Joey Bishop, The George Burns Show and The Milton Berle Show.

Basically, Bobby Rydell is a music legend and I managed to catch up with him early in 2021 to throw my crazy questions at him.

If you could be any other musician past or present, which one would it be and why?
My favourite musician is Buddy Rich. My first love was being a drummer. I feel he was the greatest in my lifetime. He did not read charts. He had a chart reader do a run through and memorised his part.

Note: Buddy Rich is possibly one of the most influential drummers of all time who started playing the drums at the tender age of two.

My favourite singer is Frank Sinatra. His phrasing was beyond compare. Who knows if the world will have another one like him. He put his own style to every song. No one else can duplicate him.

If you had to name one song from any genre that really speaks to you, which one would it be and why?
"I Gotta Be Me". It's been my philosophy my entire life.

Are you a Mulder or Scully? Do you believe aliens have visited planet earth and if so what do you think they think about mankind?
Yes I am a Mulder. I've always believed there was more than just "us" in the galaxy. I believe there is a mixed bag of beings, some good and some bad. I am sure they think we are very stupid in the way we have treated planet earth and

to tell you the truth, I am surprised they have not made themselves public to straighten us out.

What was the happiest day of your life and why?
The first time I heard one of my records on the radio. I knew my life was about to change and it would never be the same again.

If "God" (whatever your idea is on that) were stood before you now, what one question would you ask him/her and why?
I would question why we have so much hatred, suffering and challenges in life and what are we supposed to be learning from all that is put in our path.

As an expressive artist in the music industry, how does the state of the planet make you feel?
I am very disappointed and sad at the state mankind is in today. Money is the main goal, no concern for fellow man — I feel we are on a downward spiral if we as a collective do not wake up.

Do you think as a person of some influence that there is a duty on us to help influence humanity for the better?
I think every person has something to contribute to humanity — not just people with influence. If we all did our part the world would improve dramatically.

What one cause would you say you feel most associated with and why? Whether it's equality, poverty, politics, the environment or other?
I am involved with Organ Donation. I received a liver / kidney transplant in July 2012. I never really paid much attention to how important having donors sign up was — when it involves your own destiny everything changes. At every performance I tell my story and encourage the audience to sign up to be a donor. It truly is the gift of life.

If you were stood before the leaders of the world, what would you say to them?
I think most of the world leaders are so corrupt and greedy that they all should resign.

And finally my last question is in fact one written by Freddie Mercury:
If there's a God in the sky, looking down what can he think of what we've done to the world that He created?
I am sure the creator is not very pleased with how we have ended up. Our stewardship of planet earth is not something we can be proud of. I am sure there are times he would like to blow it all up and start again. Hopefully when all the dust settles from the chaos happening now we will have a chance to get it right for everyone.

Dr. Chud
The Misfits

Okay, so prepare to be utterly disgusted by a punk rock horror drummer. Yes, apparently there is such a thing and Dr. Chud is one. He is well-known for being in the punk band, Misfits, who have been around since the 1970s and are one of those bands that influenced so many things. But he's more than a drummer, he's also a songwriter, producer and now the leader of the celebrated band, Dr. Chud's X-Ward. As they say in the world of horror films, be afraid, be very... well you get the picture.

If you could be any other musician past or present, which one would it be and why?
You can turn me into Paul McCartney NOW... One of the greatest feelings in the world is creating a great song... what it must feel like to create so many...

If you had to name one song from any genre that really speaks to you, which one would it be and why?
"Limelight" by Rush. Beautifully crafted lyrics that describe some of the struggles I've always had being a performer. The music adds an incredible amount of emotion to the words... absolutely brilliant songwriting.

Are you a Mulder or Scully? Do you believe aliens have visited planet earth and if so what do you think they think about mankind?
I don't think there are aliens, Maybe alien forms of living things but nobody is visiting us, we are just bored here on earth and we are visiting ourselves!

What was the happiest day of your life and why?
I was pretty happy when my mom came to see me perform at the House of Blues in Orlando, Florida in 2000 with The Misfits. It was the first time ever she came to see me perform. She passed away shortly after, I really wish I could relive that day, she was so happy.

If "God" (whatever your idea is on that) were stood before you now, what one question would you ask him/her and why?
Ha ha. I could see it now, I'm at the pearly gates and God is standing in front of

me, I would definitely ask if he has something to do with that (pointing down to Earth) Or are you here to save me from that!

As an expressive artist in the music industry, how does the state of the planet make you feel?
From what I read and watch on TV, it looks like we take advantage of what we have and destroy it, profits over earth, animals and people... maybe make some kind of "custodian" law where one generation can only fuck up the planet just so much then leave it to the next to do the same, never making it worse then you left it! Everyone has to be in though to make it work. Seems the simplest answers aren't so simple I guess.

Do you think as a person of some influence that there is a duty on us to help influence humanity for the better?
That's the parent's job dammit! I think it's up to the individual, people are complex, brownie points if they do! Some people just might not be good at it, or just don't feel comfortable doing it it's a role for the chosen few.

What one cause would you say you feel most associated with and why? Whether it's equality, poverty, politics, the environment or other?
I love animals and I love not eating them. We are fucking up big time by destroying these beautiful creatures. Their karma is killing us everyday.

If you were stood before the leaders of the world, what would you say to them?
If I had enough influence I'd love to get them all to stop the war machine and take care of their people with all the money they saved!

And finally my last question is in fact one written by Freddie Mercury: If there's a God in the sky, looking down what can he think of what we've done to the world that He created?
Hopefully God is proud of the work in progress, and can't wait to finish it, or maybe it's just an impossible job and God is doing the best God can? God only knows!
All my bloody guts – DR. CHUD

Note: Well I must say I was expecting a little more blood, guts and decapitated babies, but that's been the beauty of doing this book, it always surprises!

Fito de la Parra

Adolfo de la Parra
Canned Heat

As a member of legendary rock band, Canned Heat since 1967, Adolfo de la Parra is a legend. He started playing drums at the age of 14 and by 1958 he was a member of the Mexican band, Los Sparks. Over the next few years he played with some of the most influential Mexican rock bands including Los Sinners and Los Hooligans.

In 1967 he was asked to join Canned Heat and never looked back. Anybody who knows anything about Canned Heat will know that they were a massive blues-rock band who played not just Woodstock but Monterey as well. They had international success with songs such as "On the Road Again" and "Let's Work Together."

For over 40 years Adolfo has played with the best, including big Joe Turner, T-Bone Walker, Albert Collins, John Lee Hooker and Memphis Slim.

I wanted to know more about how this legendary drummer ticked and so we caught up in early 2021.

If you could be any other musician past or present, which one would it be and why?
I would have loved to have been someone like Gene Krupa and be able to play with all of those great jazz swing bands.

Note: Eugene Bertram Krupa was an American jazz drummer, band leader and composer. He is known for his energy and showmanship. Most notably his drum solo on the song "Sing, Sing, Sing" brought the drummer to a new level of respect.

If you had to name one song from any genre that really speaks to you, which one would it be and why?
"Night Time is The Right Time".

Note: Also known as "The Right Time" it is a rhythm and blues song recorded in 1957 by Nappy Brown and re-recorded by numerous artists such as Ray Charles and James Brown.

Are you a Mulder or Scully? Do you believe aliens have visited planet earth and if so what do you think they think about mankind?
I do not believe aliens have visited earth lately, but I wish they would come and help us deal with our imperfect world.

What was the happiest day of your life and why?
The day Canned Heat offered me a job as a drummer was the happiest day of my life.

If "God" (whatever your idea is on that) were stood before you now, what one question would you ask him/her and why?
I would ask, God, if you really exist, how come you have allowed our world to become such a mess with all of this cruelty?

As an expressive artist in the music industry, how does the state of the planet make you feel?
Our world needs a major tune up, the destruction of wildlife and the environment will eventually destroy us too. If we don't act fast regardless of the economic impact there will be no hope.

Do you think as a person of some influence that there is a duty on us to help influence humanity for the better?
Absolutely, we in the Canned Heat have been pioneers in raising awareness of the destruction of Earth. Just look at the cover of our *Future Blues* album with the American flag upside down on the cover with the polluted Earth in the background. This record was banned in all major stores when it came out. But it became a hit anyway. Our mission continues.

Note: Right on brother.

What one cause would you say you feel most associated with and why? Whether it's equality, poverty, politics, the environment or other?
Respect and care to wildlife and our environment.

If you were stood before the leaders of the world, what would you say to them?
I would tell them the same things that Greta Thunberg said, forget economics, find a way to take care of the Earth.

And finally my last question is in fact one written by Freddie Mercury:
If there's a God in the sky, looking down what can he think of what we've done to the world that He created?
God would be disappointed and furious in the way we have taken care of Mother Earth.

Note: Let's all give a big round of applause to Adolfo and Canned Heat for taking a stand against the establishment and raising awareness of the plight of the planet. If every music band did the same, the pressure on governments and business would be immense. Bravo!

Eva Gardner

In 1993 the legendary engineer / producer Andy Johns (Led Zeppelin, The Rolling Stones, Rod Stewart, Eric Clapton) took a Pignose amplifier and bass guitar to the Hollywood Hills home of British rock bassist, Kim Gardner. Kim was a member of The Creation and The Birds with Ron Wood, was surprised when Johns handed the bass guitar to his 14-year-old daughter, Eva. Johns then goes to turn up the volume on The Kinks' classic "You Really Got Me" and proclaimed, "Now this is a solid bass line!" Eva never looked back.

Eva began performing with live bands in her hometown of Los Angeles at the age of 14. She decided to further her musical studies and attended the Los Angeles County High School for the Arts and then at UCLA, graduating with honours. Her professional career began when she toured and recorded as the original bassist in The Mars Volta in 2001 / 2002. Since then, Eva has performed and toured with numerous artists worldwide, including Pink, Gwen Stefani, Cher, Tegan & Sara, Moby and Veruca Salt.

In 2014, Eva became the first female artist to have a signature bass with Fender. It has been released for public purchase and is available worldwide. So there, now you know! And then to even greater acclaim, she put down the bass and answered my questions.

If you could be any other musician past or present, which one would it be and why?
I would be Chopin! He had such a distinct and individual style. His music is intimate and delicate, conveying so much emotion.

If you had to name one song from any genre that really speaks to you, which one would it be and why?
Jimi Hendrix, "Bold as Love." As Harry Shapiro's says, "Love comes in many hues, love is hard work and to get properly involved takes commitment and courage." Like a shift in the axis of the earth, love can change everything.

What was the happiest day of your life and why?
Happiest day of my life — playing at the Isle of Wight Festival in the UK - it truly felt like I "had arrived" as a musician. It's such a legendary festival and I met Paul McCartney backstage, as we were opening up for him (with Pink). I was

introduced as Pink's bass player and he proceeded to sing a walking baseline to me and proclaimed, "Us bass players gotta stick together!" A momentous day all around!

As an expressive artist in the music industry, how does the state of the planet make you feel?
The state of the planet often makes me feel very overwhelmed and heartbroken if I allow myself to go there. I'm very interested in history and I realise that humans have always been this way — it's all about "survival of the fittest," "divide and conquer," etc. Human nature can be quite cruel and selfish which, in turn, wreaks havoc on the planet and those inhabiting it. It feels so heavy.

Do you think as a person of some influence that there is a duty on us to help influence humanity for the better?
I think "be the change you want to see in the world" is a very powerful saying. It's important to lead by example and I'd hope that people with some influence would want to leave the world having made a positive impact. "Just as ripples spread out when a single pebble is dropped into water, the actions of individuals can have far-reaching effects." — Dalai Lama

What one cause would you say you feel most associated with and why? Whether it's equality, poverty, politics, the environment or other?
I currently support an organization called Women for Women International that helps women in countries affected by conflict and war. Their vision statement is "To create a world in which all women determine the course of their lives & reach their full potential."

Having been born and raised in a first world country, I am fortunate to have the freedoms, opportunities and access to resources that women elsewhere have not. It's important that we support and empower each other.

If you were stood before the leaders of the world, what would you say to them?
Are you in therapy?

And finally my last question is in fact one written by Freddie Mercury in the song "Is This the World We Created": If there's a God in the sky, looking down what can he think of what we've done to the world that He created?
Despite all of the devastation in the world, there is also a lot of love and beauty. There is no light without dark. It seems that it's all part of the cycle.

Chris Spedding
The Pretenders

Chris Spedding has been a member of numerous rock bands including The Pretenders, Nucleus, Trigger and even The Wombles.

His fifty-year music career has seen him have a huge hit single on his own with "Motor Bikin'" and touring worldwide as one of the most versatile guitarists.

He has recorded with Bryan Ferry, Roxy Music, Elton John, Brian Eno, Jack Bruce, Nick Mason, Art Garfunkel, Typically Tropical, Katie Melua, Ginger Baker, Joan Armatrading, Paul McCartney and Jeff Wayne amongst others, as well as producing for The Sex Pistols.

Basically, Chris Spedding is a legend to not just music lovers, but to musicians as well.

I was lucky enough to interview Chris for the book at the height of the Covid Pandemic in 2021.

If you could be any other musician past or present, which one would it be and why?
Scotty Moore. In the late 1950s every young male I knew wanted to be like Elvis. Me too, but what I really wanted to be was his guitarist, Scotty Moore.

Note: Scotty Moore formed the backing band for Elvis Presley and toured with the King.

If you had to name one song from any genre that really speaks to you, which one would it be and why?
There are many. I suppose it's between Bob Dylan's "Desolation Row" and "Going Back" by Carole King and Gerry Goffin.

Are you a Mulder or Scully? Do you believe aliens have visited planet earth and if so what do you think they think about mankind?
If aliens did visit planet earth in search of intelligent life, I think they must have been very disappointed. They probably wouldn't have stayed long.

What was the happiest day of your life and why?
I'm generally a fairly happy guy until someone actually asks me about happiness, and then I'm suddenly not so happy. So, thanks for that! (Ha ha!)

Note: You're welcome.

If "God" (whatever your idea is on that) were stood before you now, what one question would you ask him/her and why?
I'd ask him / her to go back to try and make a better job of it.

As an expressive artist in the music industry, how does the state of the planet make you feel?
Guilty. Frustrated. I think humans have overpopulated the planet and exploited it shamefully.

Do you think as a person of some influence that there is a duty on us to help influence humanity for the better?Yes. But how?

What one cause would you say you feel most associated with and why? Whether it's equality, poverty, politics, the environment or other?
I'd like to see a fairer distribution of wealth, and for the banks and financial institutions to be less greedy. It can be done. If interest rates were forgiven for a couple of years, everybody would suddenly love the banks and millions would have better lives. The banks would hardly suffer at all because the economy would bounce back immediately. Not so long ago, some first world countries forgave many third world countries their foreign aid debts. So it's not a pipe dream. Why can't this kind of thing happen more often?

If you were stood before the leaders of the world, what would you say to them?
Depends who it was. On one extreme I'd say, "Nice to meet you, Frau Merkel". If it was someone like Mr. Trump I wouldn't waste my breath.

And finally my last question is in fact one written by Freddie Mercury: If there's a God in the sky, looking down what can he think of what we've done to the world that He created?
The song title is accurate, not the rest of it. We created the world, not some deity. We created the world as it is now and — let's not forget — we also created the deities.

Burleigh Drummond

A founding member of the cult, award-winning rock band, Ambrosia, Burleigh Drummond is a drumming legend. He's also a producer, song-writer and singer. He is, in his own words, the George Harrison of Ambrosia. Burleigh was kind enough to spend some time out of touring, writing, singing, drumming and generally being a rock star to answer my questions.

If you could be any other musician past or present, which one would it be and why?
Possibly Elvin Jones, just so I could spend that much time playing with John Coltrane.

Note: Elvin Jones was a post-bop jazz drummer.

If you had to name one song from any genre that really speaks to you, which one would it be and why?
The Lark Ascending by Vaughan Williams. Recently I lost my Mother-in-law and my niece, who was my Goddaughter. I was very close to both of them and hearing this piece of music makes me feel I still am.

Are you a Mulder or Scully? Do you believe aliens have visited planet earth and if so what do you think they think about mankind?
I do believe some force has been to this planet at some point in our planet's history. I think they have been unimpressed enough not to return or maybe they live among us and we don't realize it.

What was the happiest day of your life and why?
The day my wife to be and I looked at each other and knew that we were meant to be together.

Note: Ain't that just beautiful.

If "God" (whatever your idea is on that) were stood before you now, what one question would you ask him/her and why?
How can mankind control the destructive elements that seem to torture us from within.

Note: God said, "take one of these pills twice daily and chill".

As an expressive artist in the music industry, how does the state of the planet make you feel?
I have a son and daughter. My daughter is 24 and pointed out the other day that her generation will become the first to become fully affected by the slow demise of our planet. I was ashamed.

Do you think as a person of some influence that there is a duty on us to help influence humanity for the better?
It's my duty and everybody's duty.

Note: Reader, this also means you and your mates.

What one cause would you say you feel most associated with and why? Whether it's equality, poverty, politics, the environment or other?
I would say the most pressing issue would be the environment because it is and will to a greater extent affect each and every one of us. If we could unite to save the planet, I believe we could expose the corruption of politics and the effect of poverty and inequality.

If you were stood before the leaders of the world, what would you say to them?
I would suggest to them that we should have matured beyond using warfare on other humans at this point in history. Also, to not participate in the effort to save this planet is to cast a death sentence on the very people you are entrusted to protect.

And finally my last question is in fact one written by Freddie Mercury:
If there's a God in the sky, looking down what can he think of what we've done to the world that He created?
I am not qualified to have a quantitative definition of what God is, I think sometimes the concept of God is a scapegoat for us to not take up the actions needed to save ourselves. The notion that God is on our side has probably never talked to the other side about their beliefs.

Chris Allen

The Troggs formed in 1964 at the height of the beat era. They had huge hits with songs such as "Wild Thing", "With a Girl Like You" and "Love is All Around."

In 1992 the lead singer, Reg Presley, was diagnosed with lung cancer and Chris Allen was asked to step into the illustrious role as lead singer of The Troggs.

I managed to interview Chris for the book in March, 2021.

If you had to name one song from any genre that really speaks to you, which one would it be and why?
"The Living Years", by Mike & the Mechanics. It rings true.

Are you a Mulder or Scully? Do you believe aliens have visited planet earth and if so what do you think they think about mankind?
Yes, absolutely. They would think we are savages

What was the happiest day of your life and why?
When my first child was born... obvious reasons

If "God" (whatever your idea is on that) were stood before you now, what one question would you ask him/her and why?
Why do you allow such suffering and horrific diseases like cancer?

As an expressive artist in the music industry, how does the state of the planet make you feel?
I'm horrified at how we treat the planet.

Do you think as a person of some influence that there is a duty on us to help influence humanity for the better?
Absolutely!

What one cause would you say you feel most associated with and why? Whether it's equality, poverty, politics, the environment or other?
To realise and legalise natural cures.

If you were stood before the leaders of the world, what would you say to them?
Get a grip!

And finally my last question is in fact one written by Freddie Mercury:
If there's a God in the sky, looking down what can he think of what we've done to the world that He created?
Another flood and ark!

Alan Whitehead

At only 19 years old, Alan Whitehead, turned fully professional, as a drummer. He joined Crispian St. Peters who had a No 1 hit with "I'm The Pied Piper." He then went on to play with various groups including the cult group "The Attack." In the winter of 1967 he saw an advert for a drummer in a popular music paper "Hard-working Motown group looking for a drummer".

That group was Marmalade, who were at the time the number one group in Scotland. They had decided to relocate to London and their drummer didn't, so Alan applied. Within months the band were playing at the famous Marquee club and had their first big hit, "Loving Things." This was followed up by "Wait For Me Mary Ann."

A short while later they got their number one slot with "Ob-La-De Ob-La-Da." Soon they were signed to the big record label, Decca and recorded "Reflections of My Life" which went to number one in eighteen countries. A world tour followed, with eleven top ten hits and two number ones.

As I interviewed Alan for the book, Marmalade were still, after fifty years, rocking the world.

If you could be any other musician past or present, which one would it be and why?
Stevie Wonder. I toured with him and spent many hours talking to him. His voice and musical talent were a joy and as a bonus, he was very humble. The most remarkable musician I ever met.

If you had to name one song from any genre that really speaks to you, which one would it be and why?
"Whiter Shade of Pale". A haunting melody that has stood the test of time.

Note: "A Whiter Shade of Pale" was recorded by Procol Harem and went to number one across the world. It was the most played song in the UK for 75 years.

Are you a Mulder or Scully? Do you believe aliens have visited planet earth and if so what do you think they think about mankind?
Mulder of course. Aliens have visited Earth. When in Marmalade we all stood underneath a UFO in 1978 on the way back from a gig. It was a mind blowing experience.

Note: And not one of them took a photograph.

What was the happiest day of your life and why?
Having our first hit record "Loving Things" in 1968. We had achieved commercial success at last.

If "God" (whatever your idea is on that) were stood before you now, what one question would you ask him/her and why?
I would ask God, "is this all there is?"

As an expressive artist in the music industry, how does the state of the planet make you feel?
The planet is out of sync with itself and heading for a global change. As Lao Tzu said thousands of years ago, "The Earth will wine and dine till the very last second and disappear in the twinkle of an eye."

Do you think as a person of some influence that there is a duty on us to help influence humanity for the better?
Nobody is listening anymore. There is no point.

Note: Well, let us all hope that we can make them hear us.

What one cause would you say you feel most associated with and why? Whether it's equality, poverty, politics, the environment or other?
I like the Salvation Army. It is the only charity I ever help. They are good humble souls trying to help those less well off.

If you were stood before the leaders of the world, what would you say to them?
There isn't one honest person amongst you. All of you should hang your heads in shame.

And finally my last question is in fact one written by Freddie Mercury:
If there's a God in the sky, looking down what can he think of what we've done to the world that He created?
The world is a school for souls to learn from. Hell is what mankind has created out of a paradise that we have destroyed. I have written two books for those who seek answers. The Universe talks to us all the time... sadly mankind is not listening.

Note: Mankind, listen!

Ciaran Gribbin

Hailing from Northern Ireland, Ciaran Gribbin has so far had a remarkable career. He started writing songs at around nine years old and formed small bands with his friends a few years later. He went on to study music at college and then formed the band, Leya. They put out one album and toured with Snow Patrol, Scissor Sisters, Franz Ferdinand and Embrace. Gribbin also performed backing vocals on Snow Patrol's album, Eyes Open.

In 2009 he was supporting Paolo Nutini on his Australian tour when he met Andrew Farriss, the keyboard player for INXS. They became close friends and the other members of the band were so impressed with him they asked him to audition for the position of lead singer.

In 2011 he performed his first show as lead singer of INXS in Peru before 7000 people. Only two nights later he was rocking 30,000 in Argentina.

I interviewed Ciaran with my crackpot questions and this is what he told me.

If you could be any other musician past or present, which one would it be and why?
Phil Lynott from Thin Lizzy. One, because he was Irish and, two, he was so unique. Not only black but the first real true Irish rock and roll god who toured the world in the time when rock and roll was in full swing. Rock and roll was moving, music was sweeping through the world and changing societies. I just love Thin Lizzy's music.

If you had to name one song from any genre that really speaks to you, which one would it be and why?
There's an old folk song called 'As I Roved Out'. A traditional Scottish / Irish Song, origins are unknown. It was on the first Planxty album. The lyrics of the song are about falling in love in a time of war and wishing for peace. That song like many old folk songs, speaks so well it's like poetry set to music but they connect with the common man on a spiritual level.

Are you a Mulder or Scully? Do you believe aliens have visited planet earth and if so what do you think they think about mankind?
I'm very much a Mulder. I believe aliens, or you can call them angels, have been here before. You only have to look at the old cultures like the Sumerians and their understanding of the planetary system. That's well before we get to the mystery that is the Egyptian pyramids and their precise alignment to the stars. Essentially there have been beings on this planet long before mankind that had technologies

that we simply do not understand.

What was the happiest day of your life and why?
Apart from the birth of my two sons, my happiest day was actually just recently where I had a moment looking back at my entire life and realising that I have lived many lifetimes, many dreams, and I've achieved recognition for my work. The icing on the cake is that I'm still paying my bills after 29 years in music.

If "God" (whatever your idea is on that) were stood before you now, what one question would you ask him/her and why?
What is the meaning to life and why are we here?

As an expressive artist in the music industry, how does the state of the planet make you feel?
The state of the planet saddens me. I think profit before everything else is the wrong way to do business. I think our greed and narcissism has crept into every form of government across the planet and it's what's driving countries forward. I am though optimistic; I believe there is a rise in consciousness across the planet and people are starting to realise that we have more in common than what divides us. Peacefully we can rise up and take back the planet.

Do you think as a person of some influence that there is a duty on us to help influence humanity for the better?
Yes. I think artists, musicians, poets, great thinkers need to share their thoughts, share their dreams on how the planet can look, how we can act as a society and share our unique perspective with our brothers and sisters.

What one cause would you say you feel most associated with and why? Whether it's equality, poverty, politics, the environment or other?
Pollution. Pollution of our land, our water, our air is the ultimate crime. Any corporation or human being that is doing it for profit needs to be stopped and heavily penalised. We need to encourage people to stop polluting.

If you were stood before the leaders of the world, what would you say to them?
The two-party political system that seems to be in every western democracy is simply not working. I believe we need to look at the way we govern where it's based more on a community level. Small forms of government working with the community to make the areas better. Big government doesn't work, slow to move, expensive and it's corrupted by corporations. Get money out of politics.

And finally my last question is in fact one written by Freddie Mercury:
If there's a God in the sky, looking down what can he think of what we've done to the world that He created?
He would be probably disappointed that all the wonderful resources on this planet are not shared equally. He would also be saddened about how we are divided by our leaders and how we've failed due to labels — race, religion, politics, materialism. Greed rules. But I think God would be pleased by our ability to change things in a good way.

Biff Byford

It's time to get heavy now with the lead singer of legendary heavy metal band, Saxon. The band has had international success with top selling singles and albums right through the 1980s. They have in fact sold more than 15 million albums. So Biff is not short of a penny or two. Here's what the Yorkshire rocker had to say.

If you could be any other musician past or present, which one would it be and why?
Mick Jagger. He seems to have had a magical career so far it must have been amazing in the sixties to be in the Stones breaking new ground and music.

If you had to name one song from any genre that really speaks to you, which one would it be and why?
The Who's "Won't Get Fooled Again". It's a working-class song that resonates about always feeling like your employed by bosses (management) when really you employ them.

Are you a Mulder or Scully? Do you believe aliens have visited planet earth and if so what do you think they think about mankind?
Yes I think they've visited at some point. They probably think we've fucked it up and some people are desperately trying to slow down the collapse.

What was the happiest day of your life and why?
I've had many happy days but I think getting married for the last time was a high point and the children that followed.

If "God" (whatever your idea is on that) stood before you now, what one question would you ask him/her and why?
I'd ask him if He really sent his son here to visit and prepare for something. It's a big question, religion.

As an expressive artist in the music industry, how does the state of the planet make you feel?
It's hard to change things through music. The artists that have tried have done some great things but never stopped a war.

Do you think as a person of some influence that there is a duty on us to help influence humanity for the better?
I think we have to learn from history. The mistakes that we've made and try not to keep repeating them. I think we all have a duty to question what governments are doing on our behalf.

What one cause would you say you feel most associated with and why? Whether it's equality, poverty, politics, the environment or other?
I feel for poverty. In this day and age no country who can afford to build and fund weapons should have people living in poverty and squalid conditions.

If you stood before the leaders of the world, what would you say to them?
Get in a room together and work something out for everybody to live in peace.

Don McLean

Seriously, do I have to write a bio of Don McLean? If you don't know who he is then just where the hell have you been? Okay, my publisher is looking strange at me now, so I better write something.

Don McLean is a music legend. Who, on planet Earth has not heard the song "American Pie"? Even Madonna has heard of it. Anyway, it's nearly nine minutes long and has been called a cultural touchstone about the loss of innocence. It's genius, go listen.

Of course, this isn't his only hit. The song "Vincent" was huge too (also performed as a duet with Ed Sheeran for Teen Cancer America). A beautifully melodic song about the life of Vincent van Gogh. And there's "And I Love You So" which has been covered by Elvis Presley Perry Como, Helen Reddy and Glen Campbell amongst others. Look, there's just loads of great songs by Don, go and do a search!

In 2004, Don was inducted into the illustrious Songwriters Hall of Fame. The man is nothing short of, and way beyond, the term, Legend.

I was humbled to be allowed close enough to ask him my potty questions.

If you could be any other musician past or present, which one would it be and why?
I would be Duke Ellington because he was a beautiful man with exquisite taste.

If you had to name one song from any genre that really speaks to you, which one would it be and why?
It would be "White Christmas" by Bing Crosby as I heard in the very early 1950s because it brings me back home again to a kind of perfect happiness.

Are you a Mulder or Scully? Do you believe aliens have visited planet earth and if so what do you think they think about mankind?
I am positive aliens have visited planet earth. To think that we are the only life in an endless universe is like believing the earth is flat.

What was the happiest day of your life and why?
That's a hard one since I have had many happy days. Perhaps it was getting my first Martin D28 guitar in 1963.

If "God" (whatever your idea is on that) were stood before you now, what one question would you ask him/her and why?

As a former Catholic it would have to be the Holy Trinity and I would ask Jesus if since he is God and all knowing, if he knew when he died that he would rise from the dead. Being God he would have to say yes and he would admit that he really, therefore, did not die.

As an expressive artist in the music industry, how does the state of the planet make you feel?

The chance to hold on to the natural world was within our grasp fifty years ago. Now with 60% of plant and animal life extinguished it makes me feel ashamed to be a human being with so little love for the animal kingdom.

Do you think as a person of some influence that there is a duty on us to help influence humanity for the better?

As a human being I would not want to think that my goal in life was to influence life for the worse.

What one cause would you say you feel most associated with and why? Whether it's equality, poverty, politics, the environment or other?

I am now, and have always been, opposed to war. Sometimes it is necessary certainly, but it represents the complete failure of civilisation and its expression is of the lowest kind of human behaviour. America now runs secret wars which don't upset the public so the military industrial complex which Eisenhower warned us about, can find theatres of war to try out their new killing devices and chemicals. All presidents have so much blood on their hands.

If you were stood before the leaders of the world, what would you say to them?

I would say make corruption a capital offence punishable by death.

And finally my last question is in fact one written by Freddie Mercury:
If there's a God in the sky, looking down what can he think of what we've done to the world that He created?

An earlier question was have aliens visited the earth. Perhaps the human race is alien.

James Atkin

James Atkin is famous for being the singer and keyboard player of the band EMF. Described as alternative rock, EMF rose to fame in the early 1990's, releasing three studio albums. Their first single "Unbelievable" reached the top slot in the US and their debut album made it to the number three slot.

Although EMF have often gotten back together, James has never stopped pumping out music, especially an album devised under lockdown in the Covid pandemic. I managed to get James to stop for a moment and this is the result.

If you could be any other musician past or present, which one would it be and why?
I guess being involved in some kind of late 60s Laurel Canyon or San Francisco band. The summer of love scene looked very wild — so I'll say the Grateful Dead or Frank Zappa's band.

If you had to name one song from any genre that really speaks to you, which one would it be and why?
"Papua New Guinea" by Future Sound of London — the whole essence of being lost in a field at 3am submerged in the surroundings of loud hypnotic music, pulsing lights and crazy party people.

Are you a Mulder or Scully? Do you believe aliens have visited planet earth and if so, what do you think they think about mankind?
I went through a period in the 90s where the idea of aliens was ever present. We hooked up with a load of counterculture people on our early trips to the US and got intrigued. I guess a lot of youth are searching for something bigger and answer to those big life questions — religion wasn't happening for us but beliefs in aliens seemed plausible. I've grown out of that now and it all seems a bit daft.

Note: Daft is a British term for stupid. There's a lot of daft people in the world and many of them are running our countries.

I do believe aliens are out there in the universe, just not in a bunker in the Nevada desert. I think aliens would be pretty baffled by our treatment to our planet and the way we treat each other.

What was the happiest day of your life and why?
I should say the birth of my kids, but I remember being on top of the world when we played Reading Festival in 1992. I had been bunking off school for years and hitch hiking down to the festival — finally having the chance to perform on the main stage was a true dream come true moment

Note: James we just had a message from your teachers, you have 2 years detention.

If "God" (whatever your idea is on that) were stood before you now, what one question would you ask him/her and why?
Well there is no God — so who are you?

As an expressive artist in the music industry, how does the state of the planet make you feel?
Awful — so much hatred on so many levels. From small local bigoted racists with closed minds to big corporate industries raping the earth for profit and greed. Despicable behaviour.

Do you think as a person of some influence that there is a duty on us to help influence humanity for the better?
It is everybody's duty — I do feel people feel insignificant and unable to make change happen — the people united will need to happen.

What one cause would you say you feel most associated with and why? Whether it's equality, poverty, politics, the environment or other?
Politics — we need to spread the wealth, take the power back off our overlords and establish equality for all.
Environment — people are educated on the dangers, sadly this has not made a great deal of difference, it's time to stop plundering the earth for unsustainable resources, mining and burning fossil fuels. A complete shift to green energy via whole world change is the only answer.

If you were stood before the leaders of the world, what would you say to them?
Tax the rich, spread the wealth, clamp down on corruption and greed, equality for all. Listen to experts and the young people with ideas, don't bow down to your own selfishness and need for power.

And finally, my last question is in fact one written by Freddie Mercury: If there's a God in the sky, looking down what can he think of what we've done to the world that He created?
Faith in humanity is the answer — we are fed lies and controlled by the media, the hatred fuelled by the rich people who control the media is used to their advantage and helps divide the people. A revolution of consciousness is needed now!

Note: Spot on James. And so say all of us.

© Jaymz Eberly

Jack Russell

It doesn't get more rock than Jack White. Founding member of Great White, he has toured also as a solo artist and his own band, Jack White's Great White. He's a singer, songwriter, musician and producer, but he wasn't too busy to give us a few minutes for the planet.

If you could be any other musician past or present, which one would it be and why?
Steven Tyler, because his has held up and his song writing just keeps getting better. When he performs he puts on a show, not unlike myself.

If you had to name one song from any genre that really speaks to you, which one would it be and why?
"Stairway To Heaven" because all of the melodies, lyrics, and guitar parts are hooks within themselves. And for a song to have no chorus per se, I feel it is the most successful rock song of all time.

Note: At last somebody has picked one of the best songs ever. Rock on.

Are you a Mulder or Scully? Do you believe aliens have visited planet earth and if so what do you think they think about mankind?
Mulder. Yes, I think that they have visited Earth. I believe they think that we have a long, long way to go.

Note: If anything has shocked me during these interviews, it's the sheer amount of music stars who believe aliens have visited us. Is this indicative of the general population or does all that loud noise do it?

What was the happiest day of your life and why?
The day that we played a sold-out show at Irvine Meadows in front of 18,000 people.

If "God" (whatever your idea is on that) were stood before you now, what one question would you ask him/her and why?
What is life all about? The reason which is obvious.

As an expressive artist in the music industry, how does the state of the planet make you feel?
Sad, scared, and concerned that we may not be able to put it right.

Do you think as a person of some influence that there is a duty on us to help influence humanity for the better?
Yes. Regarding issue such as earth sustainability, recycling, climate change, endanger species, caring for our oceans.

What one cause would you say you feel most associated with and why? Whether it's equality, poverty, politics, the environment or other?
Caring for our oceans because if they die, we die. There are so many species that are still unknown to us. We know more about outer space than we do the oceans on our own planet.

If you were stood before the leaders of the world, what would you say to them?
Get your shit together.

Note: And so say all of us.

And finally, my last question is in fact one written by Freddie Mercury: If there's a God in the sky, looking down what can he think of what we've done to the world that He created?
Sad, because He gave us this beautiful world and we have trashed it.

© Alan Mercer

Freda Payne

Singer and actress, Freda Payne is a legend. She is the older sister of Scherrie Payne, a singer in a little group called the Supremes and has been entertaining us from the 1960s. In the 1970s her hit "Band of Gold" was huge and since then she's starred in movies, on stage, had a talk show and much more.

But bless her, she still had time for little old me.

If you could be any other musician past or present, which one would it be and why?

I would like to have been Hazel Scott, she was an African-American pianist afflu-ent in all genres of music. She played in night clubs as well as concert halls in the United States as well as Europe. She was married to congressman Adam Clay-ton Powell. My reason for wanting to be her is that she was a true Renaissance woman. She accomplished many things and was an excellent concert pianist in the classical feel. She stood up for herself and was afraid of nothing.

If you had to name one song from any genre that really speaks to you, which one would it be and why?

"Here's to Life". The lyrics are simply philosophical and sobering, recognizing one's mortality and the desire to continue to live and accomplish more things in life.

Are you a Mulder or Scully? Do you believe aliens have visited planet earth and if so what do you think they think about mankind?

I am neither a Mulder or a Scully. Yes, I most definitely feel that aliens have vis-ited planet earth and that there are probably humanoids walking around among us. They probably think we are idiots and are stupid.

Note: Then you're a Mulder and the FBI have a file on you.

What was the happiest day of your life and why?

When I had my son. Because it was life-changing and it changed me for the better. Even my body chemistry had changed.

Note: Same for me, only it was my bank account that changed.

If "God" (whatever your idea is on that) were stood before you now, what one question would you ask him/her and why? I'd ask why are we here?

If God stood before me I would ask him why does he allow so many horrible things to happen to mankind and why did he allow this pandemic to come upon us.

As an expressive artist in the music industry, how does the state of the planet make you feel?

It makes me feel like we are not in control of anything. Life as we have known it will not be the same.

Do you think as a person of some influence that there is a duty on us to help influence humanity for the better?

Yes I do feel that most definitely. When you have the spotlight you automatically have the attention drawn to you and the words you speak can definitely influence others who look up to you, so therefore you should be responsible for what you do and say.

Note: Somebody tell Ozzy.

What one cause would you say you feel most associated with and why? Whether it's equality, poverty, politics, the environment or other?

I have not one designated cause, I like to help all of the causes.

If you were stood before the leaders of the world, what would you say to them?

I would ask them to do something to help the poor, the disenfranchised.

And finally, my last question is in fact one written by Freddie Mercury: If there's a God in the sky, looking down what can he think of what we've done to the world that He created?

When I think of the Lord God, I refer to him as Father God. God is an energy force you can't refer to God as he or she, it's a spiritual energy force. As when you pray it's a meditative energy force and prayer in numbers is even better.

Chris von Rohr

Where do you begin with a rock legend like Chris von Rohr? The man has done just about everything. He is a rock musician, record producer best-selling author and columnist, radio and TV presenter, amongst other things. But he is best known for being a founding member of the hard rock band, Krokus. And yet one rainy afternoon in May, 2021, he somehow managed to squeeze me into his busy schedule.

If you could be any other musician past or present, which one would it be and why?
Well, it would be Mozart. He had it all. To feel, compose and play like him would be another dimension.

If you had to name one song from any genre that really speaks to you, which one would it be and why?
I'm a Sixties child. There are so many great songs that mean a lot to me. From Dylan and over to Hendrix, the Beatles, the Doors, the Who, the Kinks, Procol Harum and Pink Floyd. But one of my all-time favourites remains "Satisfaction" by the Rolling Stones. It's more than a song, it was a movement and it still lifts you up anytime.

Are you a Mulder or Scully? Do you believe aliens have visited planet earth and if so what do you think they think about mankind?
I'm in contact with author Erich von Däniken and he explained to me a lot about UFOs and aliens. For me there are few doubts that they were here and smiled their blue asses off about us. There is so much more between heaven and earth than we know. When I was a young dude I experimented with LSD. It opened a whole new angle to me. Today I see the world in another light.

What was the happiest day of your life and why?
Christmas 1967 when I got the *White Album* by the Beatles and heard it. "While My Guitar Gently Weeps" summed it all up. Outside heavy snowfall, inside a warm cosy atmosphere and the sound of this masterpiece, and I was seventeen and it was a very good year.

If "God" (whatever your idea is on that) were stood before you now, what one question would you ask him/her and why?
I don't believe in a personified God-figure. For me it's rather an energy, an energy of love — God is Love — Love is God.

As an expressive artist in the music industry, how does the state of the planet make you feel?
Well mother earth, the seas and as well the air in a lot of places are in bad shape. We need to feed the soil again and learn that everything is a give and take. But I was never an apocalypse priest. I believe we will find a way to make the world a better place.

Do you think as a person of some influence that there is a duty on us to help influence humanity for the better?
This world can only be changed by example not by words. Everyone of us can do something. I try my best.

What one cause would you say you feel most associated with and why? Whether it's equality, poverty, politics, the environment or other?
I fight for more care, empathy and rights for children. It's a shame how we treat them in this world, our most precious future asset. Instead of learning from them we break them with senseless rules, stress and information. The children are the future of our planet. Let the children play, let them be in peace and give them love and understanding. There's so much coming back! With the animals it's the same, we have to start to respect them fully as creatures that feel just like us pain and stress.

If you were stood before the leaders of the world, what would you say to them?
Quit, you do a miserable job! We need urgently new blood with heart and visions. Most of the leaders in this world just care about their image and maintenance of power. They don't work for the people that elected them — it's a shame.

And finally my last question is in fact one written by Freddie Mercury in the song "Is This the World We Created": If there's a God in the sky, looking down what can he think of what we've done to the world that He created?
There is not a judging God as there is no hell. Hell is on earth created by mankind. Death means transformation and foremost, salvation. Love and peace is the only true currency.

Don Dokken

Sometime in the late 1970s, Don Dokken was a member of the band, Airborne and managed to get a record deal in Germany for a new band. He convinced George Lynch and Mick Brown of Xciter to join him and Dokken was born.

While in Germany he became friends with the members of legendary rock band, Scorpions and rehearsed with them. In 1983 the first Dokken album, Breaking the Chains, was released, followed by Tooth and Nail. Soon Dokken was famous and the rest is history. Apart from the fact that it wasn't quiet, because Don then went on to front a kind of supergroup made up of members of Europe, Watchtower, Motörhead and Scorpions.

I was lucky enough to get an interview with the rock legend, so let the drums roll.

If you could be any other musician past or present, which one would it be and why?
John Lennon because The Beatles were the greatest band in the world.

If you had to name one song from any genre that really speaks to you, which one would it be and why?
Impossible question to answer.

Note: Now come on, surely not.

Are you a Mulder or Scully? Do you believe aliens have visited planet earth and if so what do you think they think about mankind?
Mulder. It's egotistical to think that we are the only intelligent life out of the thousands of universes that exist. I believe they visited earth before modern man existed.

What was the happiest day of your life and why?
The day I signed my first recording contract.

If "God" (whatever your idea is on that) stood before you now, what one question would you ask him/her and why?
If you are omnipresent and have the power to do anything, why aren't you

guiding us into a more peaceful existence? (I understand God gave us free choice; however, it is unfortunate that history has shown that our choices have often been horrific.)

As an expressive artist in the music industry, how does the state of the planet make you feel?
Sad.

Note: You will note that Don is a man of few words. But why go over the top, when one word will suffice?

Do you think as a person of some influence that there is a duty on us to help influence humanity for the better?
No, it is not my duty. I can only bring our music to the masses and try to bring some happiness and light into their life.

What one cause would you say you feel most associated with and why? Whether it's equality, poverty, politics, the environment or other?
This is a two-fold answer: our environment and the destruction we are instilling upon it — and our constant refusal to accept equality in the world.

If you were stood before the leaders of the world, what would you say to them?
Many of you are incompetent and have gained your power through political ma-noeuvring, creating control through fear and violence. However, there are still many of you wonderful people trying to make the world a better place, and while I understand it's a daunting task, you cannot give up.

And finally, my last question is in fact one written by Freddie Mercury: If there's a God in the sky, looking down what can he think of what we've done to the world that He created?
If there is a God in the sky, he would be disappointed and saddened that we took his gift, this beautiful planet and garden of Eden, and while we should be living in a Utopian society — instead we are still being cruel to one another, our planet, our creatures and always hovering on the edge of extinction.

Eric Bell

Quite simply, Eric Bell is the man who founded and played lead guitar for that legendary rock band, Thin Lizzy. But there's so much more to Eric Bell.

Bell started out in the Belfast area of Northern Ireland playing in bands such as Them, famous for having Van Morrison as a member. By 1969 he decided it was time to do his own thing and along with Phil Lynott, Eric Wrixon and Brian Downey he started the band, Thin Lizzy. Because he liked the comic, The Dandy, he chose the name after the robot character, Tin Lizzie.

Soon they had a record deal with Decca and co-wrote many of their hits. But the pressure was on and by 1973 Eric had simply had enough. In the middle of his last concert he threw his guitar in the air, pushed over the speakers and walked off. He said he was exhausted and it was all causing him health problems. He was temporarily replaced with Gary Moore.

Eric wasn't gone for long. In 1974 he started the Eric Bell Band and was also recruited by Noel Redding along with Dave Clark and Les Sampson to form the Noel Redding Band.

In 1980 Thin Lizzy reunited to record a tribute to Jimi Hendrix. Ups and downs, lefts and rights and in the end, Eric Bell has been active ever since those crazy days.

Thankfully he wasn't too busy to talk to me! Although I did have to put some whiskey in the jar.

If you could be any other musician past or present, which one would it be and why?
I would pick Claude Debussy. He sounds totally original. his music is very dreamlike, other worldly, he sounds like he has opened some door in his imagination, very special, very emotional and breaks all the rules. I feel like I've somehow heard his music before like in my childhood. Like standing in a field, in summertime.

If you had to name one song from any genre that really speaks to you, which one would it be and why?
At the moment... it would be "I'm a fool to want you" from Billie Holiday's album, *Lady in Satin*. Her voice, so honest, singing like her life depended on it. Singing from real experience, and the music, the melody, the changes and the orchestration. Really can bring tears to the eye.

Are you a Mulder or Scully? Do you believe aliens have visited planet earth and if so what do you think they think about mankind?

Yes, I sometimes think they might see us as blind insects, all rushing around going nowhere, pushing each other out of the way to get to the top of the tree. But the big one they don't understand I think would be man's need for war, to kill each other from the days of living in caves right up to the present moment. Why!

What was the happiest day of your life and why?
Probably on one of those endless summer days when I was child around eight years old in Ormeau Park in Belfast. Just lying in the grass looking up at the sky, realising I was alive and all the senses clear and the body young and vibrant and being in the moment.

If "God" (whatever your idea is on that) were stood before you now, what one question would you ask him/her and why?
I would ask... what is the purpose of life and when do we find out what it is?

As an expressive artist in the music industry, how does the state of the planet make you feel?
To be honest, I have never had thoughts about the state of the planet, I've always taken for granted that things would carry on. I didn't think that all the resources would start to change, to run out and the way nature is slowly starting to react to us. I would love to help but in the only way I know how... to play special gigs to save the planet.

Do you think as a person of some influence that there is a duty on us to help influence humanity for the better?
Yes, but again I think I could only do it through what I do. Hopefully on a good night some people in the audience might get effected in a positive way by something I play, might inspire them in some way.

What one cause would you say you feel most associated with and why? Whether it's equality, poverty, politics, the environment or other?
My one cause would be doing away with war. Do the idiots at the top not realise that women and innocent children suffer in unbelievable ways? I remember someone saying to me once about letting the men who want the war — put them in a field and let them fight each other and leave it at that no armies, no soldiers, no weapons or stupid flags. Just let the two guys get on with it.

If you were stood before the leaders of the world, what would you say to them?
Again, I would discuss the ignorance and stupidity of war and try and get them to fully realise how long we have been living since the day of living in caves. I would say I don't understand what it is about man from those early days up until the present day that they have to fight and kill.

And finally, my last question is in fact one written by Freddie Mercury: If there's a God in the sky, looking down what can he think of what we've done to the world that He created?
I sometimes wonder why God doesn't step in and help us with all our problems and sufferings. But I believe that statement that God has given us freewill. So that we may learn from our mistakes no matter how long it may take us or how big the price.

Janiva Magness

© Paul Moore

The Blues Foundation named Janiva Magness the B.B. King Entertainer of the Year in 2009, becoming only the second woman, after Koko Taylor, to be so honoured. B. B. King handed her the award himself. In 2014 she released her first album of all originals entitled Original which earned her the award for Song of the Year.

Magness has earned seven Blues Music Awards with 26 similar nominations, and she was also nominated for a Grammy. USA Today stated, "Magness is a blues star." I happen to agree with them and that's why I asked her if she'd answer my questions. She said no, so I sent the boys round and we finally got her to agree. We released her poodle.

If you could be any other musician past or present, which one would it be and why?
Tina Turner & Etta James. I am sure there are more but those two come to mind first. It is very difficult to choose one artist simply because there are so many loves and so many influences over the course of time. Tina and Etta both for the same reasons. They survived their lives and went on to do so much more than what fate handed them. They persisted forward into their own destinies. They have had very large careers and made incredible music. They also refused to be held back by genre, sex or race. I find that not only powerful, but inspirational and deeply beautiful.

If you had to name one song from any genre that really speaks to you, which one would it be and why?
Hahaha there is the ONE choice again! In this moment, I would say "Hard Times Come Again No More" – preferably by Mavis Staples with Matt Rollins & a fantastic ensemble. For me this track encompasses the deep sorrow of the past, beckoning us to not forget life's pleasures, community and all the hope for a brighter future. It holds the full scope of the sad, fragile and beautiful human experience.

Are you a Mulder or Scully?
Scully of course!

Do you believe aliens have visited planet earth and if so what do you think they think about mankind?
Well let me put it this way, I do not deny the possibility. I will admit I have not done tons of research on this subject. I can only imagine what they might think

of humanity. I would hope they see our potential for good and the great need we have to evolve in our behaviour towards each other.

What was the happiest day of your life and why?
Again I am choosing. I believe I am blessed to have many happiest days. Choosing one, professionally speaking is May 8th 2009 — Memphis, Tennessee when BB King called my name as the winner of the BB King Entertainer of the Year Award. In chapter one of my 2019 memoir, *Weeds Like Us*, I lead with this event and the massive impact it has had on me.

If "God" (whatever your idea is on that) were stood before you now, what one question would you ask him/her and why?
Hey God, when can we talk?

As an expressive artist in the music industry, how does the state of the planet make you feel?
Deeply concerned and hopeful at the same time.

Do you think as a person of some influence that there is a duty on us to help influence humanity for the better?
Absolutely. To whom much is given, much will be required. I believe that to my core. I believe I have the debt that can never be repaid.

What one cause would you say you feel most associated with and why? Whether it's equality, poverty, politics, the environment or other?
Youth at Risk, most especially those young people on the streets suffering homelessness, abuse and multiple forms of trauma.

I am Alumni of the Foster Care system and as such, have first-hand experience I can speak to a lot of that. It is critical to use my experience to encourage and hopefully inspire people to keep moving forward. Learning to understand that whatever difficulties they may have had in their own lives, these struggles do NOT have to be the end of the story. They truly can serve as fertiliser for their own life story, into their own victories!

If you were stood before the leaders of the world, what would you say to them?
Get your priorities together NOW! Help people in need. Hold corporations accountable. Tax the super wealthy 1%. Use that tax for the greater good.

And finally, my last question is in fact one written by Freddie Mercury: If there's a God in the sky, looking down what can he think of what we've done to the world that He created?
I believe that God has much hope and many regrets. The greatest regret is what we call "freewill". The greatest hope for us is human connection and what is possible through it. Music/Art is one of those possibilities and I am eternally grateful for both. It is there most often I can feel the presence of God. It holds me and saves me every day.

Ally McErlaine

Ally McErlaine is a founding member and guitarist of the band, Texas. He has also written many songs for other bands and musicians and appeared on numerous albums as a guest.

Texas are a platinum selling Scottish rock band and they're still going strong. Their Greatest Hits album went platinum six times. Thankfully none of this went to his head and he gave up some rock star time to talk to me.

If you could be any other musician past or present, which one would it be and why?
I'd like to have been a fabulous piano player like Franz Liszt, that amazes me, the virtuosity is incredible. Wouldn't want to live at that time in history though.

If you had to name one song from any genre that really speaks to you, which one would it be and why?
There is a song called "Hero" by Family of the Year and the lines:
"While holding down
A job to keep my girl around
Maybe buy me some new strings
And her a night out the weekend."
It speaks to me because I remember when new strings were a luxury item.

Are you a Mulder or Scully? Do you believe aliens have visited planet earth and if so what do you think they think about mankind?
I do believe alien life exists in the universe but don't believe we have been visited. The distances are too vast.

What was the happiest day of your life and why?
Of course, I'm going to say my wedding to the lovely Shelly Poole. Closely followed by Celtic beating Barcelona, 2-1.

Note: Shelly Poole is a member of the pop band, Alisha's Attic and daughter of Brian Poole of The Tremeloes, who you will find in this book! Celtic are a Scottish soccer team who all wear tartan kilts whilst playing.

If "God" (whatever your idea is on that) were stood before you now, what one question would you ask him/her and why?
Why do you allow violence and war when you could easily stop it?

As an expressive artist in the music industry, how does the state of the planet make you feel?
Worried about a lot of things at the moment. Environment is in a bad state but too much energy and time wasted on useless things.

Do you think as a person of some influence that there is a duty on us to help influence humanity for the better?
Yes it's the duty of everyone to spread that message.

Note: Dear reader, this includes you, so get on with it.

What one cause would you say you feel most associated with and why? Whether it's equality, poverty, politics, the environment or other?
Looking after our old folks and also stopping animal cruelty.

If you were stood before the leaders of the world, what would you say to them?
I'd tell them their duty is to protect the world and humanity, and also to always speak the truth which our current government don't do.

Note: Politicians speaking the truth. Nobody knows where this fantasy originated, but it will never come true.

And finally my last question is in fact one written by Freddie Mercury:
If there's a God in the sky, looking down what can he think of what we've done to the world that He created?
I'm afraid I don't believe there is a God looking down, I'm willing to change my mind if science shows any evidence that God exists.

Craig Leon

© Amelia Troubridge

I was really enthused to be in contact with Craig. He's a legend in the world of music, even if it's one of those behind the scenes roles. He is in fact a brilliant composer and record producer who has launched the careers of so many great bands such as The Ramones, Talking Heads and Blondie. The man is smart and has an ear for good music, so I am very pleased to have had a chat with him.

If you could be any other musician past or present, which one would it be and why?

I don't think that I'd want to trade places with anyone. It would be great to have the playing ability of Bach or Professor Longhair, a better knowledge of orchestration and theory at the level of let's say Stravinsky. However what we are is what we get. I'm always working to develop my own talents and abilities. We all have the same ability to tap into the inspiration and drive that has inspired and driven others. Also we have to be careful what you wish for. With the abilities and talent of others comes their foibles and problems. Lots of sci-fi stories bring this point out.

If you had to name one song from any genre that really speaks to you, which one would it be and why?

The obvious knee jerk response is such and such a piece of "classical" or "electronic" music because I'm so immersed in those genres these days but it's not the case. All of those compositions are important to me and many are truly inspiring. But two that come to mind that really speak to me are both from the folk tradition.

The first is "Two Step de Bayou Teche" which is a reworking of an older folk song recording by Armedee Ardoin that was recorded by Austin Pitre and the Evangline Playboys. The main reason is that it makes me feel really good every time I hear it. The song always puts a little lightness into my step. I feel that the purpose of music and the other arts is to create a sense of being in another place or mood than what the listener, viewer, or reader was in before they encountered the work.

The other one is "On Raglan Road" which is a poem by Patrick Kavanagh set to the old Irish air "The Dawning of the Day". It gives the clearest picture that I know of as to why I was first motivated to create. The melody is beautiful as well. I've set it a couple of times.

Note: Having no idea who Craig was talking about I quickly took to google. Hands up if you just did!

Are you a Mulder or Scully? Do you believe aliens have visited planet earth and if so what do you think they think about mankind?

It's extremely likely that aliens have visited this planet. I don't know their mindset so it's hard to conceive of what they would think of mankind. I would assume there would be some curiosity about a new species that they discovered but if their sense of self-importance is anything like mankind's they probably don't think very much about us except how the new batch of organisms could be useful to them. On the other hand they could be more advanced spiritually and think that they could offer some help in clearing the clogged up neurological patterns of the species that they have found. I tend to doubt that though. Remember "How To Serve Man"?

I gave quite a bit of thought to this idea while recording the *The Anthology of Interplanetary Folk Music* which speculates on the folk music inhabitants from another planet based on the teachings and recollections of a West African tribe that has a pretty convincing story of an early series of encounters they had with aliens. They claim that the roots of their ancient religion and culture were given to them by these beings who have attributes of the "angels" in Western folklore and religion. They're quite serious about it as almost all of the art dating back thousands of years depicts only the aliens that made the huge impression on their culture or a map of where they came from.

Note: I have got to get me a copy of that recording.

What was the happiest day of your life and why?

It was actually a week when we were off from the "world" at a place on the ocean in Northern California. My partner in crime, Cassell Webb, who has a marvellously clear singing voice developed a rapport with a whale who was camped out nearby down the cliff in the ocean. Marvellous.

Actually I'm fortunate to have had many happiest days of my life and also fortunate to have had many worst days of my life. Balance is required. Sometimes I subscribe to Theodore Zelden's theory which argues that Happiness is too easily converted into self-satisfaction and complacency. Then again... sometimes I don't.

If "God" (whatever your idea is on that) were stood before you now, what one question would you ask him/her and why?

Nothing? I need to have a definition of what existed before existence. What was the raw material that was used in the process of creation and where was it found when it didn't yet exist? I'm interested in what existed before "our" universe was created but more interested in what existed before anything existed.

As an expressive artist in the music industry, how does the state of the planet make you feel?
Like the man says "same as it ever was". There have always been types who set out to control others and to "profit" from the exploitation and destruction of others and there are always artists and the like to shove their stupidity in their faces. This particular group of ridiculous leaders has led us to the precipice of annihilation (or so we think). Actually just about every generation has those who think that their world mind set is the worst one possible.

Do you think as a person of some influence that there is a duty on us to help influence humanity for the better?
I think that I can inform and point things out but that I actually have very little influence. Some of the people who I've worked with who are more in the popular consciousness have been able to influence society in general for at least a limited period of time. I'm glad to have been associated with them in their efforts.

What one cause would you say you feel most associated with and why? Whether it's equality, poverty, politics, the environment or other?
"Truth, justice and the American way." More specifically the American way as the Euclid inspired originators of the "American" system sought out to do.

If you were stood before the leaders of the world, what would you say to them?
I would point them in the direction of someone like Greta Thunberg. Then point them in the direction of a few ancient books that are relevant to everyday existence and then shut up.

A friend of mine was once asked to lecture at Cambridge University on James Joyce's Work. It was an interesting proposal as he was an alternative rock artist who was known for his irascible nature. He showed up at the lecture hall, sat down at his chair onstage and waved a copy of *Finnegan's Wake* at the audience. He tapped loudly on the cover and said "James Joyce". He then spent the next hour sitting in the chair silently reading the book to himself. After 45 minutes or so he closed the book and walked off the stage. Apparently, it had an effect on the "scholars". I hope that he got paid for the gig.

Note: If anybody would like to pay me to give such a lecture just give me a call, I'm sure I could do that.

And finally, my last question is in fact one written by Freddie Mercury: If there's a God in the sky, looking down what can he think of what we've done to the world that He created?
It's flawed but then what did you expect? Perfection would be very boring.

Dennis DeYoung
Styx

Singer, songwriter, musician and producer, you will remember Dennis as the founding member, lead singer and keyboard player for the rock band, Styx. Out of their eight top ten singles, Dennis wrote seven. He's now got a very successful solo career.

You may note that Dennis entered into the spirit of this book by taking all the questions 100% seriously.

If you could be any other musician past or present, which one would it be and why?
Wishing I were someone else is a dead end. I'd be choosing not knowing the full truth about them, remember I wrote *The Grand Illusion*. I'm comfortable being the same old goof 'cause I am accustomed to my shortcomings.

If you had to name one song from any genre that really speaks to you, which one would it be and why?
Nearly impossible to answer but "Nessun Dorma" always makes me cry and it ain't the lyrics, their in Italian. The power of melody and singers. Writers wrongly focus on lyrics cause that's their bailiwick but people remember the whole melody and forget half the words.

Note: And nobody sleeps when Dennis is around for sure.

Are you a Mulder or Scully? Do you believe aliens have visited planet earth and if so what do you think they think about mankind?
I'm more of a Sculder. Aliens most certainly are here... you should meet my uncle Sal.

Note: Somebody please abduct me.

What was the happiest day of your life and why?
I haven't had it yet, although I really enjoyed a fennel sausage pizza I had Christmas Eve in 1962 at Giovanni's pizzeria in Chicago. Thin crust, very thin.

If "God" (whatever your idea is on that) were stood before you now, what one question would you ask him/her and why?

I'd ask why are we here? God? Aliens? I need some of what you're smokin'. I have written songs about my desire to believe in a benevolent higher power but always with a healthy dose of scepticism. We believe because we feel powerless and without control and hope someone or something is way smarter than us. My question would be why us?

Note: Smoking is bad for you kids.

As an expressive artist in the music industry, how does the state of the planet make you feel?

The same way un-expressive people not in the music industry feel, very, very concerned even if I'm the CEO of an oil company. Question them on truth serum.

Note: Oh yes please.

Do you think as a person of some influence that there is a duty on us to help influence humanity for the better?

Have a duty no. My duty is like the Hippocratic oath "first do no harm". If we all try that, things could be better.

What one cause would you say you feel most associated with and why? Whether it's equality, poverty, politics, the environment or other?

Cause how this... do unto others, that a very worthwhile cause.

If you were stood before the leaders of the world, what would you say to them?

I would tell these leaders that no matter how high they climb they're still aren't going to feel that their parents loved them enough.

And finally, my last question is in fact one written by Freddie Mercury: If there's a God in the sky, looking down what can he think of what we've done to the world that He created?

I like Freddie but why him? God certainly doesn't need any questions from musicians. We're not that important. I know I've tried and I'm still on hold.

© Greg Weight

Reg Mombassa
Mental As Anything
(as you will see)

Well let's start by saying that Reg Mombass doesn't actually exist and no he's not a figment of my imagination. The name is in fact a nickname given to him by members of the band he founded, Mental As Anything. The band has had numerous top records, but for me the pinnacle for anybody is to have one of their songs featured in Crocodile Dundee.

Reg is actually also a very famous and respected artist, but I am not remotely jealous of his talent. He is a wonderful, funny and generous man who promised me one of his priceless paintings, so I let him appear in the book.

If you could be any other musician past or present, which one would it be and why?

Although it is perhaps an obvious and easy choice for someone who likes American folk and roots-based music it would have to be Bob Dylan. In my opinion he is the most influential musician of the 20th century. Elvis Presley might be more handsome and have nicer hair, but he didn't write his own songs, and John Lennon was probably more persistently politically active and engaged with the world but his tragic relatively early death limited the volume of his output.

Also, it would be desirable to be as smart as Bob Dylan. After reading his memoir, *Chronicles* and listening to the Bob Dylan *Theme Time Radio Hour* recordings he is obviously super smart with a prodigious memory and an astonishing knowledge and understanding of music art literature and popular culture.

Although I'm not sure if I believe in such concepts, he is probably some sort of shamanic avatar. Having said that, he exhibits the imperfections that all humans are prone to. The sometimes slightly spiteful crankiness, moral certainty and wilful obscurity present in his songs and writings and interviews can be unattractive. Then again, you have to excuse any aggressive paranoia from someone who has been so famous and so influential for so long.

If you had to name one song from any genre that really speaks to you, which one would it be and why?

As reluctant as I am to choose the best of anything I will select "Waterloo Sunset" by the Kinks. It has poetic 'ordinary life' and 'fondness for your locality' lyrics, a beautiful melody and a great arrangement that kicks off with a typical Kinks descending bassline and catchy guitar lines and solo from Dave Davies.

The mid-sixties is a particularly rich period of English pop with a succession of fantastic singles from The Beatles, The Rolling Stones, The Hollies, The Small Faces, The Kinks, The Animals, The Troggs, Them etc. Two other fine fondly reflecting on your childhood neighbourhood songs are "Penny Lane" and "Strawberry Fields Forever" by the Beatles.

Are you a Mulder or Scully? Do you believe aliens have visited planet earth and if so what do you think they think about mankind?

Yes I do think aliens exist and they have visited this planet. The universe is too vast and old for a race as violent irrational and self-destructive as ours to be the only sentient beings to exist. I do not believe that alien lizard creatures live under the mountains and secretly govern the earth or run pizza shop pederast rings. When you study the output of the UFO community it obviously attracts a lot of cranks, nutcases, liars, and attention seeking opportunists, but enough credible people have observed strange craft in our skies and other inexplicable phenomena for it not to be probably true.

I have heard the theory that the Earth is a prison planet for bad souls from elsewhere in the universe. I am not sure if I believe that theory but when you study our history and the present situation on earth perhaps it is the case. If true you would hope to have a cell on the sunny side of the prison planet and perhaps to have the possibility of finding some redemption or forgiveness for our many sins.

What was the happiest day of your life and why?

I have difficulty choosing the best highest or happiest of anything, but I would say the happiest days were the birth of my children. But that is three days, not one. I would prefer to choose a year and that would be 1975. It was when I met my future wife, had my first art show and began playing with the band that would become Mental as Anything.

If "God" (whatever your idea is on that) were stood before you now, what one question would you ask him/her and why?

Why did you invent the concept of suffering? I've never quite understood the sanctimonious platitude that suffering makes you stronger. A second question for a God would be why didn't you make them accept Hitler into the Viennese art school he was attempting to enrol in. He might have ended up as a cranky and bigoted old art teacher in a rural Austrian high school rather than a genocidal maniac in control of a powerful nation. And why do cats' faces have only one expression? And because humans are approaching the status of gods as we become capable of curing disease, prolonging life and creating A. I. robots, we can ask those questions of ourselves.

As an expressive artist in the music industry, how does the state of the planet make you feel?

Anxious, sad, fearful, angry! It is possibly too late to avoid a catastrophic increase in global temperature; we still have thousands of nuclear weapons in the hands of all these belligerent nation states; our persistently wilful tendency to over populate and the constant growth paradigm of ruthless capitalism is stripping the world of its resources, wild animals and wilderness areas; digital surveillance capitalism has subverted our right to privacy and computers and the Internet have made our lives busier, more complicated, and more prone to anxiety. We flounder and drown in a tsunami of pointless information and over communication. The idea that technology and robots would make our lives easier and reduce our workload was a miserable misperception.

That is a rather gloomy list of some of the problems confronting the world, but you have to hope that the persistent ingenuity and ability to solve problems of the human race will eventually prevail. But to achieve that we need to get on a little better. Unless we can transform our consciousness away from the constant bitter competition and conflict paradigm we may be doomed to extinction. I'm not sure how to achieve that. Genetic manipulation can be questionable so maybe we can just think our way into a better future. A future where we have jettisoned the ridiculous belief systems and stubborn adherence to the traditional wilful idiocy and ignorance that fuels so much conflict and bad policy.

Note: Personally, I think we're doomed and might as well just give up.

Do you think as a person of some influence that there is a duty on us to help influence humanity for the better?

I've never been convinced that art or music has the power to change people's minds to any great extent. It may reinforce or clarify positive or progressive ideas for people that already believe them, but it rarely converts those that believe the opposite. Much of our art and music reflects on the beauty of the world or on the cheerier aspects of human culture, and that is a positive influence. And much of the beauty of art and music is that it has no rules — duty sounds a bit like a rule or the right wing philosophy of duty, sacrifice, glory, patriotism, honour, etc.

What one cause would you say you feel most associated with and why? Whether it's equality, poverty, politics, the environment or other?

Those are all good causes. I am not a political activist. Any reference to these causes in my work derives from providing some subject matter; or thinking about those things creates the irritation anxiety or anger that can inspire you to create something.

Having said that, I admire political activists, it is a noble profession. I lack the courage and generosity of these brave and decent people, particularly those that agitate organise and protest in countries or localities with oppressive theocratic or totalitarian governments. They are often beaten killed or imprisoned for these activities. I have made some small contributions to some of those causes in terms of providing artwork for t-shirts and posters or for fundraisers. Mostly to do with the environment.

That is probably the most immediate problem that confronts the human race, and it affects everybody. Even those of us fortunate enough to live in prosperous countries with stable governments can see the increasing climatic instability; can see the expanding suburbs and poisoned waterways and the receding forests; and can smell and taste the dirt and soot and chemicals that are fouling the air.

If you were stood before the leaders of the world, what would you say to them?

Why do you insist on tormenting your own citizens? And to those who aren't actually slaughtering or falsely imprisoning their own people, why are your policies generally focused on your re-election and furthering the interests of powerful individuals and corporations rather than constructing a better world for all people?

And finally my last question is in fact one written by Freddie Mercury:
If there's a God in the sky, looking down what can he think of what we've done to the world that He created?

If there is a God in the sky contemplating our various activities, I would assume he/she/they would be somewhat disappointed in us. We have fouled our own nest. We have allowed the patriarchal bullies to establish and maintain hierarchical systems of control and dominance that are cruel unjust and destructive. The most aggressive selfish and violent men with their hideously bloated egos have always contrived to steal the land property labour, sexual integrity and right to self-determination of everyone else.

It is always unsettling to see photographs and footage of the millions of soldiers in the world parading proudly with their ridiculous uniforms and medals and weapons, geed up and distorted by their military training and the relentless propaganda about patriotism sacrifice honour and glory. These are the over excited indoctrinated young men who will be tricked into slaughtering each other by yet another generation of horrible old alpha males.

Note: Dude, I love you.

John Waite
Bad English

John is legendary in the world of rock. He started out as lead singer and bassist for the English rock band, The Babys, with some success. He then moved solo and started to hit big.

As a solo artist, he has released ten studio albums and had a global hit in 1984 with the single "Missing You", which reached No. 1 on the US Billboard Hot 100 and knocked Tina Turner off the top slot. She took revenge and later recorded the song herself. After all this success he then moved on to front the supergroup, Bad English, and found even more, topping the charts again. He's even been in Ringo Starr's All-Star Band. And now he's gone one better than all of that and appeared in this book.

If you could be any other musician past or present, which one would it be and why?
Jimi Hendrix is still a major influence in my life. His work is still cutting edge. No one has even come close. What he achieved and made possible on the electric guitar has never been overtaken. If I could be inside his world for an hour I'd learn something game changing even though he died fifty years ago. Who else could you say that about?

Note: Me, of course.

If you had to name one song from any genre that really speaks to you, which one would it be and why?
There are thousands of songs that have stayed with me over the years. Music seeps into your everyday decisions. One of them would be "Fast Car" by Tracy Chapman. It's beautifully written. The message is existential. It's a pop song with an unblinking view of life of the poor trapped in the system.

Are you a Mulder or Scully? Do you believe aliens have visited planet earth and if so what do you think they think about mankind?
I had dinner with Jimmy Carter a couple of years ago and found the presence of mind to ask if he knew anything about Roswell. He said there was nothing to all the rumours but that he'd seen a UFO with his own eyes. I believed him. There must be life everywhere in the stars.

Note: Yeah, Donald Trump said the same thing to me (as I was being chased off the Whitehouse lawn.)

What was the happiest day of your life and why?
When I was seventeen I took LSD. I had the whole experience over about eighteen hours. It was an ecstatic trip. What I took from it influenced the rest of my life.

If "God" (whatever your idea is on that) were stood before you now, what one question would you ask him/her and why?
I'm agnostic. Whatever is going on here is beyond human understanding. Religion seems to spark violence. Not my thing baby!

As an expressive artist in the music industry, how does the state of the planet make you feel?
I kind of wonder if we're actually evolving. Humanity just keeps repeating itself. Someone once said, "history doesn't repeat itself but it rhymes sometimes". That about sums it up.

Do you think as a person of some influence that there is a duty on us to help influence humanity for the better?
It's hard not to take sides these days. The system is flawed. We are flawed. All you can suggest is to be compassionate. That comes with wisdom. It takes a lifetime to gain wisdom so it's always ongoing.

Note: Well some of us are born with it. Just saying.

What one cause would you say you feel most associated with and why? Whether it's equality, poverty, politics, the environment or other?
The UN seems to be the only way to control war. We should all support the UN.

If you were stood before the leaders of the world, what would you say to them?
A lot of world leaders are gangsters. Politicians always seem to be open to corruption. Once in a while a "man of the people" comes along and we all feel inspired by his/her message. If I could I'd put everyone in the same room and blast out "What's So Funny Bout Peace Love And Understanding". Works for me!

And finally my last question is in fact one written by Freddie Mercury:
If there's a God in the sky, looking down what can he think of what we've done to the world that He created?
If there is meaning to existence it would behove us to live together without violence. To treat all the animals we share the planet with respectfully. War solves nothing. Violence is redundant. If Jesus returned I think he would be bemused by what we've done with religion. The money lenders are definitely in the temple.

Ian Gillan
Deep Purple

© Tommaso Mei

How on Earth do I introduce a rock legend like Ian Gillan. Well I suppose I could say, Ian Gillan is a rock legend. See, now that wasn't so hard.

Gillan is one of the things you can point to when you say England has many things to be proud of — we have Ian Gillan, so there. He is a profound singer-songwriter and probably best known as the front man for Deep Purple. Yes youngsters, there's a band called Deep Purple, go and type it into your zombie phone and see what comes back. When you hear those banshee screams coming out of the tiny speaker then you have heard Ian Gillan.

His first initial success came in that auspicious year, 1969, when he joined Purple. He stayed until 1973 but came back with his own Ian Gillan Band and then had a year as the lead singer of Black Sabbath. Eventually Deep Purple reformed and had two more big albums before he left again in 1989. Four years later, yep you got it, he returned, and has been the lead singer ever since.

There is so much more to Gillan, such as his business and charity ventures, but we all know and love him for his music. But what about aliens? I asked him.

If you could be any other musician past or present, which one would it be and why?
Cliff Bennet because; apart from my admiration for his voice, my teenage dream was to front The Rebel Rousers.

If you had to name one song from any genre that really speaks to you, which one would it be and why?
It must be two. "You're Gonna Ruin Me Baby" by Lazy Lester. Three easy chords and a simple song that taught me how to tell a story and sing my words. And "Armonias del Romane" by Tomatito because it gets me thinking more than any other piece of music; even Chopin's Mazurkas.

Are you a Mulder or Scully? Do you believe aliens have visited planet earth and if so what do you think they think about mankind?
To take an angular view at these myths or realities, it would help to read *Flatland* (1884) by Edwin Abbott and look at the bit where — in a two dimensional world

79

— Mr Square meets a sphere but can only see him as a high priest. We'd be sooner rewarded by trying to discover what an ant thinks of humanity.

What was the happiest day of your life and why?

Nice timing, I've been scribbling anecdotes and I'd like to share one which answers this question better than any of the others you've given me: I'm an eight-year-old boy at a large family gathering in Calne, Wiltshire 1953. Christmas dinner was memorable. We kids were seated in the parlour adjoining the crowded dining room where every seat was taken by the adults. After a real feast with all the trimmings we lined up again when dessert was delivered ceremonially to the table. The lights were turned off to better see the Christmas pudding soaked with brandy and all aflame that was set down next to a huge bowl of hot custard adorned with a sprig of holly.

Directly above, sellotaped to the ceiling, was a bunch of balloons. I looked up to see the *Sellotape* drying and curling away because of the heat from the flaming pudding. The balloons became detached and floated down as I watched in awe. Nothing could be done as one of the balloons landed directly upon the holly and exploded with a spectacular result. The contents erupted from the bowl and scattered outwards, splattering everyone with custard. Excellent.

The seating arrangements were the same for breakfast on Boxing Day. As we lined up again to have our plates filled, my Uncle Ivor picked up the ketchup and failed to notice that the lid was not screwed on properly when he began to shake the bottle vigorously, setting up a repeat version of the day before. The outcome was identical in every way except red not yellow. Brilliant.

It was the happiest day of my life; never surpassed.

If "God" (whatever your idea is on that) were stood before you now, what one question would you ask him/her and why?

My idea of God is Mother Nature and her great prophet Darwin through the door of Zen. She satisfies all my logical and spiritual needs; more importantly there's no nonsense about Her. For an obvious reason there is no point asking her a question and if it's not obvious I will happily explain, upon request.

As an expressive artist in the music industry, how does the state of the planet make you feel?

A lot of us — including our hero Nobel prize winner — have been writing ominous stuff about this for half a century. But now because we have, through our phones, some kind of ethereal global consciousness it may be possible to breathe for a while through fast action until — to survive — we are able to moderate our presence in this over-populated home of ours.

Other than with malice, we humans cannot kill or cull ourselves; it's just not in us, even for survival, until maybe it is too late. So, we had better find a way to live with a smaller community and make better of limited resources. It seems unwise for a parasite to kill its host.

Do you think as a person of some influence that there is a duty on us to help influence humanity for the better?
Nah... we all have a part to play. Each spoken thought creates a ripple, and the ripple becomes a swirl that meets an eddy and joins a flow that might surge or fall or bounce off a cultural wall. It's always been that way and often it is a fashionably bad idea that catches on.

What one cause would you say you feel most associated with and why? Whether it's equality, poverty, politics, the environment or other?
They are all related — I am fascinated and involved. God — Mother Nature and her great prophet Darwin — hallelujah, raise a glass to them both — shows that equality does not and cannot exist... maybe for one second, until a pickpocket gets us moving again.

A poor person can be wealthy in non-material ways (Mahatma Gandhi); poverty is subject to ethos; too complex an issue to address here, and popular analysis will keep you up all night.

Politics is suffering from Left/Right stalemate and a plague of poohbahs in a castle full of rascals. But I do prefer a rascal to a dullard who sees nothing but grey in the spectrum of life.

If you were stood before the leaders of the world, what would you say to them?
Lend us a quid, I can spend it better than you.

And finally, my last question is in fact one written by Freddie Mercury: If there's a God in the sky, looking down what can he think of what we've done to the world that He created?
God bless Freddie. My God has no feelings and no other function except to exist. Humans are inseparable from other species and our perceived dominance should be self-examined and tempered as we evolve. After all, we should not be fighting each other for survival; or should we?

Vinnie Kilduff
U2, Clannad, Waterboys

Vinnie loves to blow his own whistle. From U2 to Sinead O'Connor, The Waterboys to Clannad, the name Vinnie Kilduff has long been subtly synonymous with the cutting edge of contemporary Irish music.

Equally comfortable playing a small session or a sold-out stadium, the genre-hopping, multi-instrumentalist from County Mayo has worked with practically all the big names. But he managed to find time to talk to me.

If you could be any other musician past or present, which one would it be and why?
A few Poets/Musicians that stand out for me over the years are Bob Dylan, Van Morrison and Jim Morrison [The Doors] but its an endless list really.

If you had to name one song from any genre that really speaks to you, which one would it be and why?
"Jokerman" by Bob Dylan. It says it all and makes you listen!

Are you a Mulder or Scully? Do you believe aliens have visited planet earth and if so what do you think they think about mankind?
Probably a Scully! Yes, I think we have had visits! If I was an intelligent alien I think I would be scratching my head.

What was the happiest day of your life and why?
My first day in a professional recording studio with a rock and roll band! The place I am most at home!

If "God" (whatever your idea is on that) were stood before you now, what one question would you ask him/her and why?
Why did you create such a cruel and unequal world?

As an expressive artist in the music industry, how does the state of the planet make you feel?
Very sad. What have we done? We have made a mess of the place. We have

shaped our own destiny. So much to blame for this like religion, money, greed, politics.

Religion has divided so many people, countries, communities. How many gods are there to believe in when they keep telling you "there is only one God"? Why do we constantly insist on pushing our children into individual beliefs? Let them learn from life and learn to live together.

Our population increase is now over the brink and the planet will not be able sustain this!

Do you think as a person of some influence that there is a duty on us to help influence humanity for the better?
Yes! There is a duty on everyone and we need to start with the list in my previous answer. The Covid-19 restrictions should be a lesson/vision of what's to come. As stated in the *New York Times* — A dress rehearsal for climate change.

What one cause would you say you feel most associated with and why? Whether it's equality, poverty, politics, the environment or other?
All of them — one hundred years ago the Earth's population was around 1.9 billion people. Today its 7.8 billion. This increase needs to be seriously stabilised or nothing will be manageable.

With politics I think if everything continues on a downward curve governments will be forced into working together when it's too late. governments need to seriously start working together now to save the environment and the planet.

If you were stood before the leaders of the world, what would you say to them?
Shame on all of you, especially those of you who want to divide and conquer!

And finally, my last question is in fact one written by Freddie Mercury: If there's a God in the sky, looking down what can he think of what we've done to the world that He created?
If there's a God who is responsible for us then that God created what we've done! I just cannot see it any other way or give any other answer! In religion class in school we were led to believe, "God knows everything"

The idea of a God for me is hard to imagine. Of course I would have lots of questions for him on what I know now. I don't think a good God would create such a cruel place for mankind to exist.

Jeff Wayne

© Brian Aris

I have to admit something right now. When I heard that Jeff Wayne was going to be part of this little book of mine, I almost fell over. I have very fond memories of listening again and again to War of the Worlds as a child. And then as a teenager. And then as the old man I am now. It never fails to give me chills. It is quite simply a work of musical art and I got to interview the legend who created it. But there is so much more to Jeff Wayne than War of the Worlds. He has written pop songs, thousands of TV jingles that you would all recognise and so much more. But enough of that, what did he think about aliens?

If you could be any other musician past or present, which one would it be and why?

Mozart. Melodies and emotions that soar — and whether it was a 'small work', or an opera, he could write it all. And considering he composed his first symphony at age 8 and his debut opera age 12 — that's not bad going!

It's always hard, perhaps impossible, to truly make comparisons between a 'great' from one era to another; whether in music, or in any other area of life, like sport — 'would Joe Louis have beaten Muhammed Ali?', much less comparisons of those from centuries apart.

But when you consider Amadeus lived in an age when he only could compose and play by candlelight, with no electricity to plug modern equipment and computers into, and of course no record or publishing company to promote you worldwide, his accomplishments are astounding — perhaps proving that it is soul above all that prevails.

And if he was alive today, I'm sure he'd be highly appreciated around the world and collecting awards from all areas of the contemporary world. And while, of course, I could list many other composer/songwriters, that move me incredibly, Johann Chrysostom Wolfgang Amadeus Mozart still stands supreme.

Go Mo!

If you had to name one song from any genre that really speaks to you, which one would it be and why?

There are, of course, countless songs of genius, from so many genres and ages from composers all over the world. And it's all so very personal too, often subject to the mood we might be in at that moment in time.

But the song I'll go with, is the late Leonard Cohen's "Hallelujah". To me, it's very special and one that I've heard performed in many ways, yet no matter the interpretation, it always lifts my spirits.

Hallelujah for Mr. Cohen.

Are you a Mulder or Scully? Do you believe aliens have visited planet earth and if so what do you think they think about mankind?

They were great characters from a classic TV series. But actually, I'm neither because I'm of the mindset of an agnostic — proof always needed first.

Therefore, the best I can offer is to 'guess' as to what an alien might think of mankind — and I'd expect that he/she/it would find our planet *very* troubled along with its occupants. Once realised, I suspect they'd move on as quickly as possible hoping to find some other planet to Earth, far less alien.

ULLA!

What was the happiest day of your life and why?

Being born. With birth giving me life to unravel.

If "God" (whatever your idea is on that) were stood before you now, what one question would you ask him/her and why?

How do I know you're God?

As an expressive artist in the music industry, how does the state of the planet make you feel?

I can't imagine anyone who has chosen to be an artist of any kind, not being influenced by the world we live and bringing it into their work.

The planet has always produced a multitude of events that make us laugh, cry, celebrate or terrorise. Today we all live in a technological age where information about such events are relayed to us instantly, rather than perhaps arriving so late the impact is far less, or never even knowing about their happenings.

Over my life, my style of expressing myself artistically, has also changed — I no longer compose and score by 'hand', writing very little out, but using computers and software to assist me. My output is faster and also quite different from even 10 years ago, and comparing with when I started, it's unrecognisable.

But at the same time, the tools I use to create are just the product of our times, and I believe (or at least hope) that my soul hasn't changed, other than it's older, and what I create is still inspired by people and events from the past, and right up to the present.

Do you think as a person of some influence that there is a duty on us to help influence humanity for the better?

Like everyone, I'm aware of world-wide achievers from many walks of life, who give of their time for a particular cause. I also think there's a very fine line solely for achieving something in their professional life and representing an important cause, unless that person is actively involved within it.

Sure, it's comforting to see a household name, a beautiful person, or a high achiever from an area of life — like sport, the arts etc, fronting a TV spot or social media clip, hearing a radio ad or reading a press article aimed at gaining the widest possible support because of their participation.

But anything further, I'd like to be assured that the person representing that cause, truly knows the subject, and isn't just reading a script, and more importantly, has a genuine participation beyond that promotion.

What one cause would you say you feel most associated with and why? Whether it's equality, poverty, politics, the environment or other?

Looking back, I've been a member of CORE (Congress on Racial Equality) when I was in college in California in the 1960s, and since 1992, I've been aligned with The LTA Trust before it changed its name in 1997 to The Dan Maskell Trust, in honour of the BBC's 'voice of tennis'. I've also been a Patron to HAD (Hertfordshire Against Disability) for many years.

Both organisations provide care and attention to those disabled, and because tennis has been my sport since the age of 5, I've always felt that contributing in various ways through that sport was a natural association for me.

If you were stood before the leaders of the world, what would you say to them?

Hello! Oh, and by the way, how do you feel as our world leaders as to why humanity is still fighting, invading, destroying, and hating, just as much as from the beginning of time when humans were more like wild beasts. Only the names have changed, but so little has truly progressed.

That doesn't mean the world hasn't evolved for the better, because of course it has, and we as human beings are also able to love, laugh and learn while so much that is bad prevails in parallel.

But it does seem that it's almost impossible to expect a unified response from world leaders even from the world organisations that are meant to bring the world closer together, with actions, not platitudes needed.

Are you proud of what you have achieved? Or ashamed? Scorecards please: The Ordinary Man: 10. The Leaders of Our World: 0.35

And finally my last question is in fact one written by Freddie Mercury in the song "Is This the World We Created": If there's a God in the sky, looking down what can he think of what we've done to the world that He created?

Freddie Mercury was without doubt, a very special writer, artist and performer. Unique in every way he approached his art and what he wrote has reached so many people worldwide.

But the song and the lyrics you have asked me to comment about, leads me back to your question No. 5 — about the existence of God.

And with respect, my answer is... I have no comment! Not at least until there is absolute proof that God does exist. Otherwise, to me it's just blind faith, and I don't really see much value in that.

Until then I have to remain believing that the world we live in, with all that is great and tragic, has all been created by ourselves, Humankind.

For the moment then — WE are the Champions.

Kyle Vincent

Barry Manilow said of Kyle Vincent: "One of the best singer-songwriters to come along since the heyday of Tin Pan Alley"

Kyle is a classically trained musician, writing, singing, playing saxophone, guitar and piano. I know, he's just showing off. That's what pop stars do. His history is a good one. He was in the pop band, Candy, which, incidentally, also had Guns N' Roses star Gilby Clarke as a member. I'm sure Gilby is over the moon about being reminded of that fact.

After signing to Disney and releasing an album there was no turning back because fame beckoned. But above all of that of course, he then joined the Bay City Rollers for a US tour. You just can't beat that can you. Anyway, things got even better for him when he had me asking him questions.

If you could be any other musician past or present, which one would it be and why?
I would never want to be anyone else. I don't have the time or energy to take over someone else's issues; I'm too busy with my own. Then again, might be pretty cool to see what it was like to be Elton John on his '75 stadium tour, or McCartney running on stage at Shea. Or one of the Temptations so I could learn their dance moves. But before long I'd want to come back to being just me on my little farm.

If you had to name one song from any genre that really speaks to you, which one would it be and why?
"Me & Mrs. Jones", because I always have a "thing going on."

Are you a Mulder or Scully? Do you believe aliens have visited planet earth and if so what do you think they think about mankind?
As to the first part, I don't know what that is.

Note: Obviously Kyle is an alien himself. How else can you not know who Mulder or Scully is?

As for aliens, no, I don't think critters from another planet have visited Earth, the odds are so against that. Why, out of the entire universe, would any little green thing choose to visit our minuscule orb? However, I do know several people who I am convinced must be from another galaxy, so perhaps I need to rethink this.

Note: Names Kyle, we want names.

What was the happiest day of your life and why?

When I ran onto the stage at Shea in 1965. Oh wait, that was just a dream. I know it sounds trite, but honestly, every day that I wake up healthy and hopeful, is a happy day. They're not all that way, but I'm lucky to have a chip inside me that keeps hope alive.

Note: Can I borrow it?

As an expressive artist in the music industry, how does the state of the planet make you feel?

I would hope that everyone, regardless of what they do in life, is well aware of the condition into which we have put ourselves. I've been an advocate for the environment and its creatures since I was a child; I've written about it in songs, and I try and live as conscientiously a compassionate a life as I can. That purpose defines me and guides me, but it certainly can present a real struggle to not be overwhelmed by it all.

Do you think as a person of some influence that there is a duty on us to help influence humanity for the better?

Artists and others in the public eye hold powerful tools in their arsenal to affect change, and while it's tempting to preach on stage and in song, for me I think I just try to express a compassionate approach to the world, and hope that will help, even if only in some small way. I'm not sure people look to artists to guide their path, but if they do, I'm ready for the job of Humanity Tour Guide!

What one cause would you say you feel most associated with and why? Whether it's equality, poverty, politics, the environment or other?

I was born and raised in Berkeley, California, ground zero for political struggles at a time of great societal strife and change. My parents were extremely involved in all sorts of causes and movements, so I have activism in my DNA, and also in my real-life experiences from the time I was born. Most of the critical issues facing humanity are intertwined, with the climate emergency certainly being the most globally dire, because if we lose that battle, none of the others matter. But for someone who is simply worrying about whether or not they will have food today, whether we drive an electric car or change a light bulb is trivial — so while we need to address multiple issues at once, we also need to prioritise.

Manfred Mann

© Ron Kroon

Okay, so here's one of those short, nice bite-sized reads for you. Manfred Mann is a band isn't it? Well yes and no. It was a rock band, formed in London in the 1960s. The name came from the keyboard player, singer and songwriter, Manfred Mann. Although Manfred Mann (the band not the man) disbanded in 1969, it emerged again in the 1970s as Manfred Mann's Earth Band, following a brief jazz-rock dalliance as Manfred Mann Chapter Three.

You will know their hits of course. "Do Wah Diddy Diddy", and Bruce Springsteen's "Blinded By The Light". But do you know what Manfred Mann thinks about God? I do. Read on.

If you could be any other musician past or present, which one would it be and why?
I am not sure any of them had great lives, so none really. But if you mean quality, probably the one that most awes me is Bach. In jazz, early Miles Davis. In blues, Keb Mo. In Pop, Taylor Swift.

What was the happiest day of your life and why?
I don't believe in happiness, but I do believe in moments of joy, and I have had them most of my life.

If "God" (whatever your idea is on that) were stood before you now, what one question would you ask him/her and why?
Why is there no limit to stupidity?

As an expressive artist in the music industry, how does the state of the planet make you feel?
The question assumes that musicians somehow have a different insight into these questions, musicians are no different to anyone else. A percentage are good people, bad people, assholes and saints, no different to non-musicians.

Do you think as a person of some influence that there is a duty on us to help influence humanity for the better?
Any musician who really thinks that they are in a position of influence, outside of fashion is deluding themselves. But there is no bigger word than kindness

What one cause would you say you feel most associated with and why? Whether it's equality, poverty, politics, the environment or other?

There is no cause or belief so good that if taken to extreme is dangerous, and I see good causes every day taken over by fanatics. The best causes sometimes have some really bad people riding along on the wave, and the goodness of the cause, obscures the insanity.

And finally, my last question is in fact one written by Freddie Mercury: If there's a God in the sky, looking down what can he think of what we've done to the world that He created?

If there is a God in the sky, he/she probably is not thinking about us at all. The universe is way too big.

Peter Noone
Herman's Hermits

Yeah, that Peter Noone. Seriously. Herman's Hermits had so many hits you just have to go and look for yourself because I'm tired of typing. They existed alongside the other greats like The Beatles, The Kinks, The Who and, well you get the picture. Fully part of the British invasion. The one that didn't involve tanks and bombers. For years in the sixties, the Hermits were constantly in the top billboard charts. And blow me but I only got to interview the voice of Herman's Hermits!

If you could be any other musician past or present, which one would it be and why?
I think Louis Armstrong because he was the real thing and always enjoyed playing music.

If you had to name one song from any genre that really speaks to you, which one would it be and why?
"I Wish I Could Shimmy Like My Sister Kate". One good version is Frances Faye. Fun and bright and I never made a dance song, and this was one that made my mum and dad dance.

Note: All together now… shimmy. Dude, what's a shimmy?

Are you a Mulder or Scully? Do you believe aliens have visited planet earth and if so what do you think they think about mankind?
I am just a human from humans. Just minding my own little world one day at a time.

Note: Have you ever considered politics Peter? Evasion tactics like that would go a long way.

What was the happiest day of your life and why?
I'm hoping it's tomorrow and a surprise.

Note: Amen to that.

If "God" (whatever your idea is on that) were stood before you now, what

one question would you ask him/her and why?
Hiya G-d. Why did you choose me for all the good luck?

Note: Now if we could all say that!

As an expressive artist in the music industry, how does the state of the planet make you feel?
I am just a wayfarer. I hope to leave no damage behind!

Do you think as a person of some influence that there is a duty on us to help influence humanity for the better?
Yes and first they should all believe me when I tell them I'm Henry VIII.

Note: We believe you Peter. Nurse!

What one cause would you say you feel most associated with and why? Whether it's equality, poverty, politics, the environment or other?
I like the Salvation Army because they try to get people back to life! I have seen a few successes which make me happy for the soldiers there!

If you were stood before the leaders of the world, what would you say to them?
Politics is show business for ugly people and you aren't that ugly so how did you get involved?

Note: Dear Prime Minister, don't worry, you're ugly enough.

And finally, my last question is in fact one written by Freddie Mercury: If there's a God in the sky, looking down what can he think of what we've done to the world that He created?
My answer denies the Fifth Amendment. I hope I don't leave any damage. I have improved over time. One thing is sure "I am just the lead singer, everything you ask me to fix will end up more broken".

Maja Shining
Forever Still

Probably one of the youngest music stars in this book, Maja is lead singer of the popular Danish modern rock band, Forever Still. This is a current band with critically acclaimed albums and have performed concerts across the world. I just love their natural, earthy style and the fact they strive for animal rights and am so pleased Maja could spare the time to answer my questions.

If you could be any other musician past or present, which one would it be and why?

I would love to be in Björk's brilliant mind for a day! She has made some really inspirational music that has pushed a lot of boundaries and genre limitations accompanied by unusual and innovative visuals and it often comes with a message. She has always challenged what people have come to expect of her and hasn't been afraid to stand up for the things she believes in like feminist values and the environment to name a few. Not neglecting to mention all the things she can do with her unique and emotional voice, which still amazes me to this day. I love an artist that, when you hear them, you could never mistake them for somebody else. That's Björk to me.

Note: Bjork is that little squeely voiced one, not a member of Abba.

If you had to name one song from any genre that really speaks to you, which one would it be and why?

I'm not a person who has "all time favourites", there's way too much amazing music in the world for me to get stuck on this one track or one album. The latest song that really hit me and awakened something in me the very first time I heard it was "Borders" from Norwegian band Kalandra. It's largely vocal based and hauntingly beautiful.

Are you a Mulder or Scully? Do you believe aliens have visited planet earth and if so what do you think they think about mankind?

Having never watched *The X-Files*, I can't give a thorough answer to this question, but with the little knowledge I have of the characters, I'd probably be

95

a good mix of both. I do believe there are more things in heaven and earth than what we can see. But I'm a big believer in science in general.

Going with that I think it's highly unrealistic that we're alone in the Universe. The Universe is vast though, so whether aliens have found us yet or not, I cannot say. And what they'd think about mankind will depend largely on how different their species is from ours. Chances are, we'll probably all seem rather weird to each other.

What was the happiest day of your life and why?
Hopefully it's still to come. Once again, I'm not much of an "all time favourite" kinda gal. I try to do something every day that makes me happy and I cherish all the little things in life immensely.

If "God" (whatever your idea is on that) were stood before you now, what one question would you ask him/her and why?
Oh well, there's always the good old "why are we here?" question which, undoubtedly, would be very exciting to know. But I also feel like the answer could be somewhat unsatisfying. Maybe I'd ask, if we have a soul. I think it'd be interesting for a lot of people to know whether part of us actually "goes somewhere" after we're dead or if the end is actually the end.

As an expressive artist in the music industry, how does the state of the planet make you feel?
The initial inspiration for our latest album actually came while watching the news and realising just how much the problems we are facing right now resemble those of the dystopian futures, we read about as kids: The government in the pocket of big companies, the serious issues concerning climate change and the media preaching fear and driving us further away from one another. The state of the climate is something that worries me so much that it's still going to be a topic for me on the next release as well.

Do you think as a person of some influence that there is a duty on us to help influence humanity for the better?
People make music for different reasons, and it's not always to be in the spotlight and everything that comes with it. I feel like the world is very quick to judge and call the shots on what someone of a certain status should or shouldn't do. Demanding things from someone you don't even know seems to me as unreasonable as me knocking on my neighbours door and demanding that they speak up. As musicians we have the opportunity to reach a lot of people and I respect those who speak their mind and take a stance to try to bring on actual change.

What one cause would you say you feel most associated with and why? Whether it's equality, poverty, politics, the environment or other?
I can't give you just one cause, but I can give you three. Climate change, animal rights and female equality.

Like I mentioned, we felt the need to write a whole album centred about climate change among other things. Climate change can't be ignored and if we want a planet for our children and our children's children, we have to change our ways or we'll lose it all; I have no doubts about that.

I've always been a person with a huge heart for all living beings and have been an animal rights activist for the past seventeen years or so. It was a real eye opener, when I was young, and I realised that the reason we have some animals as pets and others as food is not because the animals are different from each other — only that our perception of them is and that it's purely cultural. It made no sense to me that stabbing a dog was animal cruelty and stabbing a cow was part of the food industry. That's when I went vegetarian as a young teenager and later vegan.

Being in a predominantly male industry, especially in heavier music, women have always had a harder time being taken seriously. I still get these comments that 'women don't belong in metal', 'go make me a sandwich' or 'take your top off'. I want to lift up other female artists as well as show young girls that there's a place for them in heavier music and that they don't have to dress a certain way to be there. That's part of why we're soon embarking on our second tour of Danish schools, which was an amazing experience that we're happy to repeat.

If you were stood before the leaders of the world, what would you say to them?
"Money won't mean a thing if there's no planet". Because that's what it all comes down to, isn't it? The costs. Which is really ridiculous to even think of, if we've destroyed the only home we have.

And finally my last question is in fact one written by Freddie Mercury in the song "Is This the World We Created": If there's a God in the sky, looking down what can he think of what we've done to the world that He created?
Well, it's sad, really, isn't it? That we've been put on this beautiful, green Earth that could have enough of everything for everyone. But instead someone decided that even that isn't enough. That they want more. And suddenly there isn't enough for everyone. And that somebody must suffer, so they can have a little more. And then suffering breeds suffering and... Well, you know where we are today. So I'm guessing a God would be saddened as well. But then again, if there is a God, they created man with all these flaws, so they can hardly be surprised.

Note: I just want to say a big thank you to Maja for giving us some things to think about. Rock on! Oh and where's my sandwich?

John Corabi
Mötley Crüe

They don't get more rock 'n' roll than John Corabi. A legendary guitarist and lead singer for The Scream and Mötley Crüe. In fact the list of mega rock bands John has been part of is rather long and I'm trying to save money on ink, so I won't name them all. Needless to say, the dude is awesome. Thankfully he came down to earth to speak to little old humble me.

If you could be any other musician past or present, which one would it be and why?
Hands down I would want to be Paul McCartney. when it's all said and done he'll have left the world the greatest body of music ever! He's so prolific, and after reading a few books on him, he seems to be pretty down to Earth as well...

If you had to name one song from any genre that really speaks to you, which one would it be and why?
I'll have to go with Queen's "Bohemian Rhapsody". That song is the genius of Freddie Mercury, on full display. I still often listen to that song and just scratch my head, and wonder if I could ever write something as brilliant as that one... It's just so amazing that he put together a ballad, with opera, and the big rock finish... amazing!

Are you a Mulder or Scully? Do you believe aliens have visited planet earth and if so what do you think they think about mankind?
I never really watched the show. I saw a few episodes but didn't really "follow" it. I did meet Gillian Anderson in Vancouver when we were doing the Mötley Crüe record. I think she stayed at the same hotel as us. I had a bit of a "crush" on her, so I'm going Scully! I wanted soooo bad to ask her out on a dinner date, but I couldn't muster the courage to ask... She was, and still is so attractive!

Note: See dropping names like Gillian Anderson is just annoying dude. Did you get her number by any chance?

What was the happiest day of your life and why?
Easily... The birth of my son Ian! Second would be getting my first record deal.

If "God" (whatever your idea is on that) were stood before you now, what one question would you ask him/her and why?

I would ask him why people are so unkind, disrespectful, intolerant with each other? I would ask how we can make the world a better place, and how long do we have on this planet? Then I would ask him/her to take a "selfie" with me... just in case everybody thought I was delirious when I told them I had a chat with God...

As an expressive artist in the music industry, how does the state of the planet make you feel?

In a word... worried! Everybody doesn't agree on the "global warming" issue but there was one statement that made sense to me in that documentary that Al Gore did. "From the beginning of time 'til fifty years ago when Al Gore was ten years old, we amassed three billion, and in the last 50-60 years we've almost tripled that number!" So just looking at that blueprint, common sense says we're using more oil, water, and natural resources, and putting much more stress on the planet... So yeah, I'm worried...

Do you think as a person of some influence that there is a duty on us to help influence humanity for the better?

Duty? No... But as a concerned person/citizen I try to do what I can. I will never tell anyone how to vote. (That's their choice)... I don't believe in telling people how to live their life, but I do believe in doing what I can to change things that bother me. There's a fine line between entertainment and standing on stage and "ranting" about the state of the world.

I think people are paying me to sing, and play music, and escape the insanity of daily life. So the last thing they're wanting is me talking about how shitty things are. I look at it like the band that kept playing music on the deck of the Titanic while it was sinking. But I also understand and respect people that are really vocal about how they feel. And it's their right to say what they want... That's why God invented channel changers... If ya don't like the program... you can change the channel... lol

What one cause would you say you feel most associated with and why? Whether it's equality, poverty, politics, the environment or other?

I just believe in being kind to everyone... period! If you can help someone in need, then help. If you can treat someone with respect... do so! Even if they're different from you. So I do totally support equality for women/people of colour/ religious freedom. I would love to figure out poverty. I would love to figure out how to make the planet a better place... I just believe in being the best human I can be each day... It's really not that difficult if you think about it...

If you were stood before the leaders of the world, what would you say to them?

"Put your dicks back in your pants and lead!" (sorry ladies, just a metaphor) It's pathetic to me how disrespectful politics have become! Nobody sees the "grey area" anymore. Nobody understands the concept of "compromise" anymore either. Life is give and take, and our leaders, and just people in general, have no respect for each others opinions!

And finally, my last question is in fact one written by Freddie Mercury: If there's a God in the sky, looking down what can he think of what we've done to the world that He created?

I have to say with an unfortunately resounding yes! It is the world we've created. Just watch the news for one day… It's full of anger, stupidity, and disrespect on a daily basis. But I still have faith in the human spirit, and believe we can pull it together and leave this world a better place for our kids, and grandkids… But that's just me…

Marcella Detroit
Shakespeare's Sister

Marcella Detroit, born and bred in Detroit, Michigan, has been involved in music her entire life. One of her earliest gigs found her opening for David Bowie. A few years later she was touring and recording with Eric Clapton, co-writing one of his biggest hits, "Lay Down Sally" and several of his most popular album tracks including "The Core", "Promises" and "Tangled in Love". She appeared live with him for "Live Aid" in Philadelphia in 1985.

She joined Shakespear's Sister in 1988 with ex-Bananarama member Siobhan Fahey. Their first two albums, Sacred Heart (1989), and Hormonally Yours (1992), both reached the top 10 of the UK Albums Chart. Detroit sang the lead vocals on their biggest hit, "Stay", which spent eight consecutive weeks at number one on the UK Singles Chart in 1992. In 2021 she rose to even greater heights and talked to me.

If you could be any other musician past or present, which one would it be and why?
I think I might choose to be John Lennon; he was such a rebel and seemed so confident and unapologetic about who he was, not to mention a musical genius. I wonder if he knew he was on the edge of something new and exciting? Completely original. I wonder what it would've felt like to be in such a unique time in rock n' roll history? If he knew that what they were about to do was going to transform rock n' roll forever.

If you had to name one song from any genre that really speaks to you, which one would it be and why?
It would have to be something from the Beatles, perhaps from *Sergeant Pepper's Lonely Heart's Club Band*. I love most of the songs on that album — still do to this day. I'd say "A Day in the Life"; it goes through so many interesting phases, really takes you on a journey, very descriptive, kind of melancholy and production wise it's fascinating to listen to, George Martin had an incredible ear and imagination; I'm sure the Fab Four were involved in that aspect as well. I love the lyrics too, the instrumentation, it's flawless.

Are you a Mulder or Scully? Do you believe aliens have visited planet earth and if so what do you think they think about mankind?

Sorry but I didn't really watch that show religiously but I respected it. I absolutely believe that aliens have visited earth. Some may call me mad, but, I was up late one night and I stumbled upon a show on the National Geographic television station here in America where scientists and that ilk were talking about our civilisation being from another planet originally, perhaps Mars. I wouldn't doubt it. In fact once, I was told that I was from another planet by someone and we were travelling in a space ship that crashed to earth. I've always felt different...

Note: I often look around me at this human species and know for certain I am not from this planet.

What was the happiest day of your life and why?

The happiest day of my life was the day my son was born. Why? Many reasons. My husband and I had experienced a few miscarriages. After that happening twice we didn't think we'd be able to have a viable pregnancy. But there it was, after my second miscarriage, five weeks later my doctor confirmed it, and this time it had a very strong heartbeat. I was hyper aware and nervous after having lost the first two but really my pregnancy was quite normal thankfully. From the minute he was born we knew he was so unique and we nurtured that from that moment onwards; he had his own little personality as soon as he came out into the world. It's elementary I guess, but it's just a wonder when you create this little person to love and to cherish, that changed my life forever, in the most positive way. And I'm very grateful for it.

If "God" (whatever your idea is on that) were stood before you now, what one question would you ask him/her and why?

I would say unto Him: why have you created the concept of colour, of racism? Why can't all people see everyone as just people, not a person who is a colour? And why do you make us love so much and then take it away from us? Why do we have to die? What happens when we do? Will there ever be world peace?

But the real question I'd ask is: why can't we all just get along?

As an expressive artist in the music industry, how does the state of the planet make you feel?

So many things about this planet concern me, aside from some of the people on it and their lack of sense of community and respect for their fellow man. For that reason I never thought I'd want to bring a child into it. But now, the way it's going I'm concerned for what I might leave my son and all children of the world; with so much denial going on about climate change and famine and very little news about it for fear of frightening the masses, I really don't know what state this planet will be in fifty years from now, let alone one hundred years. It feels very uncertain to me. I fear it's greed that will bring this planet to its knees in the end unless we heed the warnings immediately.

Do you think as a person of some influence that there is a duty on us to help influence humanity for the better?

I absolutely do! I was taking an acting class here in Los Angeles a few years after I moved here; it was not just an acting class, it was a way of life really, led by a man who was in my opinion, a visionary. His name was Milton Katselas, he was a highly lauded director famous for directing the Academy Award nominated film, *Butterflies are Free*. We were taught acting of course, but we were taught about humanity, about ethics, we learned about ourselves and how to be part of this little "community". During class one night he said, "We as artists have a responsibility to make this world a better place and need to speak up and do something about it through our art and through our work". That really stuck with me; I've written songs about social injustices, about finding the good in people, about spreading the word of love, it's part of who I am as an artist and a person.

What one cause would you say you feel most associated with and why? Whether it's equality, poverty, politics, the environment or other?
I'd say it's equality. For some reason, it's always resonated with me. My parents led by example. I was born Jewish and because I had experienced anti-Semitism, I feel I can have empathy for my fellow man, whatever colour, race or creed. I feel it in my gut when there's racial prejudice, I cannot and never will condone it and have always stood up for racial equality, sexual orientation equality and equality for women.

If you were stood before the leaders of the world, what would you say to them?
I would say, "We can do better than this! Let's work together, as a world and do what's best for all of us, for our fellow man. Let's teach it to our children ever day that we are one world, unique in our diversity, and should respect each other as such. Let's work together to show love and care towards each other; let's work together to keep our planet safe, beautiful, bountiful and habitable.

And finally, my last question is in fact one written by Freddie Mercury: If there's a God in the sky, looking down what can he think of what we've done to the world that He created?
Maybe it's a test; to see if we as humans deserve to have all this beauty, to see what we will do with it, to see if we can work together, all of us, to keep this lovely gift we were given, alive, abundant and healthy.

Note: Scores just came in from the mighty creator. We all got a D.

Courtney Taylor-Taylor
The Dandy Warhols

Where do I start with a man who has a surname that seems a silly waste of ink. I mean, just say it once and put x2 on the end. Anyway, he's a legend in the world of alternative rock as the lead singer, songwriter and guitarist of The Dandy Warhols.

But he's also written graphic novels, been an actor on a popular TV show and more. But my favourite is when the British Conservative politician and Prime Minister, Theresa May, used his song "Bohemian Like You" as she walked on to a conference stage. Taylor-Taylor wrote "Why don't these assholes have right-wing bands make them some right-wing music for their right-wing jerkoff politics? Oh, because right-wing people aren't creative, visionary, or any fun to be around."

And in the same spirited fashion Mr Taylor-Taylor answered my questions.

If you could be any other musician past or present, which one would it be and why?

I'd take a crack at being and fixing any of the legendary fuckups and sad cases like Elvis or Kurt. Those two in particular don't seem to have surrounded themselves with the right people to pursue anything but drug addictions. Such a fucking bummer. They could have gotten obsessed with using their fame, wealth and influence to help sort out a grip of issues with people's basic bad psychology or even political wrongdoings and it could very well have saved them.

Note: Don't shoot me. I just ask the questions.

If you had to name one song from any genre that really speaks to you, which one would it be and why?

"The Common People" by Pulp. There are a few by him, Jarvis, but that's the first one which comes to mind. Not for some deep meaning or answers but just cuz its perfectly clear in its writing and delivery and the production and the music all fit and flow like they've always existed

Are you a Mulder or Scully? Do you believe aliens have visited planet earth and if so what do you think they think about mankind?

When I think about mankind I like to think of it as two words: mank and ind. I don't believe aliens visit this planet. I believe they got the fuck off this rock and never looked back. They spliced us from themselves and apes so that we could mine enough gold for them to fix their ship whilst our ancestors built a series of launch pads they could try until finally they could shriek hallelujah and blast off back to a planet where they could breathe the air. Explains a lot, like why we are so gullible or programmable doesn't it?

What was the happiest day of your life and why?
The day I sold my boat.

If "God" (whatever your idea is on that) were stood before you now, what one question would you ask him/her and why?
Is this the only time I've lived through this life? Or is it a loop that I've been doing for billions or dozens of centuries?

As an expressive artist in the music industry, how does the state of the planet make you feel?
Makes me feel gross. Hopeless. I try not to obsess on the big picture but even when I look into local politics I am creeped out by the phony behaviour and the pure shabbiness which they try to disguise as "problem solving."

Do you think as a person of some influence that there is a duty on us to help influence humanity for the better?
Absolutely. And it gets harder because there are more than abundant peoples who get their pride and personal importance from inventing offences and get offended over people raising their voice in a real attempt to help. This creates a serious catch-22. Makes it difficult to care or even get started. Starting with simple obvious personal choices like buying organic non-GMO foods and not buying disposable plastic whenever possible, is something everyone can do without getting crucified on the web. I will probably never be allowed into China for saying that publicly.

What one cause would you say you feel most associated with and why? Whether it's equality, poverty, politics, the environment or other?
Because I am a native Portlander its gotta be homelessness. The low income apartments have been gentrified into boutique hotels, so we have a city of people living in the rainy muddy spaces in between. They can't all want to stay like that. Our city won't allow a local bizzillionaire to convert the old prison to studio apartments for them because some politico's ego is more important than the lives of these human beings.

And what happened to public works projects? And what about rehab? One of my friends that "camps" does it because the homeless buddy system means that you share when you've got dope or meth and when you're out someone will share with you.

One can stay high nearly all the time, which I guess beats framing or sheet rocking and having an apartment for the first couple years. He'd love a job building the next timberline lodge by this point though.

If you were stood before the leaders of the world, what would you say to them?
I would ask them how it feels to be bought and sold like a whore. Any of them who aren't, would probably have a good chuckle and the rest would be indignant. Career politicians rarely have their ideals intact by the time they buy their first home.

And finally my last question is in fact one written by Freddie Mercury in the song "Is This the World We Created": If there's a God in the sky, looking down what can he think of what we've done to the world that He created?
I think we are just unlucky that there is no god. We fucked it up and we have to fix it.

Rod Clements
Lindisfarne

Ivor Novello Award winning singer, songwriter and multi-instrumentalist of that wonderful English folk band, Lindisfarne, Rod Clements is also a bloody lovely man, which is much more important in my eyes. But for all you music fans out there you will remember that massive hit song, "Meet Me on the Corner" from 1972 and the fact that Rod was also a founding member of Jack the Lad, working with such greats as Ralph McTell.

And so to what you actually bought the book for, the interview.

If you could be any other musician past or present, which one would it be and why?
I've given this some thought and come to the realisation that the musicians, artists and writers I most admire had troubled and (for the most part) unhappy lives, while the ones who were happiest largely produced bland and complacent music. (It's the grit in the oyster that makes the pearl.) So I wouldn't want to be anybody else — just a better version of myself.

If you had to name one song from any genre that really speaks to you, which one would it be and why?
Hard to name just one, but just for the hell of it, I'll go with "This Land Is Your Land" (Woody Guthrie) for its celebration of the world's natural wonders (it's about USA but applies everywhere else too) and the fact that they are every person on earth's natural birth right.

Are you a Mulder or Scully? Do you believe aliens have visited planet earth and if so what do you think they think about mankind?
I didn't watch the *X Files* and I don't know which is Mulder and which is Scully. I infer from your question that one was a sceptic and the other wasn't. No, I do not believe that aliens have ever visited Earth.

What was the happiest day of your life and why?
This is an overly simplistic question. It's impossible to nominate (or even remember) one "happiest day" from the last 73 years. I remember happy events: meeting my partner for the first time, the birth of children, playing at big festivals,

watching the birds in my garden.

Note: Note to self, I must come up with much more complicated questions in future.

If "God" (whatever your idea is on that) were stood before you now, what one question would you ask him/her and why?

As a humanist/atheist, I consider this to be a leading question and so will decline to answer.

Note: Well that told me didn't it.

As an expressive artist in the music industry, how does the state of the planet make you feel?

I am depressed about the state of the planet but I don't think that's anything to do with me being an "expressive artist".

Do you think as a person of some influence that there is a duty on us to help influence humanity for the better?

I doubt that I have the influence that your question implies. But I feel that it is incumbent on all of us to influence humanity for the better. The problem arises when we try to define "better". After all, Hitler was "a person of some influence" who no doubt thought he was helping to "influence humanity for the better". We all need to work together on this.

What one cause would you say you feel most associated with and why? Whether it's equality, poverty, politics, the environment or other?

Firstly, I believe that the "causes" cited in your question (equality, poverty etc) are all part of the same problem. Secondly, I don't feel associated with any particular "cause" in that abstract sense. I just try to do the right thing.

If you were stood before the leaders of the world, what would you say to them?

I'd ask them to work together on an urgent united global policy to tackle the climate crisis and the worldwide social and health problems created by poverty and inequality. I would remind them of Gandhi's assertion that "there is enough in the world for everyone's need, but not enough for everyone's greed". They would then nod in agreement, then go away and do nothing about it.

And finally my last question is in fact one written by Freddie Mercury in the song "Is This the World We Created": If there's a God in the sky, looking down what can he think of what we've done to the world that He created?

God again? I don't think we need to look through the eyes of an imaginary being to see what a mess the world is in.

Note: Spot on dude.

Mick Harvey

© Katy Beal

Mick is an Australian. Yes I know, there are some famous Australians. Kylie Minogue for instance. But that aside, Mick can actually do a lot more than throw a boomerang. He can in fact play many musical instruments, compose, arrange and produce.

He formed several bands with co-conspirator and musician Nick Cave, namely The Boys Next Door, The Birthday Party and Nick Cave and the Bad Seeds. In addition to producing albums for numerous famous artists he has also managed to rack up a large number of music awards. But he managed to find time to talk to little old me.

If you could be any other musician past or present, which one would it be and why?
Beethoven, because he found the centre of the human soul and ways to express what it feels like in there (which many musicians aspire to) and he did it in such a magnificent way. Hard to find someone who did it better.

If you had to name one song from any genre that really speaks to you, which one would it be and why?
"Carrickfergus" (Irish Traditional) as sung by Van Morrison with The Chieftains. Because it has a beauty and mystery and addresses love and loss, mankind's two great emotional drivers, in a poignant way.

Are you a Mulder or Scully? Do you believe aliens have visited planet earth and if so what do you think they think about mankind?
Probably a Scully. (Is she the sceptic?) But even if I were a Mulder how would I have any idea what aliens might think about humans?

If "God" (whatever your idea is on that) were stood before you now, what one question would you ask him/her and why?
If "God" were standing before me I think everything would already be revealed.

As an expressive artist in the music industry, how does the state of the planet make you feel?
Troubled. Mostly by the environmental imbalance issues.

Do you think as a person of some influence that there is a duty on us to help influence humanity for the better?
If that's possible, yes.

What one cause would you say you feel most associated with and why? Whether it's equality, poverty, politics, the environment or other?
Inequality and the environment.

If you were stood before the leaders of the world, what would you say to them?
Work together. There is no other way.

And finally, my last question is in fact one written by Freddie Mercury: If there's a God in the sky, looking down what can he think of what we've done to the world that He created?
Problematic on a number of levels. Firstly that one is asked to interpret a piece of mediocre writing and secondly because the question is totally specious and in any case, effectively rhetorical.

Marty Wilde

© Heather Favel

So you like the bite-sized reads I hear you say, well here's a good one for you, Marty Wilde's contribution. But who is Marty Wilde I hear the folk who have been in another universe for the past fifty years. Well over eight decades Marty Wilde has been in the charts. Yes, that's right, he's a record breaker as well as being the father of pop star Kim Wilde.

Not only that but he's a Member of the British Empire and whether or not Britain has an empire is mute, the fact is he got the badge to prove it. It's pointless to name his hits, because there's so many, but let's just say your Mum and Grandmother will know them. What an amazing guy and therefore even more surprising he could be bothered to answer my questions, but he did.

If you could be any other musician past or present, which one would it be and why?
Tchaikovsky — he had such beauty in his head.

If you had to name one song from any genre that really speaks to you, which one would it be and why?
"Send In The Clowns" because it sounds like me.

Are you a Mulder or Scully? Do you believe aliens have visited planet earth and if so what do you think they think about mankind?
I have always believed in UFOs... I don't think they would be too impressed.

Note: I am constantly amazed at just how many music legends believe in aliens. Let that sink in. Can't be all the LSD can it?

What was the happiest day of your life and why?
I have had too many to pick out any particular one.

If "God" (whatever your idea is on that) were stood before you now, what one question would you ask him/her and why?
Do you sing? because I have just the song for you.

As an expressive artist in the music industry, how does the state of the planet make you feel?
Sad, because we never seem to learn.

Do you think as a person of some influence that there is a duty on us to help influence humanity for the better?
Yes, we should all do our best.

What one cause would you say you feel most associated with and why? Whether it's equality, poverty, politics, the environment or other?
Caring for animals, because they are such a joy to have on this planet.

If you were stood before the leaders of the world, what would you say to them?
Put the weapons away and start to realise all of us desperately need each other.

And finally, my last question is in fact one written by Freddie Mercury: If there's a God in the sky, looking down what can he think of what we've done to the world that He created?
If there was a God, which I don't believe there is, he very obviously would be extremely concerned, as something has gone terribly wrong with his flock.

© Paul Haggard

Jason Becker
Cacophony

Jason Becker was a child prodigy and became one half of the infamous heavy metal duo, Cacophony with Marty Friedman. They rocked the world during the 1980s and played sell-out audiences around the globe. After the pair split, Jason went to play with David Lee Roth and released solo albums. It seemed nothing could stop him. But then ALS or Lou Gehrig's Disease came along. A debilitating and life-threatening condition with a life expectancy of five years. Thirty years later Jason may not be able to play his guitar, but he's still writing, recording and releasing songs. He communicates through eye movements and spells out the words, notes and chords.

And this is how Jason answered my questions and my thanks go out to his amazing family who helped with the project.

If you could be any other musician past or present, which one would it be and why?
There are so many ways to answer this question. I could say Dylan because of the beauty of his lyrics and his awesome melodies. I could say Hendrix because of his fearless youth and playing and wild and crazy fashion. I could say Peter Gabriel because of his spiritual and mystical world view music. I could say Jeff Beck because of his beautiful heart. Then there is Mozart, Bach, Paganini, Philip Glass, Ennio Morricone, Robbie Robertson. But, honestly, I just can't think of wanting to be anyone but myself.

If you had to name one song from any genre that really speaks to you, which one would it be and why?
Man, there are so many choices. I have said "Imagine" by John Lennon because of the hope and love I wish for the world. I love "What a Wonderful World", especially when sung by Louis Armstrong. Music is such an awe-inspiring thing. It gives you goose bumps and makes you feel so good. There are several Dylan songs that make me feel that way. I hope my music makes people feel good and hopeful. My song, "Hold On To Love" makes me feel good for so many reasons. I hope I put something out there that makes people feel the same.

Are you a Mulder or Scully? Do you believe aliens have visited planet earth and if so what do you think they think about mankind?
Honestly, I did not get into *The X-Files*, like my mom, my brother and sister-in-law. But, since they did, I know who Mulder and Scully are, and I would say I am more of a Mulder in my own way. I believe in miracles because I have experienced the unexplained more than once, and I am a miracle myself. Just because we can't see something, doesn't mean it's not true.

What was the happiest day of your life and why?
I have to say the day at Disneyland with my mom, dad, my brother, Ehren, uncle Ron, grandpa, friend Elizabeth, and Aunt Dominique. We got there when it opened and left when it closed, after the fireworks. I had been diagnosed, but I was able to escape with my loved ones and have a blast.

If "God" (whatever your idea is on that) were stood before you now, what one question would you ask him/her and why?
Why are you making life so hard for me? I try to do everything I think you want me to do. I try to do the right things in life. I work so hard to give love and I want so badly to heal. What am I missing? Please tell me.

Note: Tissues are available in the auditorium. Jason, you give us all strength my friend.

As an expressive artist in the music industry, how does the state of the planet make you feel?
I wish there was more love. When you are in my position, you learn that love is all that matters. You see that little things are not worth stressing and torturing yourself over. You just want to see everyone happy and getting what they need. I keep thinking of what George Harrison said about being lucky to learn so early that fame and fortune wasn't the key to make you a happy person; it was something else. It is love; that is the key. I know that.

Do you think as a person of some influence that there is a duty on us to help influence humanity for the better?
Yes, but only through what we do, in my case make music. It is up to humanity to interpret what it means to them and to make their own contributions, or whatever to the world.

What one cause would you say you feel most associated with and why? Whether it's equality, poverty, politics, the environment or other?
Well, first of all, cure all chronic and scary diseases, regardless of how much money it can make, or how rare it is. No one should be given a death sentence without hope and help. Also, for me, it's animals. I love animals and cannot imagine how anyone could ever abuse an animal, who is totally dependent on our love and mercy. My parents had three things they wanted my brother and me to know; don't be a racist, don't ever abuse an animal, and follow your heart, even if it's business. Ha ha!

If you were stood before the leaders of the world, what would you say to them?
Hmmm... the leaders... I guess I would ask that they see humans and suffering as a tragedy to be solved and to take it upon themselves to see that there is no pain and suffering for as many humans as possible. Simply put, "do unto others..."

And finally, my last question is in fact one written by Freddie Mercury: If there's a God in the sky, looking down what can he think of what we've done to the world that He created?
He can think that we created the best and the worst, and we hope that the best will win. It is up to us.

Philip Wright
Paper Lace

Philip Wright is a member of that seventies pop band, Paper Lace, who had a string of hits, with "Billy Don't Be A Hero" hitting number one for weeks. In the USA "The Night Chicago Died" went straight to the top and won them a Recording Industry Association Award, along with millions of sales. The band has been through several incarnations but I got to interview the long term singer, drummer, Philip Wright.

If you had to name one song from any genre that really speaks to you, which one would it be and why?
Jackson Browne, prolific song writer at such an early age, his early songs were written with such insight, amazing and he was a part of the Laurel Canyon set, oh to be part of that cauldron of talent, David Crosby, James Taylor, Joni Mitchell etc.

Are you a Mulder or Scully? Do you believe aliens have visited planet earth and if so what do you think they think about mankind?
"Shine Silently" — Nils Lofgren 1974, spoke to me about a musicians life and became 'our tune' for my wife and myself.

What was the happiest day of your life and why?
I don't believe in aliens and no one has visited, if they had I think they would be pretty disappointed in mankind.

If "God" (whatever your idea is on that) stood before you now, what one question would you ask him/her and why?
Meeting the guys that would become Paper Lace and realising that I had become part of a band that I knew I was going to be in for a very long time.

As an expressive artist in the music industry, how does the state of the planet make you feel?
What is cancer all about, why have you made this awful disease which has affected so many people, what did we do to deserve such a terrible plague which has no conscience and is so indiscriminate.

Do you think as a person of some influence that there is a duty on us to help influence humanity for the better?

It makes me understand that we are not worthy of such a wonderful place, we have let ourselves down and we never learn by our mistakes, we repeatedly abuse the world we live in with little thought of the consequences of our actions.

I do think that we have to try but it is hard to have an effective voice, the power is in the wrong place, people elect a management, a government to handle things and to make decisions that should benefit everyone but money rules and generally the poorest in the world suffer this is how it is and will always be.

What one cause would you say you feel most associated with and why? Whether it's equality, poverty, politics, the environment or other?

I feel mostly associated with equality and the complete lack of it in today's world, the gap between the have and have nots is widening in front of our eyes and we as a general population seem powerless to alter things.

If you were stood before the leaders of the world, what would you say to them?

We have to unite and work together not just in times of crisis but in all things, we are all members of one race, the human race, prejudice stops here and now.

And finally, my last question is in fact one written by Freddie Mercury: If there's a God in the sky, looking down what can he think of what we've done to the world that He created?

Maybe he would think we are throwing something really precious away without a thought, I don't know, there is a lot wrong, we are ruining the environment through greed and selfishness and there comes a point where things will get so bad that the population will be on the receiving end of terrible things which we will have brought on ourselves, we need to be more considerate of others, more tolerant, more loving to the less fortunate.

Robb Nash

What has this tattooed rocker done to warrant your attention, and why has he been a keynote speaker for a Psychiatric Association of Canada conference and performed and spoken at maximum security prisons?

Found with no pulse by the first responder. They resuscitated him, and while unconscious they rebuilt his skull with Titanium. When he awoke and began rehabilitation, he frankly did not want to be alive. "My identity was lost and that brought me to a very dark place for the next two-and-a-half years," Robb says.

"Men in this society can feel like talking about our feelings or struggles is weak, so I kept it inside. But one day, I picked up the guitar and started my entire journey into music to tell my story."

For the past decade, the one-time athlete who at 17 barely survived a head-on collision with a semi-truck and spiralled into severe depression, has been telling his motivational back-on-track story to thousands of students across the Americas, changing lives, giving them purpose, erasing the stigma, and making it okay to be vulnerable and to ask for help. All the while, working on music and just made the best songs of his career.

In 2018, Nash was given the Order of Manitoba, while in 2019 he was awarded the Meritorious Service Medal by Canadian Governor General Julie Payette.

If you could be any other musician past or present, which one would it be and why?
Johnny Cash... without hesitation... he is the reason my goal was always to play prison shows. And those shows have been those most fulfilling shows I've ever played. Getting to meet inmates, hear their stories and find out that often the difference between me and them was where we started... our upbringing. Even getting to write songs with them and have them perform with us later on stage has been an amazing experience for them and our audience to hear their stories.

If you had to name one song from any genre that really speaks to you, which one would it be and why?
"One More Light" by Linkin Park. The desperation in the lyrics, music and vocals really speak to the desperation of how many lives have been stolen by suicide.

123

Are you a Mulder or Scully? Do you believe aliens have visited planet earth and if so what do you think they think about mankind?

I don't spend much time thinking about this... I feel I/we have enough shit to figure out and fix among the people already here and the mess we've made.

What was the happiest day of your life and why?

Probably the first time someone handed me a suicide note after a show when we were called to do speak and do a show at a school that had been struggling with a lot of losses. Now after more than 900 suicide notes at our shows for struggling communities, reserves and prisons... that first one is a moment I will never forget. It changed the content of every show I've performed since. It was I realised now just "what" I do... but "why" I do it.

If God (whatever your idea is on that) were stood before you now, what one question would you ask him/her and why?

I think the world already asked it everyday... "Why God, why? Every time something bad happens. I think it would be more about what God would ask us. And I think the question will be "Why did you blame me for all the shit in your life?" The way I was brought up... God would be looking down laughing as it is God that decides our fate and causes all the tragedy around us as some type of "lesson". I imagine God in tears looking down.

I always say from stage that I don't think things "happen for a reason"... I think things happen with potential. Tragedy has the potential to tear apart an individual, a family, a community or even a whole country. But tragedy also has the potential to bring people together. It involves choice in the tragedy. We are going to face enough "lessons" in life based on the world around us and the mistakes that we make.

I was once hit by a semi-truck... found with no pulse and not breathing. They had to rebuild my skull with titanium. The recovery has been brutal. People in my own family told me that "God spanked me with a semi 'cause I was a bad kid and needed to learn a lesson."

That brought me to an even darker place as I thought I was a puppet with no say on what would happen to me. Then one day someone gave me the simple truth... the "reason" I was hit by a semi was because me and my friends were going too fast on an icy road.

Shit happens... what are you gonna do when it does? One lyric I wrote was this: "Tragedy appears and people stop to pray to you... they wipe away the tears and people place the blame on you." Religion often teaches that we walk through this painful world just waiting to experience peace in the afterlife when we get to walk with God. I think we are meant to discover that peace here on earth. If you find that peace... that you can actually have an impact on the world around you. And like me... you can walk from the darkest place and go from SUICIDAL TO SIGNIFICANT... where your life has an impact on the world around you.

And I think the greatest "church experience" I have been at has been NA meetings (or AA) No one putting on a facade. You open up about your struggles at the start with no judgement. You can call the person next to you at 4:00am when you're struggling. And you pray together. I think prayer can help you through those tough times and even help you avoid them if you listen to those gut feelings you get. I wish everyone could experience a meeting like that.

As an expressive artist in the music industry, how does the state of the planet make you feel?

I often hurt seeing the pain in the eyes of so many... but the fact that we can use music as a part of someone's breakthrough is the most significant feeling there is.

Do you think as a person of some influence that there is a duty on us to help influence humanity for the better?

There's no duty or obligation... but I think everyone should experience what it is like to have your art doing something good for humanity if they haven't already. I am so grateful to be a part of this world of art that... if we allow it... can help people have breakthroughs and find out they're not alone. A song can calm you down when you need it... get you pumped up before playing a big game... and even allow you to scream along when you need to get something out of your head. A song can bring tears out of you... which is so important to do. I've always said that tears are like poison.... they're not meant to stay in your system... you gotta flush them out regularly.

What one cause would you say you feel most associated with and why? Whether its equality, poverty, politics, the environment or other?

Mental health. It's a war that we are losing. And I think we are losing some of the most gifted people on earth to suicide.

If you were stood before the leaders of the world, what would you say to them?

When I think of the leaders of the world... I think of the media. They are what dictates so much of how the world turns and our perspective on it. I would and always do beg them to share stories of hope not just of tragedy. For example... show that not every story of mental health ends in suicide... not every story of addiction ends in an overdose.

And finally, my last question is in fact one written by Freddie Mercury: If there's a God in the sky, looking down what can he think of what we've done to the world that He created?

So many people in the religious world sing "He's got the whole world in His hands" I think He gave it to us and we were supposed to take care of each other. There's enough food and water for everyone... how did we become so self-absorbed that we didn't take care of the world around us... which was our job all along.

Mike Pender
The Searchers

And now it's time to remember the good old days of pop. Mike Pender, is only an original founding member of Merseybeat group the Searchers, named after the John Wayne film. Yeah I know, sixties royalty. He sang the lead vocals on many hit singles by the Searchers, including the song "Needles and Pins" and "What Have They Done To The Rain?" Go on take a look at your sixties play list, he's on there a few times! He's also here to answer my questions.

If you could be any other musician, past or present, which one would it be and why?
Glen Frey! The Eagles! Glen wrote great lyrics and although Henley was also important, Frey was my kind of guy. In saying all that, it was Buddy Holly who inspired me.

Note: RIP Mr. Frey, we miss you dude.

If you had to name one song from any genre that really speaks to you, which one would it be and why?
"Take it to the Limit"! This song associates with what most rock/pop bands ask themselves as they carrier through their life on the road!

Are you a Mulder or Scully? Do you believe aliens have visited planet earth, and if so, what do you think they think about mankind?
The only aliens are the ones in the movies, in my humble opinion!

Note: There's real aliens in the movies? That explains a lot.

What was the happiest day of your life and why?
There are many, but probably when our one and only grandson was born.

If "God" (whatever your idea is on that) were stood before you now, what one question would you ask him/her and why?
Being a Catholic person although a lapsed one! I don't have a question for God, whatever you conceive him to be, God will say, "I gave mankind a life and free

will and what did you do?"

Note: Dear God, we messed it up. Help!

As an expressive artist in the music industry, how does the state of the planet make you feel?

I think maybe this will answer your question! I sang a song many years ago with the Searchers of course! Have a listen to the words, "What have they done to The Rain?"

Note: It's a brilliant song and it's on my "best" playlist. Go share it with everybody!

Do you think as a person of some influence that there is a duty on us to help influence humanity for the better?

I try every day!

What one cause would you say you feel most associated with and why? Whether it's equality, poverty, politics, the environment or other?

Equality comes to mind, but I'm very aware of poverty's broken communities especially in places like Syria.

If you were stood before the leaders of the world, what would you say to them?

On impulse I would tell them all to Fuck Off! But in reality I would not have any answers for them!

And finally, my last question is in fact one written by Freddie Mercury: If there's a God in the sky, looking down what can he think of what we've done to the world that He created?

For all it's sham drudgery and broken dreams, it's still a beautiful world! We are all children of the universe no less than the trees and stars and we all have a right to be here.

Ken Stringfellow
REM, The Posies

© Olli Tumelius

Ken Stringfellow is an American singer, songwriter, multi-instrumentalist, arranger, and producer. Best known for his work with The Posies, R.E.M., and the re-formed Big Star, Stringfellow's discography includes more than 200 albums. At least that's what Wikipedia says.

Nothing is ever that simple Mr. Wikipedia. Ken has an enormous musical history starting with The Posies back in the 1980s and a string of hits and national and international tours. His musical ability being what it is, he was asked to play with Big Star and tour and record with REM. He has also released several personal records and produced others. Being so prolific and busy, how on earth did he bother to talk to me. Well, he did so there.

If you could be any other musician past or present, which one would it be and why?
I don't dream of inhabiting someone else's problems or pain, even if I could glimpse their genius. The brilliant art is, in the end, made by a mundane body. Would it be fun to be a fly on the wall at various moments when my favourite albums were being made? Definitely. But to "be" those people? No thanks.

I truly believe everyone's individual journey is important, and therefore, mine must be as well. In the end, even the most talented, mind-blowing musician — say, a Prince or a Stevie Wonder — has their own personal humility to discover. We are presented with opportunities to learn and grow, and that tiny, grass-blade-like striving is a part of the grand journey of human wisdom. Sure, some of us are born into circumstances that push us into the roles of provocateurs — people who are destructive and remain so — it seems we "need" these people as well in the grand story to push the rest of us to be more compassionate and tolerant, because we can be, and evidently, they can't as easily. And by doing so, we give less fertile ground for the next generation of potential provocateurs, hopefully outgrowing the 'need' for that kind of learning at some point.

If you had to name one song from any genre that really speaks to you, which one would it be and why?
Can be many things at many times. I read a quote from Fritz Lang recently: "In all art... the supreme law is that one must be deeply moved and obsessed by one's

work. By one's work itself." So of course, I make art that really speaks to me, it has to move me first. I find myself being more moved by things closer to me in biography than further away. It's hard for me to be as excited about a 'big' song/ film/cultural moment as I may have been at a younger age.

A few years ago I oversaw the production for a posthumous release by the band Game Theory, that is, the project helmed by Scott Miller with help from various musicians over the years, most active in the 1980s. Scott had contacted me about working on a new Game Theory album in 2009, almost twenty years after their previous release, and I was honoured — yet, that was the end of the conversation. Scott eventually took his own life in 2013.

With his widow Kristine we sorted through the various songs in progress or in fragmentary demo form, and an album came from this. Scott's voice is present on many of the songs, and in some cases his friends/colleagues (Ted Leo, Will Sheff, et al) finished the implied songs just by extrapolating the demo fragments. I worked on a song called "Exit for An Opening" that has all of the highlights of Scott's brilliance — a gorgeous melody; lyrics that are at times touching and at times wilfully obscure; a completely non-standard song structure punctuated with huge shifts in tempo and rhythm that completely works as a whole, etc. Considering the end of Scott's story, the title is extremely poignant.

Are you a Mulder or Scully? Do you believe aliens have visited planet earth and if so what do you think they think about mankind?
Not so convinced they have visited and if they have, the units of time in interstellar travel are so vast, and our time here to this point so brief, there is a very slim chance it would have coincided with our existence here. For all we know, an alien civilisation could be even more barbarous than our own, or it could be so different as to make comparison — or analysis of/by these beings — difficult.

What was the happiest day of your life and why?
Easily when my daughter was born, and when I first viewed her in the incubator (she was born via a Caesarian-section so needed to acclimate for a couple hours) and saw she was healthy... when I was finally allowed to put a finger through a tiny port and she gripped it... it was overwhelming. Joy and gratitude, a vast respect for the power of life. Those first two hours where I could only look at her I just stared, tears streaming, at this new human being.

If "God" (whatever your idea is on that) were stood before you now, what one question would you ask him/her and why?
"How can I help you? What serves you best?"

As an expressive artist in the music industry, how does the state of the planet make you feel?
Well, I'm hardly in the music 'industry', any more than a grandma knitting a sweater is in the 'textile industry'. But, expressive artist, I'll take. I see the world through a lens of the powerful imposing on the weak, violently so. I have always been outraged by injustices where the powerful present untruths that the less powerful are forced to combat with a greater truth, but with less resources to establish that truth. Witch trials and other convenient distortions that end up

martyring those that were simply different or lacked the resources to resist. It's a theme that persists.

My path as an artist has been to comment on these equations of power but also to simply establish myself as defiantly 'other'. Not participating in the easy avenues to power. Of course, I have become aware that by virtue of my race and upbringing, I've been benefiting from the 'unseen hand' of privilege all along, and that just declaring myself 'other' overlooks that I am not experiencing 'otherness' the way those that have had no choice do.

Do you think as a person of some influence that there is a duty on us to help influence humanity for the better?
I don't believe anyone is exempt from this, and everyone has influence on those around them, so, yes. At least try. By getting perspective on yourself, the perspective that leads to humility, you can start that journey. Without humility, you presume entitlement to certain benefits, and that kind of thinking will lead you to believe you're exempt from participating in change — the 'specialness' of talent or fame is not a substitute for the basic work of kindness, generosity and compassion.

What one cause would you say you feel most associated with and why? Whether it's equality, poverty, politics, the environment or other?
I was deeply affected by violent bullying as a pre-teen/early teen. It's shaped my view and this kind of social cohesion by force (but with a cynical undertone of not wanting to reform the offender, just annihilate them) is a source of outrage wherever and in whatever context I see it.

If you were stood before the leaders of the world, what would you say to them?
Good heavens. I have no idea. I don't presume to dictate to them any kind of incredible insight. I don't really see that as a circumstance I would find myself in.

And finally, my last question is in fact one written by Freddie Mercury: If there's a God in the sky, looking down what can he think of what we've done to the world that He created?
If there is a divine creator, they have written all of the misunderstandings, conflicts and divisions into the plan. It is up to us to crack the very simple code implied by the fact we are composed of different languages, races, customs, religions etc. All that's needed is to look at those who appear different or 'strange' without fear or contempt, and with the compassion of understanding.

After looking at different groups with that kind of thinking, then the next step is to look at individuals, to discover that really no one is fully in a category determined by those larger aspects I described above. We are a planet of individuals, who deserve recognition as such, as opposed to just being biproducts of a culture. It's more work to look at each person, top to bottom, get to know them... we sort them out of laziness. And yet we have ample tools for assessment and observation.

Note: Note I didn't have to put any notes in because Ken basically said it all, and besides, I couldn't get a word in.

Toni Baker
The Dakotas

In the 1960s there was a little band who had a lead singer called Billy J. Kramer. That band was called The Dakotas. They are freaking legends of the era. Of course their true claim to fame is that Toni Baker of The Dakotas wrote the music for TV shows, Phoenix Nights and Max and Paddy. I know, you're an American and you have no idea what I'm talking about, but seriously it's not my fault you're not cultured. And so, with that in mind it is time to hear what Toni has to say.

If you could be any other musician past or present, which one would it be and why?
I've always admired Eric Clapton for his skill and for what he's been through. At one point he was a total addict but now is totally clean and playing better than ever.

If you had to name one song from any genre that really speaks to you, which one would it be and why?
"The Cat's in the Cradle" by Harry Chapin. It's a warning to parents about losing the kids.

Are you a Mulder or Scully? Do you believe aliens have visited planet earth and if so what do you think they think about mankind?
Not really.

Note: Toni is not known for long speeches.

What was the happiest day of your life and why?
Probably the times I held my new-born children the first time.

If "God" (whatever your idea is on that) were stood before you now, what one question would you ask him/her and why?
Why do you allow terrorists to kill innocents?

As an expressive artist in the music industry, how does the state of the planet make you feel?
Sad. People are so uncaring.

Note: See, told you he didn't like long speeches.

Do you think as a person of some influence that there is a duty on us to help influence humanity for the better?
Absolutely. We can lead by example.

Note: Get Ozzy on the phone.

What one cause would you say you feel most associated with and why? Whether it's equality, poverty, politics, the environment or other?
The environment. Without it nothing else can exist.

Note: Simple and yet so true. Zen Toni.

If you were stood before the leaders of the world, what would you say to them?
Deal with the earth not politics.

And finally, my last question is in fact one written by Freddie Mercury: If there's a God in the sky, looking down what can he think of what we've done to the world that He created?
He must be embarrassed to have thought mankind would do the right thing.

Brad Walsh

© Anna Hafner

Pop star, singer, songwriter, record producer and artist, Brad Walsh has sold millions of records and is a regular at the top of the charts. He's even done tunes for TV shows such as The Oprah Winfrey Show. What more do you want? Oh yes, the interview.

If you could be any other musician past or present, which one would it be and why?
I would be Madonna. She changed pop music and artist presentation forever and mastered the concept of reinvention for longevity. And now she's a rich bitch still making headlines. She can and does do whatever she wants, without harming others.

Note: Dear reader, we'd all love to see you do a photoshop making Brad turn into Madonna please.

If you had to name one song from any genre that really speaks to you, which one would it be and why?
"Crucify" by Tori Amos. She always captures the futile optimism of relationships so perfectly.

Are you a Mulder or Scully? Do you believe aliens have visited planet earth and if so what do you think they think about mankind?
I have actually never seen *The X-Files* I believe the universe is full of aliens but I doubt they have visited us in our lifetime. But I also know that I know nothing. If they watch us, they must be so embarrassed. Like when I watch the *Real Housewives*.

Note: Seriously, who the fuck watches that?

What was the happiest day of your life and why?
Maybe the day I bought my house. Maybe the day I first had sex with someone I loved. Maybe it was a random day when my serotonin spiked. I hope the happiest day has yet to come.

If "God" (whatever your idea is on that) were stood before you now, what one question would you ask him/her and why?
Why do our sex organs double as waste disposal? That's kinda fucked up.

Note: How true. Of course, if Apple had invented us we'd have just the one port for everything as well. Maybe God is an Apple?

As an expressive artist in the music industry, how does the state of the planet make you feel?
I am thrilled to live my small life amid the chaos of impending climate apocalypse. If it all ends tomorrow I will have had a great time today.

Do you think as a person of some influence that there is a duty on us to help influence humanity for the better?
Absolutely yes. It's everyone's responsibility to leave things better than when we arrived. People with "influence" may have louder mouthpieces, which doesn't make their opinions more valuable, but there is a duty to advocate for improvement and better and humane treatment all around.

Note: Somebody tell the Trump family.

If you were stood before the leaders of the world, what would you say to them?
Go fuck yourselves. Every day that you don't actively end suffering is a day wasted, and it's most days for you.

Note: Hands up if you'd love to see Brad at the UN going for it.

And finally, my last question is in fact one written by Freddie Mercury: If there's a God in the sky, looking down what can he think of what we've done to the world that He created?
I can't believe in a God that created us, and this world for us, who wouldn't intervene as we destroy it and each other. I'm not saying I don't believe in a higher power, but I can't believe in the fairy tale of a human-like God who administers "tests" and has primitive emotions like sadness and rage.

© Tony Mcgee

Carol Decker
T'Pau

No, Carol Decker is not a Vulcan elder from Star Trek. She is in fact the gorgeous redhead lead singer from the band T'Pau. She's quite mad, which is why I love her so much. T'Pau had their first big international hit with "Heart and Soul" and followed up with the massive "China in Your Hands". The album, Bridge of Spies, reached number one and in fact went quadruple platinum. See, I can spell. It was a cold March morning when Carol Decker put a spell on me.

If you could be any other musician past or present, which one would it be and why?
I'd be Debbie Harry. She was stunning & sexy but never came across as any man's plaything or a helpless little woman. She fronted her band and was perceived as a strong leader and absolutely essential focal point. I believe that our sexuality is part of our humanity and don't have a problem with a good-looking person making that gift part of what sells the band a long with of course credible music and a great voice. Debbie was a big influence on me.

Like Debbie, I too was in my late twenties when I got my break and thirty when "China in Your Hand" was at number one, but only in my dreams am I that cool!

Note: 99.99% of red-blooded males have to agree with me when I say Carol Decker is just as hot as Debbie Harry.

If you had to name one song from any genre that really speaks to you, which one would it be and why?
This is hard one as on a different day I might pick another song, but today I pick "Running Down A Dream" by Tom Petty. The relentless drums, the super cool guitar lick. It's one of those songs that gets you bopping, you can't not tap your foot! I like the space in the song. There are big chunks with no vocal, but the instrumentation still keeps you hooked. I've never been able to write a song like this as I'm not a player, I'm a singer, so I fill a song with words. I always play air drums to this song especially the outro, that just sails on into infinity. I imagine it still playing in the ether after the fade. May I add I was particularly gutted when he died. It was huge loss to music.

Are you a Mulder or Scully? Do you believe aliens have visited planet earth and if so what do you think they think about mankind?
Never really watched it! And I know that's like saying I've never seen *Star Wars*!

Note: Carol, that is just like saying you've never seen Star Wars. Jeez.

What was the happiest day of your life and why?
With apologies to my husband and children I would say my first *Top of the Pops*. I had been trying for years to get a record deal. I was in my late twenties and I felt time was running out. Finally we 'made it' with our first hit "Heart and Soul". I had grown up watching *Top of the Pops* and it was an institution. Every age group watched it, It was a unique programme in that way. To appear on it meant you had a hit on your hands, Well I nearly burst with pride!

If "God" (whatever your idea is on that) were stood before you now, what one question would you ask him/her and why?
There is no God.

Note: Yeah, but what if there was?

There is no God.

Note: Okay fair enough, just asking.

As an expressive artist in the music industry, how does the state of the planet make you feel?
I never took any notice of the state of the planet when I was young. I was very focused on my own little life but now I'm older and I have kids I feel like I have skin in the game and I am more aware. I do feel huge concern for how we ruthlessly decimate it. I do what I can. I want to be a conscientious world citizen. But it is hard to live a modern life blame or guilt free.

Do you think as a person of some influence that there is a duty on us to help influence humanity for the better?
Yes, but without hypocritical lecturing. I'd start by saying do what you can locally, recycle, pick up your litter, take your shit home after your picnic, research how things impact your world and do the best you can to live responsibly. Educate your kids but have fun with your life! You can't save the world every day!

What one cause would you say you feel most associated with and why? Whether it's equality, poverty, politics, the environment or other?
For me it's disabilities and especially kids with them. Life can be hard enough when you're able bodied and have full mental capacity. Since I became a parent I feel a stab in my heart when I see a kid with very real problems to overcome.

If you were stood before the leaders of the world, what would you say to them?
Stop all the rhetoric and fucking do what you said you were going to do to get elected.

And finally, my last question is in fact one written by Freddie Mercury: If there's a God in the sky, looking down what can he think of what we've done to the world that He created?

Mother Nature created the world and we are abusing it — quite a lot.

© Thomas Ertmer

Blaze Bayley
Iron Maiden, Wolfsbane, Blaze Bayley Band

Leader of the band, Blaze and the Blaze Bayley Band, he now also performs solo. But Mr. Bayley was also the lead singer of rock band, Wolfsbane, for ten years and lead singer of some small rock band called Iron Maiden that you've probably never heard of. So just like a highly bread canine, he has pedigree. Blaze managed to stop screeching over the noise of crashing guitars just long enough to answer my questions.

If you could be any other musician past or present, which one would it be and why?

That is one of the most difficult questions ever in the history of music. I have tried for many years to be happy where I am and with what I have got.

I realised how many great moments I trivialised and did not appreciate. I let things slip by me while me and my ambition looked at the top of the mountain. Now I celebrate every small success and try to squeeze the juice out of the moments. So my choice can only be superficial. I believe that in most cases, great art comes from pain. I do not want the pain and challenges of those musicians I have come to admire but I will take the fluffy nice bits.

Bill Withers for his voice and songs. James Brown for his impossible achievements and innovation. Elvis Presley for his influence on popular music and his voice. But the artist whose journey I would be most interested in taking would be Jimmy Page. With Led Zeppelin he created a sound that became the expression of my teenage soul and the sound of my adult passion. The modern equivalent of the Greek god Apollo with all his powers, but with command of demons and electricity as well as the sun and music.

If you had to name one song from any genre that really speaks to you, which one would it be and why?

That question is literally insane. No one who loves music will willingly name one song. It is a wicked question. Songs that bring memories of my first kiss. Songs I clung to as my broken heart tried to heal. Songs that filled me with a dark power that raised me to my aching feet and made me try once more to master my own voice and destroy any predetermined destiny. It cannot be done. But... there is one that takes me to a beginning. A song that changed my life and set me on a path that I still tread. Black Sabbath, "Children Of The Sea". Written in 1979 by Tony Iommi and Ronnie James Dio. Released in April 1980 as part of the *Heaven and Hell* album. That song.

Are you a Mulder or Scully? Do you believe aliens have visited planet earth and if so what do you think they think about mankind?

I am Scully. They took me away and experimented on me in a laboratory on a train. Aliens are not responsible for any of the technology available on earth. Aliens are time travelling humans. Humanity right now is the most advanced intelligence in this universe. We will be gently side-lined by the silicone and diamond and quantum life forms that are gestating in our phones. The satellites we choke our space with will give the self-destructive nature of humanity every assistance in destroying itself. I will be standing on a desolate world looking at Fox Mulder saying… "I told you it wouldn't be aliens!"

What was the happiest day of your life and why?

No. there can be no happiest 24 hours. Something always seemed to go wrong. And my philosophy demands that I value every day available to me. But yes there have been some truly magnificent moments in my musical life that stay with me. Wolfsbane opened up for Ozzy Osborne at Wembley Arena and it was broadcast live on Radio One at a thing called the great British music weekend. Thirty magical minutes where we believed we could not be stopped.

If "God" (whatever your idea is on that) were stood before you now, what one question would you ask him/her and why?

"Why haven't you updated the Ten Commandments? Or at least sent an appendix." We need things about fake news and too much sugar and global warming now. Can we change graven image for something to do with recycling and emissions?

As an expressive artist in the music industry, how does the state of the planet make you feel?

I'm hopeful. The technology exists to change things. If the same political will that has been applied to the situation with coronavirus, is applied to environmental problems, things could go well in the future. In my life I have learned that most people are basically good. It's those few power-hungry selfish psychos that cause most of our problems.

Do you think as a person of some influence that there is a duty on us to help influence humanity for the better?

It is so nice that you think of me as a person of some influence. I am not. I'm a small underground heavy metal singer supported by my fans. As an artist I have tried to show truth. A deeper spiritual human truth. I don't feel it is any artist's duty to do anything except be honest to themselves.

Fans make things popular not artists. In the scheme of things I am not popular. I have a few wonderful fans that support me in my dream of being an independent artist. If I have a duty it is to them, not humanity. For my fans I do my best. They are the people that inspire me and support me.

My message is simple.

    Try to be a good human being.

    Try to be a good person.

    Try not to tell lies.

    Try to be fair.

And don't give up. Even longest darkest night will end with a dawn.

What one cause would you say you feel most associated with and why? Whether it's equality, poverty, politics, the environment or other?

I'm most associated with singing and songwriting. I hope that my work can help my fans to feel better and help them through difficult times. If every person helped every other person and tried to help themselves, I believe all the problems of the world could be solved. Some may say I'm a dreamer, but I'm not the only one.

If you were stood before the leaders of the world, what would you say to them?

"Selfish bastards. Isn't it obvious what's wrong? If it's not obvious I will have to take over!"

And finally, my last question is in fact one written by Freddie Mercury: If there's a God in the sky, looking down what can he think of what we've done to the world that He created?

"I had to flood them out last time they got this bad. Maybe try a virus this time?"

Brian Poole
The Tremeloes

Born at the height of World War Two, Brian Poole was brought up in the East End of London like thousands of others. But by 1960 he was the lead singer of the popular beat band, The Tremeloes.

In 1962 record label, Decca, were on the hunt for a new beat band and auditioned two aspiring bands — The Tremeloes and a Liverpool group called The Beatles. Decca chose Brian Poole and The Tremeloes.

They formed in 1958 after being highly influenced by the rock and roll world around them. By 1963 they had a hit with "Twist and Shout" followed quickly by "Do You Love Me" which knocked the Beatles off the top slot.

Since his days in The Tremeloes, Brian has played Royal Gala Performances and in 1988 got together with Reg Presley of The Troggs, Mike Pender of the Searchers, Tony Crane of The Merseybeats and Clem Curtis to form The Corporation. He has toured with other sixties stars around the world.

I was honoured to get my interview with Brian in March 2021.

Before I get into these questions, I would like to thank Phil G for asking me and I must explain that some of my answers consist of two or more parts. I found it hard to answer in the singular because things have changed so many times over my 79 years!

If you could be any other musician past or present, which one would it be and why?

As a musician, listening to songs written by my daughters Karen and Shelly, I often think 'where did that thought or idea come from?' I'm pretty sure it wasn't from me or my wife Pam, but sometimes it can be very profound. They are both prolific songwriters. Look them up! #KarenPoole, #ShellyPoole, #AlishasAttic.

Following on from this it makes sense that for my choice of artist that I would have liked to have been is Bob Dylan. Great ideas about his life and times come through with humour and sensitivity. So as a simple singer and musician, I do not pick another musician but a writer, which is what I always wanted our children to be. It was a choice between people like Carole King, Buddy Holly, James Taylor etc. but I went for the 'poet' of our times.

If you had to name one song from any genre that really speaks to you, which one would it be and why?

The song that still speaks for me is "In My Life" by John Lennon. As the Tremeloes we had the pleasure of touring with the then unknown 'Beatles'. We were never 'best friends' but this song says everything about our times. My favourite version is by Bette Midler who sings this simply and does not try to own the song.

Are you a Mulder or Scully? Do you believe aliens have visited planet earth and if so what do you think they think about mankind?

I don't think aliens are here... yet, but when they do arrive I think that the earth would be a pretty fine place to live. I think that people like *Greenpeace* etc are, although not yet extremely successful, well on the way to making the Earth sustainable in our galaxy. One little thing also. With the recent exploration and documentation that is being undertaken by many countries we can now see what a beautiful place we live in. The photos taken from space show this wonderful blue planet which would be very inviting to anyone, Alien or otherwise.

What was the happiest day of your life and why?

I have had a life of so many great days to remember, so I cannot just pick only one. These two memorable days are connected. My wife Pam and I had two wonderful and talented daughters and the birth of these two, Karen and Shelly, were great days. Another great day was, when walking in the Milton Keynes Shopping Centre a few years back we were passing HMV and saw two massive 6-foot-high cardboard cut outs of our daughters as Alisha's Attic. Pam turned to me and said, 'I reckon they made it then.'

If "God" (whatever your idea is on that) were stood before you now, what one question would you ask him/her and why?

I have three favourite arch angels. Raphael, Michael and Gabriel. I would ask God why, when they are about, there is a distinct smell of oil and wet leather and are they really as big and powerful as they seem. I was taught to be cautious, so mostly I keep these thoughts and allegories to myself, but hey...

As an expressive artist in the music industry, how does the state of the planet make you feel?

At my age, slightly more tired, but have plenty to do, even though semi-retired. I totally love the Earth, it's a great place to be. For millions of years there have been ice ages and then global warming periods, so nothing has really changed there, and it's nice to know that people who can, are trying to keep our great planet safe. I am very pleased that this is happening even though there is not much constructively I can do. (Yes, keep an eye on it)

Do you think as a person of some influence that there is a duty on us to help influence humanity for the better?

I do not presume to have any real influence on these massively wide issues and hope that nobody thinks they are powerful enough to influence a whole planet (even with hit records)... (joke). Of course people must try though.

What one cause would you say you feel most associated with and why? Whether it's equality, poverty, politics, the environment or other?

I support the cause of charity and over my lifetime have demonstrated this. I was greatly honoured to appear on a Royal Variety Show in the eighties. In fact at the age of 79 I can honestly say that I support all of these causes and none of them. Hope that's an honest answer that is appropriate at this time.

If you were stood before the leaders of the world, what would you say to them?

I hope in this question we are talking about the whole world and not just the major countries, but if I had a PA system big enough to address the whole worlds' leaders, chiefs etc. the thing that comes to mind is, ask everyone to look after our planet, stop the misleading advertising and news and knee jerk reactionaries making everyone's lives a misery. Listen to the real people, not the demonstrative minority.

And finally, my last question is in fact one written by Freddie Mercury: If there's a God in the sky, looking down what can he think of what we've done to the world that He created?

No matter how many people argue about who created this and that, all using their own agendas (sometimes well disguised), to influence ordinary people by their celebrity. This Earth is there, and we live on it. It takes all kinds and usually, over the millions of years it has survived all that is thrown at it, it is the most beautiful planet in the solar system (as far as we know). Enjoy it.

Monty Oxymoron
The Damned

I know, you're all thinking, why didn't he change his name? Well if that's what you're born with, sometimes it can make you stronger. Monty is in fact a psychedelic punk rocker like so many others. He's also a keyboard player in the British punk band, The Damned. So this interview ought to go just fine.

If you could be any other musician past or present, which one would it be and why?
Well I feel honoured to be keyboard player in the Damned: I was a fan and it was the answer to a wish I made when I heard them start using keyboards. I guess if I had another choice I'd like to have been in Miles Davis' electric band Like Keith Jarrett and Chick Corea (RIP), as I love spontaneous improvised music.

If you had to name one song from any genre that really speaks to you, which one would it be and why?
So many songs! Iain McGilchrist suggests (in *The Master and His Emissary*, great book), that we as a species sang before we talked. Right now I'm thinking of that cheerful ditty with a lyric both wise and profound: "It 'ain't what you do, it's the way that you do it".

Are you a Mulder or Scully? Do you believe aliens have visited planet earth and if so what do you think they think about mankind?
I keep an open mind: I have a problem with belief itself. There was a time when people had beliefs: now beliefs have them. The world is full of people who are ready to carry memes of all sorts, to proclaim them, define themselves by them and live by them. Worst of all, they feel they are better than those who don't share them. Perhaps we should choose beliefs with more care. If your belief inspires you to be better than you were then keep it up, if worse, abandon it! It seems to me the height of narcissism and arrogance to assume your beliefs are "Truth". Besides "the truth is in here" as well as "out there": otherwise the aliens get there first!

What was the happiest day of your life and why?
I've had so many happy days (and lots of not so happy). I think it's when there's a feel of rightness and "fit" with the universe are the happiest moments. My friend Daevid Allen of Gong wrote the song "Now is the happiest time of your life": now there's the key!

Note: Own now.

If "God" (whatever your idea is on that) were stood before you now, what one question would you ask him/her and why?
If I, was to be confronted with the Absolute,...the Being of Beings,... the beginning and the end of the All... the ultimate Mystery... what could I say?? I'd be reduced to silence. Maybe, "How can we move from ignorance to knowledge, from darkness to light: from death to life?"

As an expressive artist in the music industry, how does the state of the planet make you feel?
The danger is to despair: I have to avoid nihilism. I've never known a good government. They are probably a rare and fleeting phenomenon.

Do you think as a person of some influence that there is a duty on us to help influence humanity for the better?
It's difficult because "The road to hell is paved with good intentions". I read a fantastic book by John G Bennett, a follower of Gurdjieff, *Hazard: The Risk of Realisation*. In it he says we are all subject to the "law of hazard: whatever we intend can go wrong." He even suggests that God is also included because there is only meaning in creating if that creation can go wrong!

Otherwise, the perfect complete and finished thing is already there in the mind: why bother? I love improvising music in the moment; it can go wrong, but it can also surprise! I guess you have to try, while realising people may well misunderstand you: history is full of misunderstood and misapplied teachings. It's when the left hemisphere misrepresents them and thinks it understands them all (McGilchrist again!)

What one cause would you say you feel most associated with and why? Whether it's equality, poverty, politics, the environment or other?
So many great causes! It's like we know the "what" of WHAT needs to be done (save and preserve the planet and the life on it; develop a less oppressive and financially unequal society; eradicate bigotry...) but we don't know the HOW. I think THE cause for me would be to promote understanding. It's so odd how we now know through psychology and neurology about "emotional" and "social" intelligence, and yet we are collectively less empathic than we have ever been: why? Is it our use of technology? It seems worse than in the last century. No one wants to understand "the others": THEY are "the problem". As a psychiatric nurse I've spent time trying to understand people who no one else can understand: what is it LIKE to have those beliefs and experiences? These days I work with people with dementia: what is that like? Yet the gap between so called "normal" people gets wider and wider: only if we can understand one another can we even

begin to solve problems.

If you were stood before the leaders of the world, what would you say to them?
"Have you considered that your desire to be where you are might indicate you are unfit to be there?"

And finally, my last question is in fact one written by Freddie Mercury: If there's a God in the sky, looking down what can he think of what we've done to the world that He created?
Well the worst thing might be seeing how religious teachings themselves have caused the problems: "Have in dominion the earth and all in it"; "Go forth and multiply": well we've surely done that big time: now what? Did "He" really say that? What did "He" mean?

Note: See, Monty is an Oxymoron.

Cy Curnin
The Fixx

© Heimo Reifetshammer

As lead singer of the new wave band, the Fixx, Cy has himself co-written over a dozen songs that hit the Billboard Charts. As a solo artist he has released singles, albums and EPs. And I take no pride whatsoever in pointing out he was born in the UK, like so, so many other great musicians. Just saying.

I'm not going to go on and on about how he's a Brit, honest, but he did manage to spend some time out of his busy superstar world to chat to another Brit.

If you could be any other musician past or present, which one would it be and why?
Nat King Cole. His timbre and timing were second to none. His lyrical resonance connected with people above and beyond the political prisons of the day. He comforted an age of war and strife, racial disparity with his gentle nature. As I sit at my piano in the dark of night, I often emulate his style and would love to surprise and audience with the power of gentility.

Note: Please release an album, we'd love to hear that!

If you had to name one song from any genre that really speaks to you, which one would it be and why?
David Bowie's "Young Americans". This song really captures the times of its day. The fracturing ideology of democracy and the path of self-destructive excess unfolding before a clueless generation. Even today, it's relevance matures and the irony bites deeper.

Are you a Mulder or Scully? Do you believe aliens have visited planet earth and if so what do you think they think about mankind?
I'm definitely Mulder! Humanity and it's imagination has only been a blip thus far.

Maybe we shall discover one day, beneath the sediment, clues to extra-terrestrial life forces. Even if we don't, I feel the arrogance of our limitations blinds us from understanding that statistically there must be many, many forms of 'life' out there. Just see how big the universe is!

Note: Big. An adjective meaning of considerable size or extent.

What was the happiest day of your life and why?

It's hard to narrow or track happiness to just one day. For me this is a constant source of light shining. Indeed all emotions are constantly ebbing and flowing all at once. The hue of any particular day is then reflected as an instant rush of adrenalin in three dimensions only to then be stored as a memory without a heartbeat.

Note: Now ain't that one of the deepest answers for that question so far. Deep man (said in a distinctly Woodstock era tone.)

With that said I'd have to say that this day that I'm typing is the happiest. I can feel true love and enjoy every second of it while the awareness of its vulnerability reminds me to never take it for granted. There's a gratitude that exists that only until recently evaded me. I used to confuse detachment with peace which I now realise is false. True joy is found in the arms of love.

Note: Amen brother.

If "God" (whatever your idea is on that) were stood before you now, what one question would you ask him/her and why?

God is the edge of our imagination. As animists we have created myths to help us connect and conquer our fears only to drive us mad with the instinct that we know deep down we are failing to be our own saviours. That said, I say to 'God' "do the washing up and take out the trash."

As an expressive artist in the music industry, how does the state of the planet make you feel?

As an artist with a gift for expression I'm alarmed at the sound of Bedlam. The art of listening seems lost to the deafening cries of madness. Political unspeak and corruption is depressing. They say cream rise to the top. Unfortunately so does shit.

Note: Obviously not all politicians are shit. Some of them are too stupid to be shit. I mean, shit can be quite good on the allotment tomatoes. Although I can't think of any politicians good enough for my tomatoes. I'd imagine they'd leave a foul taste.

Do you think as a person of some influence that there is a duty on us to help influence humanity for the better?

Along with journalists, I believe artists are cultural watchdogs who can and should bring to humanity's attention the possibilities of true social revolution and wrongdoings all over the world. A darker view of this is; we serve as canaries in the proverbial coal mine warning the unaware and somnambulist world with alarms. Unfortunately, money has suppressed the urges of many true voices which in turn incarcerates them in a prison of complicity.

Note: Hell yeah!

What one cause would you say you feel most associated with and why? Whether it's equality, poverty, politics, the environment or other? The most important existential threat facing humanity is climate change. The planet will survive without us but we cannot survive without it's balanced environment. Again our myopic mindset cannot handle the size of the pending disaster therefore we choose to ignore it. At our peril.

If you were stood before the leaders of the world, what would you say to them?

I would say, "You are the servants of destiny. Now serve well or be gone. Place yourselves in the hands of truth and science. Forget your short-term legacies because no one will be alive to remember you anyway. Act as if you have only one short term in office. Do your best and move on. Collaborate, designate higher intelligence to do your thinking and delegate your attention span to the watchful eyes of your populace. A day, not too far off will arrive when you will be held accountable."

And finally, my last question is in fact one written by Freddie Mercury: If there's a God in the sky, looking down what can he think of what we've done to the world that He created?

We are the masters of our own demise. To call on God is an abdication of our responsibility. There is no God to redeem us, just as the only evil that exists is in our own minds. In my humble opinion anyway.

I wait to be proved wrong with an open mind and heart.

Note: Dude, that was awe inspiring. You got my vote.

Tony Moore
Iron Maiden

Singer, songwriter, musician and radio presenter. Oh yes, he was also a member of that eighties band, Cutting Crew, and some unknown rock band called, Iron Maiden.

It was 1977 and Tony saw an advert in a Melody Maker for a keyboard player for a new London band. He responded and got the gig. Iron Maiden was the band. And thus it proves that learning to read is a good thing. It can open doors. Well, not literally obviously.

And yet, Tony decided he didn't fit in and in the eighties was invited to play keyboards for new wave group, Cutting Crew. They went on to international fame. Today Tony tours solo around the world, but I caught him and made him answer these questions.

If you could be any other musician past or present, which one would it be and why?
Prince. There was something so ethereal and yet very grounded in his spirit and personality. I truly believe he was one of the greatest musicians, writers and performers to have ever lived and made everything he did joyous, inspirational and fun. Yet there was no doubt his work ethic would terrify those of a more laid-back disposition.

Note: No tea breaks then?

If you had to name one song from any genre that really speaks to you, which one would it be and why?
"Imagine" by John Lennon. The genius simplicity of the lyric, and melody that managed to encapsulate a generation's dream of peace and brotherhood of man.

Note: We're still imagining.

Are you a Mulder or Scully? Do you believe aliens have visited planet earth and if so what do you think they think about mankind?
I actually never watched a whole episode, somehow the *X Files* passed me by. I have a sneaky feeling they are here (aliens that is, not Mulder and Scully) and always have been, that maybe we were brought here.

Note: Am I the only person who ever watched that show? Jeez.

What was the happiest day of your life and why?
Corny though it may read, I try to make every day, the best day of my life, and find happiness in many things around me. One of the happiest days was only

a few weeks ago, after live streaming almost 200 shows since March 2020 and having the anniversary show filled with messages from people located all over the world telling me how much the community that grew up around the webcasts has impacted their lives so positively in such dark times.

Note: Yep, corny. But nice all the same. Don't tell anybody I said so.

If "God" (whatever your idea is on that) were stood before you now, what one question would you ask him/her and why?
Why is it all so short?

As an expressive artist in the music industry, how does the state of the planet make you feel?
I am deeply concerned by the division and dark energy that seems to be manifest across the planet right now and do everything I can to put light and love into the world via my music and my personal energy.

Do you think as a person of some influence that there is a duty on us to help influence humanity for the better?
I actually think it is incumbent on all of us to take responsibility for being positive role models and being open to debate, to be tolerant of different ideologies and to strive to be the best we can be. We have to make changes "upstream" and that means guiding the next generation with love, acceptance and wisdom to live lives that are meaningful, purposeful and honest.

What one cause would you say you feel most associated with and why? Whether it's equality, poverty, politics, the environment or other?
I would say the most important cause is the one for truth — there can be no greater ideal than that of working to share the truth, the whole truth and nothing but the truth

If you were stood before the leaders of the world, what would you say to them?
You have the power to change the world, so use that power to "empower" others. Don't make more laws, create healthier environments. Don't treat your citizens with contempt when they disagree with you, but respect the lives, values and dreams of those precious souls over whom you have executive authority. Power is a privilege not a right and should be held as precious and a gift from the people.

And finally, my last question is in fact one written by Freddie Mercury: If there's a God in the sky, looking down what can he think of what we've done to the world that He created?
We didn't create this world, we created the chaos, beauty, madness, anger and everything else that makes up our different societies which straddle the world and define the lives we lead. "If there's a God in the sky, looking down" then he is saying… "Come on guys, just do the right thing". "What can he think of what we've done" He will love us no matter what, he doesn't discriminate "to the world that He created?" We have freewill, but will we be free?

Ted Nugent

© Brown Photography

Well, where do I start with Ted Nugent? Oh boy. Guitar shredding showman who has sold over forty million records, played to nearly seven thousand audiences and broke so many attendance records I've lost count. It could be said he's been fairly successful then.

Already a rising star in the Motor City, Nugent started to catch national attention with a feisty cover of "Baby Please Don't Go". But it was the Amboy Dukes' psychedelic Journey to the Centre of the Mind that kicked Young Ted's career into hyper drive.

He then broke out as a solo artist, signing with Epic Records and he soon earned the title Motor City Madman. His amazing career spans six decades of multi-platinum hits. And yet, when I wanted to interview him he just stretched back in his big black chair and stroked his white cat and said okay then.

If you could be any other musician past or present, which one would it be and why?
Though I admire an endless list of musicians, I cannot imagine the desire to be anyone but myself.

Note: I've always fancied trying out being Doris Day for a bit, but I suppose that's just me.

If you had to name one song from any genre that really speaks to you, which one would it be and why?
There are hundreds of amazing songs that would qualify but "Street Fighting Man" by the Rolling Stones due to its pulse, groove, energy and spirit.

Note: Never heard it. Are they big then?

Are you a Mulder or Scully? Do you believe aliens have visited planet earth and if so what do you think they think about mankind?
I am much too busy figuring out mankind to bother considering alien beings.

What was the happiest day of your life and why?
Today, because I am alive, in touch with my loved ones and fellow man, and vigorously celebrating life, liberty and the gonzo pursuit of my American Dream happiness.

If "God" (whatever your idea is on that) were stood before you now, what one question would you ask him/her and why?
What's with skunks?

Note: That answer stinks dude.

As an expressive artist in the music industry, how does the state of the planet make you feel?
I celebrate the endless good while fighting to reduce the bad and ugly.

Note: I do believe you may have met my sister-in-law.

Do you think as a person of some influence that there is a duty on us to help influence humanity for the better?
All caring people who seek knowledge and wisdom develop varying degrees of influence, but truth, logic and common-sense regardless of who delivers it will ultimately influence others in a meaningful way.

Note: Wow. See just because these rock stars destroy your ears doesn't mean they ain't deep.

What one cause would you say you feel most associated with and why? Whether it's equality, poverty, politics, the environment or other?
Truth and the evidence to support it.

If you were stood before the leaders of the world, what would you say to them?
I would arrest them all and try them for power abusing crimes against humanity.

Note: Can I help please?

And finally, my last question is in fact one written by Freddie Mercury: If there's a God in the sky, looking down what can he think of what we've done to the world that He created?
Of course it is, in all its good, bad and ugly glory.

Robert Berry
Rock Legend

Guitarist, singer and record producer, Robert Berry is a legend in the industry. In 1988 he formed the band 3 with Keith Emerson and Carl Palmer of Emerson, Lake and Palmer fame. A hit single, album and tour followed. His band, Alliance, is a supergroup of other rock greats and he has worked with tons of other rock superstars as a musician, songwriter and record producer. I got to chat!

If you could be any other musician past or present, which one would it be and why?
Very interesting way to start off Phil. This took some thought. There are so many aspects of the music business I love that there isn't one guy that seems to cover them all. I'd love to be Sammy Hagar. Great singer, great songwriter, member of one of my favourite bands, successful business man with so many ventures. But then again, he isn't the studio guy that I also love being. Maybe an Alan Parsons fits the bill better. Covers most of the basis that I think I relate to. Artist, great musician, songwriter, engineer, producer (not as much fun as Sam though). But then again — I like that Paul McCartney does all this and is the most comfortable person in his own skin I have ever seen. Okay done! It's Paul. I've also always wanted to write and record a few songs with him.

Note: Oh really? I turned him down.

If you had to name one song from any genre that really speaks to you, which one would it be and why?
I love a story that hits the heart. The song "Walking in Memphis" really hits it. But then again there are songs or total albums like "The Lamb Lies Down" by Genesis that really resonate with me. As you can tell, I don't have one, clear answer to any of your questions. Music is not as much about perfection to me as much as it is about doing "the real deal" in whatever style you resonate with. A good ole' on the porch blues song done the right way with the bumps, squeaks, and out of tune sounds making it real does it for me too.

Are you a Mulder or Scully? Do you believe aliens have visited planet earth and if so what do you think they think about mankind?
It's hard for me to think that they haven't. As much as we know there is so much more to learn. My current band mate Greg Kihn and 90s band mate Sammy Hagar have both had the pleasure of alien ship sightings. Hard for me to believe though as I have not. But they must be out there. Or in here.

What was the happiest day of your life and why?
My life is a happy place. Everyday I get to do what I love and spend it with people that I love. I also get to work with musicians in my studio that are doing what is special in their life — recording their newest song, or as I like to say, birthing their next baby. If I had to hone it down to one, I would say the birth of my children. Alexandra and Robert III. Of course there was that first lunch with Keith Emerson. That was quite a happy day.

If "God" (whatever your idea is on that) stood before you now, what one question would you ask him/her and why?
I would ask if he was aware of everything I had done and everything I had said (especially the bad stuff lol). Then I would know how to defend myself when God asked me a question back. I often feel this invisible guideline in my life. Do the right thing, be the guy I strive to be, and make a difference in the world. I feel like everything has a reason and a purpose in my life. I respect everything that I come across. And of course there is the age old question I might ask — uh, could I borrow a million dollars? Or is that if I was standing before a Genie?

Note: I've tried it. Didn't work. Don't bother.

As an expressive artist in the music industry, how does the state of the planet make you feel?
I live in California. We have the world's seventh largest economy, we are all over cleaning up air pollution, we have plenty of jobs, and dreams are always available to achieve here. But — we have a terrible homeless population. It is hard for me to think the planet is in good shape when the seventh largest economy in the world can't take care of that problem. Sure, our politicians have a good speech, but seriously — this is a problem that can and should be solved, but it's been going on for so long. So how do I feel about the state of the planet? Hopeful, mad, sad, and sincere.

Do you think as a person of some influence that there is a duty on us to help influence humanity for the better?
I believe that everything you do, everything you say, effects your circle of influence whatever that may be. For some it is a few family and friends. For others it is fans across the world. Neither is more important than the other. How you effect your fellow man (or woman) brings the ebb and flow to life. I always feel it is much better to bring a positive to every situation. You must realise that every negative can be solved with a positive. It may not be the solution you like the best, but it can be solved and you can move forward. My motto is what good can I accomplish tomorrow? Today is set. I must be able to make a difference in some way tomorrow!

What one cause would you say you feel most associated with and why? Whether it's equality, poverty, politics, the environment or other?

My life includes equality. Music is the universal language. The yelling and screaming that there is not equality in the U.S. just makes me shut it down. I see more people of all races and economic levels that can do more good to help their inner circle of influence. It's hard for me to explain but the solution is to just do something positive in every way. Not make it this big media hype that just divides people. This is a touchy subject and I am not really getting my thoughts across here. I guess that's part of my philosophy. Do something — don't just talk about it. Equality doesn't have to be a problem.

Poverty is at the top of my list. I have already talked about the homeless situation in California. I have a band called December People that goes out each November and December and plays concerts to raise money for the hungry and the homeless. We believe that if each city or town (smaller circles of influence) took care of their own hungry and homeless, the problem could be wiped out. Sounds simple but when you visit food banks and see how far $20 goes to buy food and how many empty building there are that could house people it all makes sense.

Politics is off the charts and off the discussion. My thought is that if I can at least partially understand why you would think something opposite of me then I have the right to a strong opinion of my own. If I just rant and rave about my point of view and don't consider how and why you believe a different way, then I have no right to discuss it. Hard to understand why people on both sides of the isle think the other side is a bunch of idiots. Successful people with good families on both sides but the other side considers them ignorant. I don't get it.

Environment is a tricky one. I believe that we in the U.S. are doing a great job of moving forward in all areas that effect our environment. I also know that other countries like China are completely ignoring the problem. The balance has to be made over the whole world because the U.S. alone can't solve the problem. This is a difficult question and solution.

If you were stood before the leaders of the world, what would you say to them?

I have spent time with many famous people. I learned early on that they live in a different world than we do. They are catered to in every way and have the financial means to do just about anything they choose to do. That makes their expectations and their reactions different than the average people. Right or wrong, this is what I've seen. So to speak to the leaders of the world would be tricky. Some like it soft spoken and non-confrontational. Others want to be challenged. Let me ask — could I choose to not stand before the leaders of the world please? LOL.

I do have an observation though. I believe if I could have a big lunch or dinner with all their wives I could learn more about how to handle certain personalities and then — stand before the leaders of the world fully armed with the protocol that would open the door to a meaningful conversation.

And finally, my last question is in fact one written by Freddie Mercury: If there's a God in the sky, looking down what can he think of what we've done to the world that He created?

I believe every human has their own definition of love, life and success. I also believe if there is a god in the sky he is not so narrow of a thinker that everybody has to be judged by the same criteria. My wife Rebecca is a second grade teacher. If she has a problem with a student she always wonders what is going on in their world. Their home life, their circle of friends, their outside influences of any kind. She tries to find the bigger picture and then work on the smaller problem. That is the way I believe a god would judge us and think about how we have affected the world.

© J.D. von Lerber

John York
The Byrds

John has a long history as a bass and guitar player with bands such as The Bees, Sir Douglas Quintet, The Byrds, the Mamas and the Papas and Gene Clark's touring band. He has released several solo albums and is a legend, which is why I was so happy to get him in the book.

If you could be any other musician past or present, which one would it be and why?
Maybe Vivaldi. He left so little evidence of his personal life, so we have to get to know him through his music.

If you had to name one song from any genre that really speaks to you, which one would it be and why?
"Create in Me a Clean Heart" (from Psalm 51)

Are you a Mulder or Scully? Do you believe aliens have visited planet earth and if so what do you think they think about mankind?
Don't have a TV... haven't watched it in years. I haven't had any alien encounters, but I do know several people who have. Maybe they pity us.

Note: We found somebody who has not watched TV for years! Imagine that. Nope, I can't. I would never have seen Star Trek: Enterprise. It just doesn't compute in my mind.

What was the happiest day of your life and why?
I hope it's today.

If "God" (whatever you idea is on that) were stood before you now, what one question would you ask him/her and why?
I'd prefer to keep my mouth shut and just pay attention. If a question was required, I'd ask if our being clueless is part of the plan.

As an expressive artist in the music industry, how does the state of the planet make you feel?
The planet, which includes us, is overly ripe right now. Either we make something wonderful together, or we all just become compost for the next crop.

Do you think as a person of some influence that there is a duty on us to help influence humanity for the better?
Of course. We should spread the love around.

Note: Hands up if you want to spread your love around.

What one cause would you say you feel most associated with and why? Whether it's equality, poverty, politics, the environment or other?
Music as a healing art.

Note: I recommend Megadeth.

If you were stood before the leaders of the world, what would you say to them?
"Get a real job..." or maybe, "Don't follow leaders, watch your parking meters."

And finally, my last question is in fact one written by Freddie Mercury: If there's a God in the sky, looking down what can he think of what we've done to the world that He created?
God is weeping...

Eric Bazilian
The Hooters

At the age of only 16, Eric Bazilian started writing songs for his first band, Evil Seed. It was an age of Summer Love and Woodstock's and Evil Seed would play at some of the infamous "be-ins" in Fairmount Park. I'm fairly confident there was no LSD floating around.

In the 1970s and after completing his Bachelors in physics, he met Rob Hyman and started a band called Baby Grand, releasing two albums. When the band disbanded Bazilian and Hyman decided to try something new and started The Hooters in 1980. Their debut album sold two million copies and three top 40 singles.

The band grew and grew throughout the 80s and 90s. In 1985 they opened Live Aid in Philadelphia. In 1986 they played the Amnesty International Conference at Giants Stadium. Following a brief hiatus, The Hooters came back strong and toured the world.

And so, who better to ask some crazy questions to than a major rock star?

If you could be any other musician past or present, which one would it be and why?
J.S Bach, just to know what was going on in that mind as he was writing his repertoire of transcendent genius.

Note: You only needed to ask Eric, I could have told you.

If you had to name one song from any genre that really speaks to you, which one would it be and why?
"I Want To Hold Your Hand". Just because.

Note: The song is by some minor beat band from Liverpool.

Are you a Mulder or Scully? Do you believe aliens have visited planet earth and if so what do you think they think about mankind?
I'm a Sculder. Or a Mully. I'm not averse to the theory that at some point an intelligent species visited Earth and worked a little genetic manipulation magic on some primates.

Note: There are in fact many people who actually do believe that thousands of years ago aliens came down to Earth and genetically engineered mankind. They cite fallen angels, watchers and all-manner of myths from ancient times. Well, I suppose it's as good as ripping out a rib from Adam.

What was the happiest day of your life and why?
The happiest days are often the saddest. And vice versa. Of course I could pick out specific personal or professional victories but if 'happiness' is about feeling fully alive then life's tragedies provide the same function. But, okay, meeting my wife, marrying her, the birth of my children, their milestones in life, this concert or that concert, this song or that song. But it's all part of the same symphony.

If "God" (whatever your idea is on that) were stood before you now, what one question would you ask him/her and why?
That's my line, you're welcome.

Note: Don't you just love folk who like to mess with your head.

As an expressive artist in the music industry, how does the state of the planet make you feel?
The state of the world looks pretty scary right now. But, then, putting it into a historical perspective, compared to the wars, revolutions, plagues, and natural disasters our species has survived in the past, things actually look pretty good.

Do you think as a person of some influence that there is a duty on us to help influence humanity for the better?
There is a duty on every person to influence humanity for the better. Duh.

Note: Take note every person reading this. He means you.

What one cause would you say you feel most associated with and why? Whether it's equality, poverty, politics, the environment or other?
It's all the same cause.

If you were stood before the leaders of the world, what would you say to them?
What's for dinner?

And finally, my last question is in fact one written by Freddie Mercury: If there's a God in the sky, looking down what can he think of what we've done to the world that He created?
This is the world that we created that created us. Et cetera.

Note: I have nothing further to add.

Kenney Jones
The Who

© Mike Lawn

Kenney Jones is, yes you guessed it, a legend. I know that term is being used a lot in this book, but hey, it's a book about interviews with... legends.

Kenney's history is long so I shall try my best to keep it as short as possible, because basically you ought to know already if you're into music. I mean, he was the drummer for The Who.

In around 1965 Kenney Jones and his friend Ronnie Lane became founding members of the English rock group Small Faces. They were early Mods in many ways and had a string of hits including "All or Nothing" and "Itchycoo Park". They were so famous that London's Westminster Council erected a commemorative plaque in 2007.

Jones said on the BBC: "To honour the Small Faces after all these years is a terrific achievement. I only wish that Steve Marriott, Ronnie Lane and Don Arden were here to enjoy this moment with me".

When Steve Marriot left the band in 1969 a certain Rod Stewart stepped in along with Ronnie Wood on guitar. They then became the Faces.

In 1978 The Who needed a drummer. Pete Townsend sought out Kenney and the rest is, as they say, history. (Who says that? I mean, you hear it a lot, but where did it all start? Anyway, who cares.)

After ten years drumming for that little band Kenney formed The Law with former members of Free, Bad Company and The Firm.

In 2001 Kenney formed The Jones Gang, named after... erm, himself. Kenney has had a very interesting music career and recorded with copious music stars including The Rolling Stones, Rod Stewart, Joan Armatrading, Jerry Lee Lewis, David Essex and Wings.

Now, see, that's why he's called a legend. But even legends can't escape me.

If you could be any other musician past or present, which one would it be and why?
Either Elvis Presley or Otis Reading. Elvis was a great rock and roll singer and Otis was a great soul singer.

Note: Have you noticed how many legends ignore the question and choose more than one?

If you had to name one song from any genre that really speaks to you, which one would it be and why?
Willie Nelson, "Stardust". I love the emotion in his voice.

Are you a Mulder or Scully? Do you believe aliens have visited planet earth and if so what do you think they think about mankind?
I think I'm a bit of both. Absolutely. I do believe we aren't alone.

What was the happiest day of your life and why?
The day I met my wife Jayne.

Note: Dear Jayne, I think he deserves a kiss for that one don't you?

If "God" (whatever your idea is on that) were stood before you now, what one question would you ask him/her and why?
I would ask — why are you pissing about with life? Why do you allow us to get it wrong all the time? Can't you let us be a bit more peaceful. There's so much temptation out there for people.

As an expressive artist in the music industry, how does the state of the planet make you feel?
Very sad but it's something we can put right. It's going to take a lot of time to do and to make an impact though.

Do you think as a person of some influence that there is a duty on us to help influence humanity for the better?
Yes, that's what I'm striving to do every day.

What one cause would you say you feel most associated with and why? Whether it's equality, poverty, politics, the environment or other?
Wrap them all up into one. I think all of the above are equally important to me.

If you were stood before the leaders of the world, what would you say to them?
I would say — fix things.

Note: Dear politicians of the world, the drummer of The Who said fix things, so bloody well get on with it.

And finally, my last question is in fact one written by Freddie Mercury: If there's a God in the sky, looking down what can he think of what we've done to the world that He created?
He should know, he created it.

Lowell Levinger
The Youngbloods

Okay guys and gals, a short one. I do like to provide small bite sized chunks for those in a hurry. Lowell Levinger, otherwise known as Banana. One of the founding members of the critically acclaimed American rock band that formed in the mid-sixties, The Youngbloods. If you like your rock with a slight Woodstock, psychedelic feel, then go and check them out!

Levinger, brought a lot to the band and could play the piano, banjo, mandolin, mandola, guitar and bass. Previously he had played in the Proper Bostonians and the Trolls and played mainly piano and guitar in the Youngbloods.

Since the breakup of the band, Banana has gone on and carried on making sweet music and touring to packed audiences. But where did the name "banana" come from you ask? Okay maybe you didn't but I'm gonna tell you anyway. He said, quite simply and elusively, that it made sense at the time. Well, why not? From now on I shall be known as Orange.

And so it was that Orange asked Banana a few fruity questions.

If you could be any other musician past or present, which one would it be and why?
I would not want to be any other musician, thank you very much. I've got my hands full just being myself and that looks comparatively easily when looking at others.

If you had to name one song from any genre that really speaks to you, which one would it be and why?
Thank goodness I don't have to. I relish the vast repertoire that constantly circulates through my head and despise the thought of pairing it down.

Are you a Mulder or Scully? Do you believe aliens have visited planet earth and if so what do you think they think about mankind?
Don't know what either of those things are. Although Scully made tape recorders. I've never thought about what potential alien visitors might think. Their previous visits are dubious.

What was the happiest day of your life and why?
So many happy days. What if my sweetie reads this? Better say wedding day, right? Although today is a pretty good day.

If "God" (whatever your idea is on that) were stood before you now, what one question would you ask him/her and why?
I don't accept a "God" who answers questions, sorry. And if there is one, I wouldn't want to bug her with my stupid questions.

As an expressive artist in the music industry, how does the state of the planet make you feel?
Scared.

Do you think as a person of some influence that there is a duty on us to help influence humanity for the better?
Yes.

What one cause would you say you feel most associated with and why? Whether it's equality, poverty, politics, the environment or other?
Peace.

If you were stood before the leaders of the world, what would you say to them?
Ciao a tutti, Per favore ascoltate a Greta Thunberg.

And finally, my last question is in fact one written by Freddie Mercury: If there's a God in the sky, looking down what can he think of what we've done to the world that He created?
There is no "God in the sky looking down", sorry. It's what we think of what we've done that matters and what we're going to do about it matters even more.

Peter Beckett
Player

Best known, according to Wikipedia, as the lead singer of the band, Player. Peter is much, much more. In fact his first recording was written by Ray Davies of The Kinks called "All Night Stand". Soon afterwards he joined the band, Paladin and recorded two albums. It wasn't too long before he'd formed Player and "Baby Come Back" was at number one. After four albums the band split and Peter went on to write hit songs for Janet Jackson, Olivia Newton-John, The Temptations and Kenny Rogers.

After some solo work, Player got back together, released a new album and toured. He's written songs and music for TV shows and films and toured world-wide. He's a legend so there. And, even better, he talked to me.

If you could be any other musician past or present, which one would it be and why?

I've never wanted to be anyone but myself. There are a few musicians I really admire like Paul McCartney, for being ridiculously talented and creative all the way down the line. Paul Rodgers, the best rock singer ever. Elvis for bringing sexy to the music started by Chuck Berry, Little Richard etc (post the blues classics). Beethoven, for writing such amazing music while going deaf (which seems to be happening to me… what?)

Note: Please Peter, I'm the joke man.

If you had to name one song from any genre that really speaks to you, which one would it be and why?

Well, *right now*, after the debacle of the last four years, topped off by a pandemic and an attack on the capitol and the constitution itself… I just did a small performance for an L.A. based charity to help health care workers and first responders, and I sang the Beatles "Here Comes The Sun." It speaks for itself.

Are you a Mulder or Scully? Do you believe aliens have visited planet earth and if so what do you think they think about mankind?

If they showed up fairly recently, they probably took one look at this mess and turned right around.

173

What was the happiest day of your life and why?
Two days. The day my son was born healthy and beautiful, and the day I found out "Baby Come Back" had made it into the top 100 on Billboard were both amazing days that gave me a great sense of accomplishment and purpose.

If "God" (whatever your idea is on that) were stood before you now, what one question would you ask him/her and why?
I'd ask what happens to our souls once we leave this world. And maybe "What is the meaning of life?" but Monty Python made that very clear.

As an expressive artist in the music industry, how does the state of the planet make you feel?
Happy to be leaving this planet *relatively* soon, as I've run out of adjectives to describe this mess. Having said that, things are looking a little brighter and saner now. Here comes the sun.

Do you think as a person of some influence that there is a duty on us to help influence humanity for the better?
I think everyone has a duty to help influence humanity for the better. My wife Eden makes me do it all the time.

Note: We all got one of them dude.

What one cause would you say you feel most associated with and why? Whether it's equality, poverty, politics, the environment or other?
Mine is the environment because we owe it to our children and the animals to leave them a habitable planet.

If you were stood before the leaders of the world, what would you say to them?
No matter how much power you have or how much money you make, it won't change the fact that you are going to die, so start making decisions that help mankind, not yourselves.

And finally, my last question is in fact one written by Freddie Mercury: If there's a God in the sky, looking down what can he think of what we've done to the world that He created?
"Well... that went sideways" I feel hopeful right now, but the monsters are still out there.

Jim Pons
The Turtles

Jim Pons played bass guitar and sang for some of the most legendary bands of the sixties and seventies. The Leaves, Mothers of Invention and of course, The Turtles, who gave us such classics as "Happy Together". He was also a film director and even designed the logo for the New York Jets. Well of course he did.

How could I not ask Jim my lame questions?

If you could be any other musician past or present, which one would it be and why?
A very difficult question to answer. The list of those who have inspired me ranges from Fats Domino to Bill Monroe. I guess I would have to say Paul McCartney. I actually did want to be him when I started my first band.

If you had to name one song from any genre that really speaks to you, which one would it be and why?
How about "Rhapsody In Blue"? That has been a favourite for the longest time in my life.

Are you a Mulder or Scully? "What does this mean?" Do you believe aliens have visited planet earth and if so what do you think they think about mankind?
I do believe life exists throughout the universe, so it seems like it could be possible given the almost infinite number of planets and galaxies. If anyone has visited here they undoubtedly saw that were are still a very immature species.

Note: So there we have it, I managed to actually find somebody who has never heard of The X-Files.

What was the happiest day of your life and why?
Too many to quantify. Today would be one of them. Just because I am alive and healthy and still able to enjoy what I do with my family.

Note: Awe, bless. How many of us would have said that?

If "God" (whatever your idea is on that) were stood before you now, what one question would you ask him/her and why?
My idea of God is not a him or her that I could stand before. God is the life force existent in all of us.

Note: I agree, therefore I am.

As an expressive artist in the music industry, how does the state of the planet make you feel?
Concerned. We have not taken good care of it and are beginning to suffer the consequences.

Do you think as a person of some influence that there is a duty on us to help influence humanity for the better?
Yes. Absolutely. Thank you for the opportunity to be heard.

What one cause would you say you feel most associated with and why? Whether it's equality, poverty, politics, the environment or other?
Spirituality. All of our problems stem from a mistaken idea of who God is and who we are – the proper understanding of which could still save us – and bring about the kind of peaceful world we dream about...

If you were stood before the leaders of the world, what would you say to them?
I wish I knew the technology of social media better so that I could be heard. I would remind them that we are one human family and that we all exist on a tiny piece of rock third from the sun in a galaxy among trillions of others in the known universe. There has to be a way for us to wake up to that fact and be able to live together peacefully and lovingly.

And finally, my last question is in fact one written by Freddie Mercury: If there's a God in the sky, looking down what can he think of what we've done to the world that He created?
There is not a God in the sky looking down on us thinking about what we are doing. That mythological belief has done more damage to the human race than anything else. It has separated us from God, from each other, and caused fear and anxiety that breeds competition, anger, violence and war. We need to get over that childish myth and accept our own responsibility when it comes to taking care of our planet, and each other. The church has crippled us with the belief that God is coming someday to fix everything. We must wake up and move on from such beliefs before they kill us.

Note: Don't shoot me, he said it. I just happen to agree wholeheartedly.

John Anthony Helliwell
Supertramp

Saxophonist, keyboardist, singer and much more John Anthony Helliwell is a member of that truly super group, Supertramp. Not to name drop or anything, but he also played with Pink Floyd on their album, A Momentary Lapse of Reason, and to be honest, just go do a web search, because he's into just about everything with everybody. How on earth he managed to find time to answer my questions I don't know, but I'm grateful he did, or the book would have been too thin.

If you could be any other musician past or present, which one would it be and why?
Julian "Cannonball" Adderley, because of his musicianship, soul, artistry, and sheer ebullience.

Note: Cannonball Adderley was an acclaimed saxophonist in the 50s and 60s.

If you had to name one song from any genre that really speaks to you, which one would it be and why?
"You've Got A Friend" sung by Donny Hathaway, from his album *Live*. A great song, great sentiments sung about, the best voice, a wonderful audience who sing like angels, a crack band — just one track from the very best live album ever!

Note: A crack band is not one of those 60s psychedelic bands getting high on too much powder.

Are you a Mulder or Scully? Do you believe aliens have visited planet earth and if so what do you think they think about mankind?
I lean towards Scully and if aliens ever visited Earth, I don't think that they would have been too impressed with us.

What was the happiest day of your life and why?
Yesterday — I have lived nearly 40 million minutes, and my heart has beaten about 2.5 billion times, and I am grateful for having survived that long.

Note: How on Earth did you manage to keep count?

If "God" (whatever your idea is on that) were stood before you now, what one question would you ask him/her and why?

"Why do you allow such pain, death, and disaster to be perpetrated by evil people on the world's populace?" I cannot countenance such bringers of war and catastrophes.

As an expressive artist in the music industry, how does the state of the planet make you feel?

Most of the planet's people are fine, things can get easily spoilt by a few insensitive people.

Do you think as a person of some influence that there is a duty on us to help influence humanity for the better?

I don't think that everyone can do it, but my mission, as a musician, is to help to raise people's spirits.

Note: You're doing a damned fine job of it old boy.

What one cause would you say you feel most associated with and why? Whether it's equality, poverty, politics, the environment or other?

Music education for the young.

If you were stood before the leaders of the world, what would you say to them?

Try your best to bring peace to the world please.

And finally, my last question is in fact one written by Freddie Mercury: If there's a God in the sky, looking down what can he think of what we've done to the world that He created?

They would be disappointed, but it would be their fault!

Paul Shortino
Rock Legend

Musician, rock god and lead singer for Rough Cut, The Cutt, Quiet Riot, Bad Boyz and Shortino. He's recorded with J. K. Northrup, written songs for Sega games and recorded lead vocals in the heavy metal Hear 'n' Aid benefit along with Dio, Dokken and a host of rock legends.

And yet, his hearing was till good enough to be able to answer a few questions from me.

If you could be any other musician past or present, which one would it be and why?
John Lennon. Great songwriter, a legend.

If you had to name one song from any genre that really speaks to you, which one would it be and why?
"In My Life". This song says it all in the lyrics. There are places I remember all my life though some have changed, some for good and not for better. Some have gone and some remain.

Are you a Mulder or Scully? Do you believe aliens have visited planet earth and if so what do you think they think about mankind?
Mulder. Yes aliens have been to Earth They are right here still. I believe they think we're full of ourselves especially with social media. It's all about how many likes humans can get.

What was the happiest day of your life and why?
That's a tough question. The day my son Paul Jr was born. He was born to "Whole Lotta Love" by Led Zeppelin, one of my favourite bands. Also the day I married my Soulmate Carmen. We eloped to Las Vegas.

If "God" (whatever your idea is on that) were stood before you now, what one question would you ask him/her and why?
Why did you create human beings? The most destructive creatures on the planet. We could learn a lot, just from dogs. A definition of gratitude.

Note: I have watched my dogs and I still have not managed to scratch behind my ears with my hind legs yet. Still trying. Much to learn.

As an expressive artist in the music industry, how does the state of the planet make you feel?
I believe the planet goes through cycles like the seasons. We don't have any control over it. I do believe mankind has abused the planet. I feel sad that there are animal species, plants, whales, fish going extinct. I feel we need to have a balance between mankind and nature. I fear if this doesn't happen soon it will be too late.

Do you think as a person of some influence that there is a duty on us to help influence humanity for the better?
I believe everyone who lives on this beautiful planet has a duty to show respect, treat our planet with love and not abuse it.
Note: Damn right.

What one cause would you say you feel most associated with and why? Whether it's equality, poverty, politics, the environment or other?
I'm very involved with saving animals, homeless folks and Veterans. My wife Carmen and I try to get more people involved in helping by doing events to bring awareness.

If you were stood before the leaders of the world, what would you say to them?
I would say I'm tired of broken promises. I'm tired of them using race to keep us divided and the endless wars. We came into this world innocent not hating each other. This hate is taught to us.

And finally, my last question is in fact one written by Freddie Mercury: If there's a God in the sky, looking down what can he think of what we've done to the world that He created?
God who created the universe and all life is looking at an evil corrupt world. "For God so loved the world that He gave His only begotten son, that whoever believes in Him should not perish but have everlasting life." -John 3:16.
   Caring for others is the tie that's binds. The work of God on this earth is unstoppable. God will work everything together for the advancement of His kingdom, and He will not leave you behind. His work cannot be halted or hindered.

© Andy Goodwin

Robbie Fulks

Grammy nominated country singer and songwriter, Robbie Fulks, has released more than a dozen albums over the course of a thirty-year history. He has a wonderful clean and yet rough style that stands out amid the technical wizardry that seems to take over these days. Jim Fusilli of the Wall Street Journal said that "a world in which Fulks isn't a household name is somehow upside down." In an upside-down world, I happen to agree, so I spoke to him and this is the result.

If you could be any other musician past or present, which one would it be and why?

You caught me at a moment when I'm researching songwriters of the Middle Ages, so those largely obscure figures — Troubadours, in a word — are occupying most of my musical attention and curiosity. The subgroup called *Trobairitz* were women who roamed around a wide swath of southern Europe in the 12th and 13th centuries; they're the first women in history to have composed secular music. Among them was a figure called Ysabella. Of her almost nothing is known, including whether she was flesh-and-blood or an invention of another composer. If she did exist, there are multiple theories about her identity, all of which link her by blood or marriage to powerful rulers. So I'd like to be her, if only to find out if she was real, who she was, and what on earth it was like to lead a life like hers in the 1200s. That said, I'd want a two-way trip for the experiment, returning quickly to the air-conditioned present.

Note: You will be happy to know that Robbie gave me such full answers I won't be adding anything in.

If you had to name one song from any genre that really speaks to you, which one would it be and why?

There are really hundreds, so to single one out is false, but one I've been playing at home almost every day for the last few months is "Goin' Back To The Blue Ridge Mountains" by the Delmore Brothers. It has some things in common with a lot of the songs that resonate with me: some melancholy in the tone, lyrics that verge on meaninglessness ("you can't be my little baby, you can't be my sweetheart now"), and a simple singable melody. Almost all the value that can come of a tune like this is in the performance, which calls on you to invest yourself fully.

What was the happiest day of your life and why?
It sounds a little self-centred, but the day I was born was a red-letter day for me. For most of my life (which has admittedly been an easy ride compared to most lives) I've managed to take strong and conscious pleasure in the simple fact of existing, and I do feel gloomy about the prospect that one day it will all end.

If "God" (whatever your idea is on that) were stood before you now, what one question would you ask him/her and why?
Why did you create a universe with so little evidence of your Hand? What do you have to say that explains this species of mammal who strives to locate, know, describe, and worship you, but who in learning ever more about the natural world have ever more reason to exclude you from the universe?

As an expressive artist in the music industry, how does the state of the planet make you feel?
I see the atomic work done during World War Two as an opening of Pandora's Box and the beginning of the end for us. Sadly, the place is rigged to blow up, and there's no erasing the knowledge that got us to this point. On the plus side, it does seem likely that the planet itself, and its ability to regenerate some kind of organic life, will continue. And it does seem likely to me that among the innumerable other habitable planets out there, life is going on and will go on.

Do you think as a person of some influence that there is a duty on us to help influence humanity for the better?
This is tricky, because before you arrive to influence others, they already have an idea of the direction in which they'd like to be influenced. In recent American life we've experienced the dire effects of a particular influencer. This gnawed away at me to where I eventually felt an irresistible need to do things I had never done before — donate to activist groups, play fundraisers, and, wildest of all, disclose to my audience my political stance. The results were mostly predictable. I put a tiny drop into an enormous bucket, enraged and alienated some of my fans who disagreed with my views, and earned a bump in esteem and some cheap online praise from the others.

Besides its being unclear whether all this constituted a net gain or loss for me personally, I have no very sure sense of having contributed to the bigger outcome. I think the outcome, meaning the presidential election, would have been the same if I'd done nothing at all. By comparison, on occasions when I've helped a neighbour, consoled a grieving friend, or given food to a homeless person, there's been an immediate and perceptible payoff for both parties.

I talked to a musician friend the other day who told me that she's coming out of the Trump era with renewed resolve to be an agent of this sort of very local and practical service. This is an inspiring route because it's available to people of no particular influence, and it gets around the problem of setting yourself up as an irritating, look-at-me, public opinionater. But it leaves open the question of moving bigger dials. There I suspect the best way forward is through the idea of "effective altruism" as defined by Toby Ord — a data-based leveraging of the wealth of privileged societies. I guess the implication of that, to bring it back around to the question you asked, is that there is more power and influence in systematic social behaviours than in all the celebrity statements on earth.

***What one cause would you say you feel most associated with and why?
Whether it's equality, poverty, politics, the environment or other?***
There's no shortage of ways to better poorly functioning systems by tinkering with embedded incentives. What's stopping that from happening? What keeps us from making immediate improvements in the performance of, for instance, our public schools, elected representatives, police, health-care systems? First, that people's financial incentives are in line with the systems as currently configured. This area is way beyond my IQ, but I'll press forward anyway: one of the biggest social changes in my lifetime is the prevalence of cigarette smoking. When I was born, in 1963, 42% of my countrymen were smokers. Now it's 15%. That's a radical change that was achieved against powerfully entrenched interests — not to mention the entrenched desires of many millions of addicts! — but 58 years, believe me, is a long, long time.

The other piece of the puzzle, it seems to me, is the attraction of terrible ideas. Tribal attachments that override the fact of our species' biological sameness are an evolutionary inheritance that makes for some awful outcomes. It seems to me that most of the sufferings we're able to inflict so self-confidently on others stand exposed as mere brutality once the intoxicating ideas that support them are stripped away; so the ideas make for excellent targets. Among the bad ideas — I say this fully aware of your resumé, Philip! — religious faith tops the list for me... but I'll leave it there.

If you were stood before the leaders of the world, what would you say to them?
Too many men, more women please.

And finally, my last question is in fact one written by Freddie Mercury: If there's a God in the sky, looking down what can he think of what we've done to the world that He created?
That's a big "if," but if there is one, then the explaining that needs done is not one-directional.

Steve Hackett
Genesis

Oh my, where do I start with a man like Steve Hackett? Musician, singer, songwriter, producer and all-round grand chap. Most folk will have heard of that little prog-rock band called Genesis. Well, Steve was in that. In fact six studio albums, three live albums, seven singles and one little old EP. In 2010 he was, with the other members, inducted into the Rock and Roll Hall of Fame (it's a little place round the back of the Red Lion).

There aren't many people who can claim to have influenced Eddie Van Halen or Brian May, but Steve's amazing musical ability is beyond compare, so we won't go there anyway. His solo work is vast, so vast it would turn this book into Lord of the Rings, so go and do a web search thingy on that phone glued to your hand.

So he's a god of music and I managed to get an audience with him up in the lofty clouds.

If you could be any other musician past or present, which one would it be and why?
It would be Bach. He was extraordinary skilled as both musician and composer, and ahead of his own times.

If you had to name one song from any genre that really speaks to you, which one would it be and why?
It would be "MacArthur Park", written by Jimmy Webb and sung by Richard Harris. It's because of both the power of the sentiment combined with the orchestration, and sensitively sung. An homage to lost love.

Note: Now kids, Richard Harris is a legend in the acting world and he sang this song which took us all by surprise, pleasantly. It'll be on YouTube I'm sure. Have a look.

Are you a Mulder or Scully? Do you believe aliens have visited planet earth and if so what do you think they think about mankind?
I can't remember the details of the characters, but it was a thought-provoking series. I doubt if they have visited Earth, as it would take them so many light years to reach this obscure part of our galaxy. But if they did and if they'd reached a high state of development, I guess they'd see us as flawed, irresponsible

creatures, easily manipulated by narcissistic leaders.

Note: I must be an alien, because that's exactly what I think! Nanoo nanoo (okay so if you're under fifty you won't get that).

What was the happiest day of your life and why?
The day I married my wife Jo because I'd finally found my true love and soulmate, and it was a perfect day.

Note: And now Jo, you have it in print, give the man a hug.

If "God" (whatever your idea is on that) were stood before you now, what one question would you ask him/her and why?
I would ask the question, "Why?"

As an expressive artist in the music industry, how does the state of the planet make you feel?
Despondent. In fact, Jo and I have just written a song which expresses ecological concerns. It'll be on my next album.

Do you think as a person of some influence that there is a duty on us to help influence humanity for the better?
Yes I do. I wish deeper concerns were more a part of today's music culture, and we ideally need to support humanitarian efforts.

What one cause would you say you feel most associated with and why? Whether it's equality, poverty, politics, the environment or other?
All those causes concern me, but perhaps most of all the environment, because without protecting the planet, we've all had it in every way.

Note: Vote Hackett.

If you were stood before the leaders of the world, what would you say to them?
Plan long term, think globally, feed the family of Man and do your part to take care of the entire planet.

And finally, my last question is in fact one written by Freddie Mercury: If there's a God in the sky, looking down what can he think of what we've done to the world that He created?
He, She, It or The Force which links us all would be pretty disturbed at the current state of everything. We all need to do our bit to heal the world's wounds.

Ric Sanders
Fairport Convention

Apart from the fact that Ric Sanders is an extremely nice man, he's also a music legend. Yes he is. The people he has played with is amazing. Rick Wakeman, Dave Cousins of Strawbs, Jethro Tull, Robert Plant, Roy Harper, Gary Brooker of Procol Harum, Pentangle, Gordon Giltrap, All About Eve, The Mission, to name but a few.

But his day job is as a member of the folk-rock band, Fairport Convention. And that's how I tracked him down. I shall not be putting in notes because Ric has given us plenty to read and besides, you have to be getting bored of me by now.

If you could be any other musician, past or present, which one would it be and why?

I've never felt confident about singing. Sometimes if the mood takes me I might scat sing in unison with the notes I'm playing on the violin. It would be an exaggeration to say that this sound has proved popular with audiences unless they've all had one or three glasses of Shiraz too many, under which circumstances it has occasionally gone down quite well. So I've always been an instrumentalist, and although I'm best known for being, since 1985, the fiddle player in Fairport Convention, my background is that of blues, jazz, and rock, and the players who have influenced me most come from those genres.

It would be next to impossible for any jazz fiddle player of my generation not to be influenced by the great Stephane Grappelli and Jean-Luc Ponty, but in fact Don 'Sugarcane' Harris, who played with, amongst others, John Mayall and Frank Zappa, has I think been my main influence, because nobody has ever brought the fiddle closer to the blues harp than he, and the blues is at the heart of everything I do. I've never aspired to sound like anyone but myself though. Couldn't really.

I've been influenced by many non-violinists too. Working with the mighty guitarist John Etheridge in Soft Machine and 2nd Vision taught me a lot. Still haven't answered the question yet have I? Past or present you say? Well, from the past it would have been something to have been Percy Grainger, just to experience occupying the mind of such an amazing composer. But from the present (final answer alert!), there is no musician I enjoy listening to more than Jeff Beck, so there's my answer – it's Jeff!

I

If you could name one song from any genre that really speaks to you, which one would it be and why?

I recently saw Paul McCartney in a 2018 interview with Jarvis Cocker in front of a live audience at The Liverpool Institute, and a member of the audience asked Macca if there was one song by another songwriter that he'd wished he had written. He chose the beautiful 'Fields Of Gold', by Sting.

One of the many joys of being in Fairport over the years has been having the opportunity to write instrumentals for the group. My instrumentals have loosely fallen into two categories. Firstly, up tempo, whimsical, folk influenced jaunts, often with a jazzy twist, which John Shuttleworth would describe as 'fun tunes'! Secondly, and much more difficult to write, are the folk influenced ballads, again with a (hopefully) more subtle jazzy twist — tunes like 'Portmeirion', 'The Rose Hip', and 'Precious Time'.

There are few things in the art of composition more difficult than writing a simple but beautiful folk-like melody that touches people's hearts. Nik Kershaw is a brilliant songwriter with a great gift for such melodies, and in 2012 I was delighted to play on his lovely song 'Red Strand', which also has beautiful lyrics, from his album *EI8HT*. In my case I don't have to worry about lyrics.

The lyrics of 'Fields Of Gold' are beautiful too, as are the lyrics of the song I have chosen, which is by Macca, from his 1997 album *Flaming Pie*, and is called 'Calico Skies'. The melody is wonderful, and the lyrics speak of personal and universal love. Gets me every time. In the trio I have with Vo Fletcher and Michael Gregory we have often played these songs as instrumentals, and they work beautifully.

Are you a Mulder or Scully? Do you believe aliens have visited planet earth and if so what do you think they think about mankind?

I love science fiction, and as a kid read lots of H.G. Wells, Isaac Asimov, Arthur C. Clarke, and many of the other classics. Most recently I have been enjoying the brilliant steampunk novels of Colin Edmonds in his *Steam, Smoke & Mirrors* series. I became an immediate fan of *The X-Files* when it first aired in 1993, and I'm a Mulder and a Scully.

Like Fox Mulder I believe we can't be the only sentient life forms in such a vast universe, but the sceptical Dana Scully side of me thinks, from the little I know about physics, that to travel the immense interstellar distances needed to find other civilisations, or for them to find us, makes it pretty unlikely. The little I do know about physics has been gleaned from the two Brians (or the two brains!), Cox and May.

I do have a GCE O-Level in physics, Grade 4, but we never got as far as manipulating the fabric of the space-time continuum to create transwarp conduits. Had I worked harder and got a Grade 1, I might have a better grasp of all this stuff, but it was 1967, I was fifteen, had heard 'Sergeant Pepper' and 'Magical Mystery Tour', discovered Miles Davis, decided to be a jazz rock fiddle player, and had the shades and a fuzz box to prove it! Science took a back seat, and to this day I think string theory is something to do with ukuleles!

As to what aliens might think about mankind had they visited Earth, I imagine they'd think, 'shows promise, pity about Donald Trump'. I'm assuming here of course that these aliens would be benevolent and enlightened. But perhaps

Trump himself is an alien. He does have an uncomfortably reptilian look about him. I'm not being fair on reptiles here am I?! I don't even like to speak the name of the former president anymore, and should he crop up in these answers again I'll simply use one of Jimmy Kimmel's nicknames instead. 'Uncle Scam' is a favourite, as is 'Fibberace', as is 'Golfie McNugget'!

On reflection, I think that I lean more towards being like Scully — a great fan of the empirical. I'm always fascinated and entertained by ideas of aliens visiting Earth millions of years ago and suchlike, but when it comes to the conspiracy theories proposed by the lunatic fringe of The Republican Party, the theories which stop people wearing masks, getting vaccinated, and makes them believe that elections were stolen, I see danger lights flashing very brightly! Even Mulder and Scully would have trouble getting their heads round these nut jobs!

What was the happiest day of your life and why?
I'm guessing I'm not the only one to say that I'm hoping it hasn't happened yet! On a personal level it's the day I met the love of my life. On a broader level, I remember the day of Live Aid — Saturday July 13th 1985. I'd recently played on my first Fairport Convention album, and plans were afoot to go on tour — plans which would change my life. So I was in an optimistic mood when I settled down in front of my little telly in Birmingham, cranked the volume up to 11, and heard The Quo kick into 'Rockin' All Over The World' — fantastic! I watched the whole show, feeling proud to be part of a music industry that was making such a difference.

Whilst still lamenting that governments should do more, and sad to hear the voices that want to cut foreign aid, I always support Children in Need and Comic Relief, because surely a function of any art form should be to remind us of those less fortunate than ourselves. One of the best things about being a musician is to be able to do a bit of fundraising. Although after such events I do sometimes think, in the immortal words of Major Dennis Bloodnock from The Goon Show, as written by Spike Milligan and voiced by Peter Sellars, 'It's the least I can do — a quantity I specialise in!'

If "God" (whatever your idea is on that) were stood before you now, what one question would you ask him/her and why?
Firstly we need to clarify — is it him or her, and how do we find out? Well, more often than not God is referred to as He, which is a gender-specific personal pronoun, meaning that if there is a Mr God, there must therefore be a Mrs God, otherwise God is an It, i.e. a gender-free entity or one which embraces all of the genders, however many that may be, and remember we're not talking just of this planet here — there could be millions of them (see Question 3).

So why is God usually called He? Probably because most religious books were written by men, being the more dominant of the species and always more than happy to subjugate women, other men they could bully, animals, and anything else they could think of! You could probably be forgiven now for thinking that I have a problem with religion, but it's not that simple.

I describe myself as an atheist humanist Christian Buddhist who also has a well-worn copy of *The Bhagavad Gita*. You could probably be forgiven now for thinking that I'm a confused person, but it's not that simple. The atheist/humanist part of me simply can't believe in the, for want of a better word, supernatural aspects of religion — an all-powerful omnipresent all-knowing being just doesn't ring true. The phrase 'God made Man (male again!) in His image' doesn't make sense either, as the reverse seems much more likely. Nor does any afterlife or concept of a heaven where you can live eternally without evolving. As for the concept of a hell, that's so medievally off the scale to me that it's not worth discussing, but if you want it, it's on Freeview Channel 70, The Horror Channel. You can also get *Star Trek* on there too, which is good to know!

You could probably be forgiven now for wondering how I could in any way describe myself as any sort of Christian, but it's not that simple. I come from a Salvation Army family, and I remember them as good people, who got out and about to help others. They had good brass bands as well — my dad played tenor horn in one when he was young. Then in the war years he swapped the Sally Army uniform for an RAF one and discovered Duke Ellington and Ella Fitzgerald. I was very grateful to hear his collection of shellac 78s as a nipper — still love them. Still got them! I have a lot of Christian friends now, in fact friends of many faiths, and whereas I may not believe in all the stuff they do, they're all very tolerant and nice people. I'm most familiar with Christianity of course, and the good stuff about Christianity is very good. So I think Jesus, though not the son of a god I can't believe exists, was a wonderfully good and kind man, and I celebrate him as such.

To me it's beyond tragic how his teachings have been misrepresented over the centuries. There are many religions that I know very little about, but I feel sure that they all have goodness within them. To put it mildly it's such a shame when a perverted version of a faith is used for power and cruelty. In the case of Christianity nothing in our contemporary world demonstrates this much better than American TV evangelists like the horrific Kenneth Copeland who scams those vulnerable enough to put their trust in him, and has become so immensely rich that he has a private jet he calls 'A Preaching Machine', and then uses it to go on hunting holidays in Texas so he can be proudly photographed with two beautiful axis deer that he's bravely shot. And he's not the only one. These TV evangelist scumbags bang on about Satan, who doesn't exist, but if he/she/it did you'd find him/her/it pretty close to home, you evil sods!

And so to Buddhism, which deserves a new paragraph after my little rant! Buddhism is the religion which appeals to me most, probably because it doesn't have a supreme deity — Buddha was a man, not a god. I like the idea of aspiring to find awareness, enlightenment, higher consciousness, and compassion. And if there is an existence beyond this life, I find reincarnation to be the most plausible, so I'm pinning my hopes on it. And so to my copy of *The Bhagavad Gita*. I've had it since about 1972, when I learned Transcendental Meditation, which I practise to this day. I liked the fact that I was told I didn't have to believe in anything in particular for it to work, which proved to be true. It was described as The Science Of Creative Intelligence. I've never had much to do with the TM organisation, or any other organisation connected in any way to religion, for no other reason that it's a personal and private thing.

We have George Harrison to thank for doing so much for Indian music and spirituality all those years ago. I loved listening to Ravi Shankar, saw him at Birmingham Town Hall, which was magical, and these days I love listening to his daughter Anoushka Shankar. In the seventies John McLaughlin fused Indian music with his own wonderful style of jazz and rock with The Mahavishnu Orchestra and Shakti. Shakti toured with Soft Machine around 1976, and it was a fantastic experience meeting those guys and hearing them play. Their violinist was the incredible L Shankar — and he just couldn't have been nicer to me! So, at long last, what question would I ask God if he/she/it were standing before me now? I could do no better than the one posed by the inimitable comic Steven Wright. I'd say 'God, if you dropped acid would you see people?'

As an expressive artist in the music industry, how does the state of the planet make you feel?

It's hard not to be anything but very worried about the state of the planet — the environment, the rise of the far right and white supremacists, especially of course in the USA. And so much conflict everywhere you look. Nobody seems to agree about anything! But there are lots of good, tolerant, and kind people who just keep the world turning. We don't have a spare planet, so better look after this one, and if anyone can, it's those kind people, who couldn't be better represented than by our wonderful NHS who have worked tirelessly to help us through the nightmare of Covid-19.

Do you think as a person of some influence that there is a duty on us to help influence humanity for the better?

Music and indeed all art forms can work on many levels, and sometimes needs to do nothing more than simply lift your spirit. Music certainly does that for me, and comedy too. Whatever the artist or performer feels is fine by me — I wouldn't want to inflict a sense of duty on a juggler or magician or trapeze artist. Their great talents give more than enough just in the amazement and delight they bring! Music can make you groove or touch your heart. Poetry, drama, dance and the visual and conceptual arts can make you think about life in new ways — there's so much that art can do and yes, in many ways help influence humanity for the better and make the world a kinder place.

What would you say you feel most associated with and why? Whether it's equality, poverty, politics, the environment or other?

I've always been an advocate for kindness to animals. It's a cause very close to my heart. Animals don't have a voice of their own, they need human friends to help them. I was born in 1952 and from the moment I found out where meat came from, I couldn't believe it. I remember at primary school learning that there were words which had the same sound but different meanings, so if we had lamb for lunch I thought it couldn't be those beautiful little animals we'd been shown living happily on farms. I discovered there were places called slaughterhouses, and I was horrified.

I tried to go vegetarian when I was seven or eight, but we had a dinner lady who had been trained by the SAS, so that was not an option. I became vegetarian in the early sixties, and that was my first step in not conforming to how society wanted me to be, and becoming a musician followed on from that, because I wanted to be part of that sixties counterculture that was not just entertainment but sought to say things about the world. Yes, it was teenage idealism I know, but I've never lost it, and still to me why I play music is even more important than how I play music.

Compassion is my favourite word. In some ways it's an even better word than love, because you can show compassion to someone you don't love, or even dislike intensely! I may say some very caustic things about politicians and TV evangelists, but I would never do them any harm. I would show them the compassion they most certainly would not show to me. It would be nice to see Golfie and Kenneth banged up in prison though. Nothing draconian — they could share a nice comfortable cell and plan all the scams they could do together if they ever got out!

I became vegan about ten years ago, after seeing some PETA films and reading an article by the musician Julian Cope. The cruelty in much of the dairy industry is less obvious to people I think. I know there are organic farmers who do have higher standards of animal welfare, and good for them — any move in that direction is a step forward. But I have no doubt that even with the most heartless factory farming, animal products will not feed the ever-increasing population in this world. Going plant-based is healthier, and kinder to the environment that we all depend on. And now here's a couple of answers to the questions I've been asked many times in 55 or so years of being veggie, by people trying to catch me out!

Animals eat other animals though, don't they?
I've always felt compassion towards animals but have never, ever, even for one moment, wanted to behave like one.

You care about animals more than people don't you?
Just not true. Kindness has no limits. You can be kind to people, animals, and the planet.

By the way, I hope it doesn't sound like I'm preaching! Many of my dearest and closest friends are not vegetarian, and I still love them!

If you were stood before the leaders of the world, what would you say to them?
Take global warming very, very seriously. Believe in science. Try to take on board that as long as the gap between the very rich and the very poor is as vast as it is now, then we will never live in a conflict-free world. It's much better, and much easier, to be kind rather than cruel. Find tolerance and love, not bigotry and dogma, in whatever your faith or politics may be. Oh, and never lose your sense of humour! My favourite world leader, The Dali Lama, has never lost his, even during a lifetime in exile.

And finally, my last question is in fact one written by Freddie Mercury: If there's a God in the sky, looking down what can he think of what we've done to the world that He created?
It's a beautiful song. We're still creating this world — and it's up to us. If things go wrong we only have our own species to blame. If things go right, then we will have found goodness by looking no further than our own hearts. Love, Peace, and Evolution.

Parthenon Huxley
ELO II

Parthenon, yes that's his name, is an American musician, singer, songwriter and producer. Probably because he gets bored or something. His name by the way is his stage name. He loves Greece and Aldous Huxley, the writer. So now you know.

He is known for his solo albums and for his involvement in ELO Part II and The Orchestra. He has also made cameo appearances in several films including Dragon: The Bruce Lee Story and The Flintstones. Why you ask? Because he's famous, stupid.

If you could be any other musician past or present, which one would it be and why?
Jimi Hendrix and John Lennon both died too young and suffered so much pain from their parents, it's tough to choose either of them. I'll go with Paul McCartney, the most successful musician of the twentieth century and deserving of every accolade he gets. All his success aside, I admire Paul because he is first and foremost a creator. I don't love everything he's created, but I know there'll always be more coming down the pike, because *create* is what he does, and that's what I believe is our mission on Earth: create (as opposed to destroy.) And, of course, at his peak, McCartney was arguably the greatest creator we've ever had, not to mention an amazing singer, bassist, guitarist, drummer, pianist, lyricist, arranger, band leader and live performer.

If you had to name one song from any genre that really speaks to you, which one would it be and why?
Loads of songs absolutely move me to tears, including "Starting Over" by John Lennon, "A Long December" by Counting Crows, "I Can See Clearly Now" by Johnny Nash, "America" by Simon & Garfunkel, "The End" by The Beatles, but if I had to choose one, then, today at least, it would be "Don't Dream It's Over" by Crowded House. It's a melodic and lyrical marvel with a never-ending appeal to my sensibilities as a creator, as a dreamer, as a writer and artist. "Don't Dream It's Over" ought to be humanity's rallying cry in the face of global threats to our existence.

Are you a Mulder or Scully? Do you believe aliens have visited planet earth and if so what do you think they think about mankind?
My dad saw a UFO once, a big silver shape, hovering over his backyard. He was a no-nonsense chemical engineer, former Marine, so if he said he saw one, that's good enough evidence for me.

I always imagine aliens watching us and marvelling at our sleep habits. "Earthlings do the strangest thing. They lay horizontally and become inactive whenever the Earth spins away from the Sun. When the Sun's light returns, they rise and often claim to have experienced odd adventures that make little sense."

What was the happiest day of your life and why?
Two days: the birth of my daughters, Fiona and Imogen. And every day since has been an echo of my two happiest days.

If "God" (whatever your idea is on that) were stood before you now, what one question would you ask him/her and why?
Where did you come from, God? What existed before everything began? If the answer is nothing, then how and why did nothing become something?

As an expressive artist in the music industry, how does the state of the planet make you feel?
I hold out hope we won't overrun the planet and destroy ourselves, but logic says it's nearly inevitable. I believe it will take some massive mind-altering events to turn us into better planetary caretakers. These events could be inspired by amazing leaders, catastrophes that force our hands to take action, viruses that wipe out populations, who knows? The human story is being written every day *and it's a mixed bag of progress and tragedy.*

Do you think as a person of some influence that there is a duty on us to help influence humanity for the better?
I have no illusions that I'm influential or duty bound to decide what's best for humanity. One can influence others mostly by personal example. In that light, despite my faults and shortcomings I hope I've lived my life in an overall positive, creative, loving way. There is some evidence that my music speaks to people's better sides and moves them in a loving way. I think I'm most impressed with young people like Greta Thunberg, Malala and Emma Gonzalez. They have already done more in their young lives to reach people than a hundred of me. They give me a lot of hope.

What one cause would you say you feel most associated with and why? Whether it's equality, poverty, politics, the environment or other?
I financially lend to support to three groups: Black Lives Matter, Democrats and 4Ocean. I'm particularly hopeful that we can clean up the oceans. It seems achievable through new technology and stricter environmental laws. Cleaning our water is also relatively non-political. Who doesn't want clean water? Who is not outraged by nation-sized patches of plastic bottles bobbing on the ocean? It seems possible to make a difference.

If you were stood before the leaders of the world, what would you say to them?

At this crucial juncture in the history of mankind, we must think in terms of *planet first, sovereignty second.* There are no such things as American car exhaust, Chinese coal emissions or Brazilian fires from deforestation. They must be seen as borderless, human actions that endanger all nations. For nations to respect the internal affairs of other nations, internal affairs must remain internal. Therefore, to ensure sovereignty, nations must replace coal, gas burning engines, deforestation and other non-localized activities with technologies and policies that eliminate harm to other nations.

And finally, my last question is in fact one written by Freddie Mercury: If there's a God in the sky, looking down what can he think of what we've done to the world that He created?

She'd probably say, "I knew they'd muck things up. I suppose I'd better get down there."

Jon Carroll
Starland Vocal Band

© Julian Parker-Burns

At age just 18 years old, Jon Carroll was a founding member of Starland Vocal Band, and recorded the number one hit "Afternoon Delight". The group went on to win two Grammy Awards.

Since then, he's not slowed down as a performer, composer, arranger, producer, songwriter and musician. His works have appeared in films, commercials and episodic dramas and comedies, and he is highly sought after studio session performer appearing on many recordings.

His songs have been covered by artists such as Linda Ronstadt, Tom Jones and Kenny Rogers. He's also the long-time keyboard player and vocalist and band member with Mary Chapin Carpenter, with touring stints for countless others including Rodney Crowell, Dixie Chicks, Peter Wolf and Eric Lindell. He's also a true gentleman and had time to answer my questions.

If you could be any other musician past or present, which one would it be and why?

That's a fabulously profound question, although it begs the temptation to bring many non-musical informative aspects into its answer. For instance, in experiential terms, I'm more curious about the salient respective cultural realities within the "story universes" of say, Little Richard, Nat King Cole, Paul Robeson, Chuck Berry, or even someone in their band... Johnny Johnson, perhaps. But to be a Black artist in their time, what wondrous elixirs I could retrieve and further impart to others. A woman, a Josephine Baker or Marion McPartland, perhaps, would offer some grand juxtapositions, to be sure. So, there's a bit of a "would you want to experience the consciousness of that being, who happened to be a musician?" I'm hard pressed to choose what would transcend which.

So, in light of all that being a particular person would entail and reveal to me, I suppose I'd choose a player/producer/arranger/performer to cover as much musical ground as possible, then fervently follow them into their cultural realities. What they had in their toolkit, what they knew about how to use those tools, whom did they encounter and with whom and how did they collaborate? Tough one. But all considered, including the music played, written, arranged, performed, I'd be Ray Charles. What more possibly could be wrought from that life and artistic world as a perspective broadener is anyone's guess. It's actually a bit frightening to ponder. On third thought, yeah… Brother Ray.

If you had to name one song from any genre that really speaks to you,
which one would it be and why?
Please. This hurts. Too many. But… I've performed (and recorded) Bob Dylan's
"Tight Connection To My Heart" over the years, and I often say it's my favourite
of his. It's one of those brilliantly told tales within a three-act structure that (to
me) speaks so tenderly of the realities of life: the challenge of reconciling innate
personal dignity with the inevitable threats to self-esteem, and how we must rely
and concentrate on the former to prevail over the latter. It's a wonderful gospel to
me, all wrapped up in that justified definition of humanity — longing.

Are you a Mulder or Scully? Do you believe aliens have visited planet earth
and if so what do you think they think about mankind?
I have one tattoo, and it's a simple rendering of a crop circle that appeared in
Sept 2001 near a spot in the UK where (I later learned) historians theorise may
have been the site of a series of battles that eventuated the fall of the Roman
Empire. Of course, that's not why it spoke to me. I was ignorant of any of such
history. I just liked it, as I do most of those beautiful crop circles that, although
many "experts" have proffered, haven't been convincingly explained.

They're beautiful, harmonically perfect, and I believe that human intellectual
arrogance knows no bounds in light of so many boundaries that define our
perception. All the while, so much exists beyond what we can physically perceive
or intellectually conceive. That's to say, if we can come to terms with say, that
fruit fly's obliviousness to say, us… why then do we find it so difficult to accept
that we humans are merely another step of consciousness along on that grand
stairway that leads to/from who knows where? We're intelligent enough to have
that intellectual facility with which we hone a conveniently articulated manifest
version of existential desperation. In other words, I'm a Mulder. Were those
circles and halos in ancient renderings really space helmets? Sure, why not?
Because really… I don't know shit.

What was the happiest day of your life and why?
There we are again, with a profoundly indefinable word: Happiness. The question
also begs to consider a day as a unit, much like a bolt of fabric, if you will. I don't
believe, or desire to believe, in "good" or "bad" days, "happy" or "sad"… every
breath is magical, and every moment precious. I do recall not days, but moments
within them that held great import. I had a moment after leaving a friend's house
where I had been hanging out with a particular group of personalities that enabled
me to, for the first time, have an independent sense of my own personality and
spirit, knowing what I liked about those people, and an inkling of maybe what
they liked about me. I share that memory with younger folks who are deciding
whether to commit to a long-range agreement of some sort — marriage, for
instance. Because at that time, I was 27 years old and it was six years after my
first marriage, five years after the birth of my son, which was truly humbling, holy,
whole and soul justifying.

There've been accomplishments and reaching various ego-gratifying
destinations are certainly worthy of celebration. Finishing a song. Releasing

a record. Proudly finishing a creation. None of those outshines the immediate gratification of easing someone's pain, of boosting another's outlook, helping one who's feeling the fear of desperation. Sharing experience, strength and hope. That to me brings the most soul-felt glow of righteous purpose and spiritual resolve. There are a handful of memories of times when I was having so much fun with a group of friends —I mean laughing until I seriously thought I would pass out. One of those days was when I was eleven. Another was when I was in my forties, I think, on a tour bus with one particularly wonderful group of people. That's pure celebratory joy. A great show on a tour that I'll know I'll remember forever. The feeling of love, understanding, forgiveness and hope. That's the God I strive to know better and hang out with more often. Today. Today is the happiest day of my life.

If "God" (whatever your idea is on that) were stood before you now, what one question would you ask him/her and why?
I would, and do often, ask for the wisdom to know the difference between the things I could bravely try to change for the better, and the things I'd be wise to merely accept as a tolerable reality. Because I'm a dumbass.

As an expressive artist in the music industry, how does the state of the planet make you feel?
As an artist, I feel a responsibility to follow a spiritually well-informed muse and trajectory, though there's ever the consideration of what one must do in order to sustain the facility with which to express oneself as an artist. Being aware and in-step with the spiritual rhythm around us and within us is crucial. When American society is rife with meritocratic constructs, we must be brave and silence the superficial. There is a flame of truth always burning at our centre. Stillness and reflection will open the windows to help clear the smoke and fog that shroud those things that are merely burning.

Do you think as a person of some influence that there is a duty on us to help influence humanity for the better?
Each of us is a person of influence. That fact perhaps is one that escapes many folks who are caught up in the machinations of their own "bane of existence". That's so unfortunate, for it lulls us, perhaps batters us, into a sense of personal insignificance, and nothing could be more untrue. We affect everyone we meet, see, smile at, shout at, share a moment with to every infinite degree. I do believe an equality and justice-oriented stance is crucial, and I believe that folks are ever increasingly aware of the bravery required to maintain it. That requires seeing to your voice being heard in an original, but resolute way.

Righteous indignation goes a long way, when being "right" is the ammunition to counter what may be doing many people "wrong". We must look after each other. For we are each other. We must each and all Stand Up! Our fear fosters further intimidation, and there are forces whose raison d'etre is to capitalise on those fears — of loss, of harm, of respect. They are bullies, and they must be opposed.

Spirits become emboldened when it appears all other measures have or will fail. To maintain, retain, our theoretical democracy here, bravery must be implemented well prior to that point. In terms of holy flesh, Jesus walked, did not cower, all the way to Calvary. All appropriated historical moralising and liturgical sensationalism notwithstanding, that is inspirational to say the least. Human rights and justice warriors should not, have not and will not cower.

If I had one wish for our human race, it's that we'd all learn somehow to be more interested and curious in the lives and works of others. We've been around long enough on this little space-ball to have discovered, learned and had many causes that affected much and many. A mere humbly sincere interest in the multitudes of our historical pasts is awesome. The gift of inquisitiveness keeps on giving to one and all throughout it. Knowledge is power.

What one cause would you say you feel most associated with and why? Whether it's equality, poverty, politics, the environment or other?
To live, work, play, breathe and create in a way that will embody and convey an appreciation and celebration of our being one of many glorious species on a unified planet. Universality. One love.

If you were stood before the leaders of the world, what would you say to them?
"Each of us, our legacies, our cultures — have profoundly more similarities than differences. It's important to emphasise that fact, which can be accomplished by articulating those similarities, then be inspired by that aforementioned curiosity to appreciate and celebrate those differences through open-eyed gained insight."

Perhaps I would tout, then quote our American author Harper Lee whom, as the character Scout in *To Kill A Mocking Bird* says "just standing on Boo Radley's porch was enough." We all must be willing to make the effort to leave our own yards to catch a glimpse of the inarguable perspective of another. I wrote a short essay on this.

And finally, my last question is in fact one written by Freddie Mercury: If there's a God in the sky, looking down what can he think of what we've done to the world that He created?
Although very much a devotee of all causes that endeavour toward higher spiritual ground, I adamantly do not believe in the anthropomorphised or even conceptually personified and judgmental "God" on high.

In fact, I've recently become somewhat obsessed with the legacy of a manifest patriarchy that has indeed informed, throughout historical eras, societal systems and various theocratic sub-strains therein. I find it interesting, the constructs of deities, forces and all things larger than ourselves that we seem arrogantly hell-bent to explain into existence in order to provide for ourselves the convenience of obeisance and certainty. The irony of the arrogance of contextual thought achieving righteous humility is remarkable.

On the other hand, the palpably elevational joy that we're enabled to experience through thought, deed, creation (music, art, prose, all the muses) seems very much, to me, a verifiable proof of what lives and dynamically seethes among, beyond and through us individually as well as collectively. So often does our wariness obstruct true awareness, which is born from our innate animalistic nature. We are challenged as a species to rely upon our facilities for our very survival. It is the Eden we've created as one worthy of creation.

We only need achieve the stillness of self and strive toward the desquamation of these earthly indoctrinations to see the true light that shines within us all. I believe that particular light is divine and was endowed upon us by something much larger than our brains will enable us to understand in terms of this world. You might accidentally step on that ant. Unless physically disturbed, he has no sense of your presence, and he's no clue about you or your nature. But if his fate allows, and you happen to step over him, he will strive on and do his part to help himself and his community survive. He's smart that way. Most of what he builds within his community is advantageous to his survival.

We humans are another animal. We brilliantly create things with an intelligence and ingenuity we see as exclusively our own (note: there were no "right angles" before us) that could indeed bring about our own demise. Yet we also have more than enough intelligence (note: we have conquered our atmosphere, can uniquely create a sustainable environment anywhere within it) with which to invent and implement systems and devices that would enable us to avoid our own destruction. I wish more of us could see that as "God-given", that the positive action enabled and emboldened by it as a form of prayer. We are a species of highly venerable potential. If we're rationally smart, and humble, enough to survive.

Justin Sullivan
New Model Army

© Julian Parker-Burns

No, John Sullivan is not a member of Oliver Cromwell's army. New Model Army is a sort of punk rock band that has stood the test of time and still draws huge crowds. They even recorded a single with Tom Jones, so if that doesn't give them street cred nothing will. Their music is quite eclectic, with folk, rock, pop and all-manner of influences. The beauty of them is that they stay true to themselves. They didn't go around getting 80s haircuts or going all smooth in the 90s. They stayed punk cool. Justin will hate me for this of course, but he is the ultimate in cool punk rocker.

If you could be any other musician past or present, which one would it be and why?
I'm not sure if I'd like to be him, in terms of how his life was, but just to step inside that incredible musical sensibility for a few minutes or hours would really be something — James Jamerson, Motown bass-player and my all-time favourite musician.

If you had to name one song from any genre that really speaks to you, which one would it be and why?
I can't name one — there are so many songs that speak to me — rather like gods (in the Greek or Indian sense), there are different songs for different moods and different states of consciousness.

Are you a Mulder or Scully? Do you believe aliens have visited planet earth and if so what do you think they think about mankind?
Oh, definitely a Scully. Although I quite like the idea that classic movie 'aliens' are super-evolved versions of us from the future — big eyes, big brains, pointy fingers and not much else.

What was the happiest day of your life and why?
Whoah! I've had 64 years — that would include a lot of good days.

If "God" (whatever your idea is on that) were stood before you now, what one question would you ask him/her and why?
God is stood before me now — and yesterday and tomorrow. But if I ask questions, he/she/it just smiles and the weather keeps rolling in.

As an expressive artist in the music industry, how does the state of the planet make you feel?
Desperately sad.

Do you think as a person of some influence that there is a duty on us to help influence humanity for the better?
I'm not sure if artists actually have the kind of influence you suggest. We're just little people who do the best we can.

What one cause would you say you feel most associated with and why? Whether it's equality, poverty, politics, the environment or other?
All of them.

If you were stood before the leaders of the world, what would you say to them?
Please burn all those bloody flags — or maybe I'd just look at them, laugh and shake my head.

And finally, my last question is in fact one written by Freddie Mercury: If there's a God in the sky, looking down what can he think of what we've done to the world that He created?
Oh, he/she will simply get rid of us soon enough.

Sonique

Sonique, is a British singer, musician and DJ. She first came to public attention as a member of the 90s dance band S'Express. Even greater success was ahead when she went solo in the early 2000s. She hit big with songs like "It Feels So Good", "Sky", "I Put a Spell on You" and "Can't Make Up My Mind". She won the 2001 BRIT Award for British female solo artist. Even better she got to answer my questions.

If you could be any other musician past or present, which one would it be and why?

I would have loved to have been Josephine Baker because she was an entertainer at such a glamorous time.

Note: So basically you want to be an American born French woman who was a wartime resistance fighter and civil rights activist, who also managed to be extremely sexy and sing like a songbird. Fair enough. Me too.

If you had to name one song from any genre that really speaks to you, which one would it be and why?

"What's Going On" by Marvin Gaye. I love the innocence of him asking his mother and father why is life not what he expected it to be when he was a child.

Are you a Mulder or Scully? Do you believe aliens have visited planet earth and if so what do you think they think about mankind?

I don't believe in aliens.

Note: Me neither.

What was the happiest day of your life and why?

The best day of my life was when I won my BRIT award but the best part about it was my best friends, my family and everyone that I loved was around me at that moment and I seriously felt blessed.

Note: Of course getting an award with the word BRIT in it would make anybody happy.

If "God" (whatever your idea is on that) were stood before you now, what one question would you ask him/her and why?

I talk to him every day so I wouldn't really have any questions to ask him.

Note: What's he doing on Saturday? I've got some questions.

As an expressive artist in the music industry, how does the state of the planet make you feel?

I am disappointed in the way that we treat the planet, but you have to educate everyone all at the same time to be able to fix a problem like that.

Do you think as a person of some influence that there is a duty on us to help influence humanity for the better?

Yes I do believe that as an artist we should be influencing people to treat each other and the planet better.

Note: Get Ozzy on the phone, I need a word with him.

What one cause would you say you feel most associated with and why? Whether it's equality, poverty, politics, the environment or other?

I'm passionate about homelessness. No one should be homeless.

If you were stood before the leaders of the world, what would you say to them?

If I was in front of the leaders right now I would most probably say how can I help?

Note: They sure as hell need it.

And finally, my last question is in fact one written by Freddie Mercury: If there's a God in the sky, looking down what can he think of what we've done to the world that He created?

God is definitely not happy about how we've treated each other and the planet and animals and everything.

Dee C Lee

A singer in her own right, with plenty of singles and albums to her name, Dee C Lee has also been a backing singer for Wham! and a member of The Style Council. In fact she has worked with so many music legends over the years that I don't want to waste ink stating that she has worked with members of Level 42, been in movies and was even married to Paul Weller. So I won't. She did however take the time to answer the questions from some lame author.

If you could be any other musician past or present, which one would it be and why?
I have worked with so many fantastic vocalists and musicians, that I had to really think who I could choose. I would say the late Donald Byrd.

Note: Donald Byrd was an American jazz and rhythm & blues trumpeter and vocalist.

I was blessed to work with him on Guru's Jazzmataz tour in the UK, Europe and Japan alongside another idol of mine Lonnie Liston Smith.

Note: Lonnie Liston Smith is an American jazz and funk artist.

Donald Byrd told me that my voice was like the jazz singers he worked with back in his early days. Hanging out with him was one of the many wonderful moments of my musical life. He was such a great, humble, funny and talented man, RIP.

If you had to name one song from any genre that really speaks to you, which one would it be and why?
Funnily enough I thought this question would be unanswerable for me, so many to speak of but one that started my love of vocal melodies, passion and the theatre of music is the first track that showed me the class of soul and jazz vocals was Ms Diana Ross with "Ain't No Mountain".

Are you a Mulder or Scully? Do you believe aliens have visited planet earth and if so what do you think they think about mankind?
I'm a Mulder, yes I do believe aliens exist, But some things will always be beyond our knowledge.

What was the happiest day of your life and why?
This is a hard one to answer because I have so many happiest days but I would say the first day in order would be the day I got married, then the birth of my children.

If "God" (whatever your idea is on that) were stood before you now, what one question would you ask him/her and why?
Absolutely nothing because I believe everything happens for a reason.

As an expressive artist in the music industry, how does the state of the planet make you feel?
Sometimes the state of the world can evoke strong and powerful emotions that can inspire the song writing process for me. However there are times when the world can be very dark and hostile which also can influence how you write, but I choose to take away the positive as much as I can. I still believe very much that love is the answer.

Note: It is after all, all you need.

Do you think as a person of some influence that there is a duty on us to help influence humanity for the better?
I believe we should all lead by good example. I don't think it's important whether you're a person of influence or not.

What one cause would you say you feel most associated with and why? Whether it's equality, poverty, politics, the environment or other?
There are a lot of causes I associate with just on a human level. But I feel very strongly about the abuse of children in all its forms, it's particularly heinous to me.

If you were stood before the leaders of the world, what would you say to them?
I would ask some of the leaders or people in power, how do you sleep at night? That's all I'm saying.

Note: Smiley face.

And finally, my last question is in fact one written by Freddie Mercury: If there's a God in the sky, looking down what can he think of what we've done to the world that He created?
I believe that the higher powers would understand that humans make mistakes and for the small amount of evil acts there's an awful lot of good in this world. I think our purpose is to learn and grow. Life is such a gift!

Robby Lochner
Jack Russell's Great White

In 1997 Robby Lochner was nominated as guitarist of the year because, well, he's a brilliant guitarist. And yet he is actually self-taught. Having said that, he has the distinct advantage of being a direct descendent of Robert Schuman the classical composer.

After winning the Jam Trax LA guitar battle, he was selected by Rob Halford of Judas Priest to play in his band, Fight. By 1996 he was in the LA band, Treason and won the Best of the Best guitar competition by Music Scene International. By 1997 he had released his own album with a host of stars for his band. Well, to be honest he has a long history of working with greats, including being in the band, Jack Russell's Great White. I managed to track him down.

If you could be any other musician past or present, which one would it be and why?

I've never thought about being anyone else ever though in the spirit of the question I would go with Bach because of the sheer genius of his composing. However since I have no concept of how his life would've been in those times I will go with Van Halen. His journey was incredible! Reshaping the musical landscape and influencing generations of musicians is truly astounding! So many of the musicians before him looked down upon him as he came up but eventually couldn't deny what was happening. Having some of your heroes dissing you in the formidable years would be a bummer though the ride to the top must have been something else.

If you had to name one song from any genre that really speaks to you, which one would it be and why?

"Go Your Own Way" (Fleetwood Mac) comes to mind. What a great song that speaks to what I think everyone goes through at sometime in their lives. They captured lightning in a bottle not only on that track but that entire record.

Are you a Mulder or Scully? Do you believe aliens have visited planet earth and if so what do you think they think about mankind?

I don't know the characters enough to answer the Mulder, Scully part of the question. As for aliens visiting Warth? There is more and more evidence of aliens having visited or actually living here somewhere. I couldn't say for sure but definitely not beyond the realm of possibility. The nearest solar systems with potential life is so far away they'd either have to travel through a worm hole or have mastered time. Any alien that could get to Earth would be far beyond our technology. They'd look upon us as a whole as a primitive species. Spiritually I think they would have to respect that we're all from the same source so probably would have that level of respect. Beyond that they probably think we are foolish little children.

What was the happiest day of your life and why?
The day my daughter was born. I was there for her birth and also cut the umbilical cord. Leading up to that moment I was excited about her arrival and did talk to her in the womb, however the moment I was able to hold her changed me for the better instantly forever!

If "God" (whatever your idea is on that) were stood before you now, what one question would you ask him/her and why? I'd ask why are we here?
I feel we are returning to complete wholeness so why go through the trials and tribulations of life? Is this an experiment? What good are lessons if we are going to return to a place of bliss?

As an expressive artist in the music industry, how does the state of the planet make you feel?
I always want to feel hopeful and optimistic that things can and will evolve in a positive direction. However not to have my head in the sand it's clear to see things have been going backwards. Four steps back, five steps forward? I do have definite opinions on what is good or bad though, thinking something is good or bad is what makes it good or bad in our minds though may not be so.

Do you think as a person of some influence that there is a duty on us to help influence humanity for the better?
Yes, though this does go along the lines of what I perceive to be good may not be for someone else. I try to make decisions based on what my body tells me is the correct thing to do. Uneasiness in the body is a good indication the decision is not the correct choice although ego can jump in and complicate things. I do my best to treat everyone with respect. I don't follow the old adage "you must earn my respect". Everyone deserves respect just by being human/soul. Strangely, some people misinterpret kindness as weakness. That respect can be lost quick.

To answer the question completely all people have a duty to influence humanity for the better. Everyone is important whether they know it or believe it or not. Let someone cut in traffic, help someone who can't lift their baggage at the airport, hold open a door, feed someone who's hungry etc. Everyone's input makes a difference. People come into what we may perceive to be "power" and lose that "power" all the time. There's always a shift happening. I will say there's nothing worse than some douchebag who's famous being a tool because he or she thinks they're better than others. I've seen it plenty, and the truth is no one is better than anyone else...

What one cause would you say you feel most associated with and why? Whether it's equality, poverty, politics, the environment or other?

Equality is a good one. I think everyone should be treated the same (respect, dignity etc) up until the point of them making a decision that adversely affects another. I do know you can't give everyone the same things and expect an equal outcome. Everyone has different talents, it's a matter of everyone finding their role. Give two people a thousand dollars and one will turn it in to10k and the other will be broke, however the broke individual may be happy during and after their spending spree while the 10k may person could be bitter and unhappy. It's unrealistic to expect equal outcomes by the very nature of how humans are. Give everyone equal footing and help guide them to their path and the true success in life will follow. In my opinion the result is joy, happiness and love... now you have equality!

If you were stood before the leaders of the world, what would you say to them?

What I'd like to say, would say or could get away with saying are different things. I could have a laundry list of things to say and wouldn't be allowed to say or may lose my nerve to say. If I could do it freely without regard, it would be something along the lines of: stop lying, cheating, stealing, don't be so greedy, ease up on the power grab. Treat all people as brothers... brothers you like. Be fair, be open up, lighten up, get off your superiority complex and do something that actually helps people/humanity not just you and yours

And finally, my last question is in fact one written by Freddie Mercury: If there's a God in the sky, looking down what can he think of what we've done to the world that He created?

My knowing on this is we are living in an illusion of time and space. From the perspective of spirit this doesn't exist. God is not a deity sitting on a throne scolding everything we do. We live in this world where forgiveness and love are the two most important things. They help us in every aspect of our lives if we allow them to. Forgiveness will no longer be needed when we transition, love lasts eternal. So I think for many it'd be, "job well done" for others it'd be go back and try again. For someone with power, riches and what is perceived as a life of privilege if they abuse it, they'll be coming back without any of that.

Ryan Newell
Sister Hazel

Originating from Gainesville, Florida, Sister Hazel is comprised of five gifted, seasoned musicians whose well-spring of natural talent has been called "one of the Top 100 Most Influential Independent Performers of the last 15 years" by Performing Songwriter Magazine.

Song "All for You," topped the adult alternative charts during the summer of 1997 and the success propelled their album to platinum status. Since then, the band has become firmly established not only in rock and alternative music, but now in country with four back-to-back Billboard Top Country Albums Chart entries along with making their debut on the most revered stage in country music, the Grand Ole Opry. Ryan Newell managed to find time for our project. Yee haw!

If you could be any other musician past or present, which one would it be and why?
I would say Paul McCartney. He was a driving force in, arguably, the most influential band of all time. He's a brilliant songwriter and multi-instrumentalist and he wrote/sang some of the best melodies I've ever heard. He seemed to satisfy his creative drive throughout his whole life which was/is a blessing for him as well as all of us.

If you had to name one song from any genre that really speaks to you, which one would it be and why?
"Imagine" by John Lennon speaks to me because it is brutally honesty. Although his fictitious world could never be a reality, it is nice to think that we could make a better place for everyone to live without the barriers of social and political constraints.

What was the happiest day of your life and why?
I have three days that I would consider the happiest. The day I married my wife and the birth of my two children. All three days changed my life forever and I'm blessed in every way to have experienced so much love.

If "God" (whatever your idea is on that) were stood before you now, what one question would you ask him/her and why?

There is no way I could narrow it down to one question because the answer would cause more questions. I also feel that if God wanted me to know the answer, he/she would have already let it be known. I might not want the burden of carrying that information and I have a feeling God feels the same way.

As an expressive artist in the music industry, how does the state of the planet make you feel?
I think being an artist in the music industry makes me one of the least qualified to know what is really happening to our planet. Everything I've heard from people who are qualified to speak on the subject has told me that we are simply not sustainable. This makes me concerned about the world my children will have to endure. I think there needs to be major change worldwide. If we just keep going, future generations will be cursing our legacy.

Do you think as a person of some influence that there is a duty on us to help influence humanity for the better?
I think it all starts with the family unit. We all have major influence on humanity whether you are an "influencer" or not. When people teach their children first-hand and do not put so much weight on celebrities telling them what's important, I think it has a longer lasting effect. Not just a fad. That being said, I do think it's great to be inspired by famous people in positive ways. You do have to know that some people want direction from outside sources. There is a responsibility to use the gifts you have been given for the greater good.

What one cause would you say you feel most associated with and why? Whether it's equality, poverty, politics, the environment or other?
Sister Hazel and myself have always been involved in cancer charities. We have our own charity called Lyrics for Life and we have raised millions of dollars for cancer research. I have had cancer rip through my family and friends and it's impossible to sit back and do nothing to help. I have been blessed with opportunities to help on a personal level as well as a financial level and feel driven to continue this seemingly never-ending quest to beat this monster.

If you were stood before the leaders of the world, what would you say to them?
War means you are not smart enough to come to an agreement. Be smart.

Suzi Quatro
Rock Goddess

Suzi once said that she would retire when she went on stage, shook her ass and there was silence. There are plenty of red-blooded males who have screamed at the shaking of Suzi's ass and still do. Suzi will be forever.

American by birth, but chosen by the British as their own, Suzi Quatro had a string of hits in the 1970s with songs such as "Can the Can" and "Devil Gate Drive". She has been a regular on our TV screens on various shows, but most famously on Happy Days.

In fact Suzi has released no less than fifteen studio albums over the years and sold over fifty million records.

I like to think of Suzi as a friend, but I'm amongst a million other blokes who like to think that as well, but I got to interview her, so tough.

If you could be any other musician past or present, which one would it be and why?

Carlos Santana. Because when I jam a long with CDs which I often do. I always play the exact same bass lines as his bass player. Also he is the only guitar player who can do non-stop solos. And I am never bored or fed up with it... Just love him. Inventive, melodic, and great. Would love to share the stage with him and show him 'my' chops.

If you had to name one song from any genre that really speaks to you, which one would it be and why?

I would have to pick two, "Blowin' in the Wind" by Bob Dylan, because of the profoundness of it. It makes me smile, it makes me think, it makes me cry, every single time. Also, "When I Fall in Love", by Nat King Cole. This song for me covers the entire range of emotions available in life to each and everyone of us, if we care to wear it.

Are you a Mulder or Scully? Do you believe aliens have visited planet earth and if so what do you think they think about mankind?

I think it is egotistical to think there are no other lifeforms. The universe is unlimited and never ending. Yes I think there have been lots of visits and that they, somehow, live amongst us. A closely guarded secret. And what do they think. Who knows? It's all alien to me!!

215

What was the happiest day of your life and why?
That's a hard one... really hard. I don't know if I can pick out one happiest day... I don't think like that. I have been blessed with many happiest days. Would not like to choose one.

If "God" (whatever you idea is on hat) were stood before you now, what one question would you ask him/her and why?
Are you lonely?

As an expressive artist in the music industry, how does the state of the planet make you feel?
Obviously we all need to be more aware of Mother Nature. We do take for granted our environment and it can turn on a dime. Lots of good organisations are around making us all more aware. I do what I can.
Note: Do we?

Do you think as a person of some influence that there is a duty on us to help influence humanity for the better?
One million percent. I always try to be inspirational in everything I do. I aim to ease the pain, talk through the heartache, and argue the toss. I am a communicator from my toes up.

What one cause would you say you feel most associated with and why? Whether it's equality, poverty, politics, the environment or other?
Equality for sure. I don't do gender. I don't do race, I don't do religion. I just do 'equal'. We are one race of people. End of story.

Note: Well, that's that then. End of book here. What more is there to say? Oh yeah, them there leaders.

If you were stood before the leaders of the world, what would you say to them?
Get your shit together!

Note: All together now.

And finally, my last question is in fact one written by Freddie Mercury: If there's a God in the sky, looking down what can he think of what we've done to the world that He created?
Well I would not like to assume what Freddie meant. I only hope he knows. I am not that negative. I think God created some magical things. But for every good there is bad. I am an optimist through and through, and I believe in magic.

Simon Phillips
Toto

An extremely talented jazz, pop and rock drummer, Simon has the illustrious title of having been the drummer for Toto. But that's not even half of his amazing career. He's also drummed for Jeff Beck, Gary Moore, Bernie Marsden, Jon Lord, Nik Kershaw, Mike Oldfield, Judas Priest, Mike Rutherford, Tears for Fears, Brian Eno, 10cc, Big Country, David Gilmour, Whitesnake and The Who. So small fry then.

Of course, he's also released two albums through his own band, Ph.D. He's also an extremely nice bloke who took the time out to answer my questions.

If you could be any other musician past or present, which one would it be and why?
Frankly I wouldn't want to be another musician. I'm really happy being myself and I prefer to admire all the great musicians I know or know of. Being a musician is not about perfection or being someone else. It's about learning from all your idols and peers and coming up with innovative, inspiring music whether played or composed.

If you had to name one song from any genre that really speaks to you, which one would it be and why?
I cannot answer that question because there are so many songs and tunes I love from all genres. It's a bit like being asked who's your favourite child, if you happen to have a few. The list would be long!

Note: I'm pretty sure I will be able to pin him down soon. Hang in there...

Are you a Mulder or Scully? Do you believe aliens have visited planet earth and if so what do you think they think about mankind?
I used to think that there are entities from other planets which have visited us. However, the older I grow I begin to doubt the possibility of visitors. Not because I don't believe they exist but more because the chances of humans overlapping with another planet of beings is so small given the time restraints of the universe. Our whole existence over thousands of years is a blink of the eye in universal terms.

What was the happiest day of your life and why?
That's really tough to answer as I'm sure there were many such days in my younger years. However the most recent "happiest day" would be moving into my newly re-built house after three years of dealing with all the issues of losing my house to the Thomas Fire of 2017!

If "God" (whatever your idea is on that) were stood before you now, what one question would you ask him/her and why?
Where do we go after we die?

As an expressive artist in the music industry, how does the state of the planet make you feel?
Exasperated! There are so many things that our governments could be doing to help the problems we face. Politics is our main enemy and waste of money that could be used to change the world and make it a better place.

Note: I do hope there are some politicians reading this book. They sure as hell are not getting a good press.

Do you think as a person of some influence that there is a duty on us to help influence humanity for the better?
Definitely. Even if it's a small contribution like making people happy by making them feel good on a day to day basis. For example — simple manners, politeness and respect. Thanking someone for a simple gesture. Opening a door for someone. Helping someone to cross the road or with their luggage in an airport or a plane. It doesn't cost anything other than being aware.

What one cause would you say you feel most associated with and why? Whether it's equality, poverty, politics, the environment or other?
I do have strong opinions on gun laws here in the US. I think it may have to do with growing up in England where gun laws are extremely strict, as they are in most countries. I am not against the ownership of guns but the attitude and lack of law here is asinine. Driving a car on a public road requires a tough test. The drinking laws here are tough but obtaining a firearm is ridiculously easy. There are no tests to pass — no safety regulations given by the NRA — no control over the types of firearms allowed to be sold. It's basically still the Wild West when it comes to firearms. Hence there are so many accidental deaths every year!

If you were stood before the leaders of the world, what would you say to them?
"Fellas — you're losing your heads" to quote Orson Wells.

Note: There is a precedent for us to get out the old chopping block again for our so-called betters. Revolution baby!

And finally, my last question is in fact one written by Freddie Mercury: If there's a God in the sky, looking down what can he think of what we've done to the world that He created?
"Good grief" to quote Charlie Brown!

Simon Kirke
Bad Company

Simon is a rock drumming legend, having been a member of two of the most iconic and classic rock bands, Free and Bad Company. The weird thing is, as I type this, Bad Company's "Can't Get Enough" came up on my playlist. Now I'm totally distracted. Where was I? Oh yeah. All right now, you get the picture? He's a rock god. Oh and of course, he's also toured with Ringo Starr's All Star Band and you don't get into that unless you're a... well... star. I interviewed him and had to shout because well, all those years banging his own drums and all that.

If you could be any other musician past or present, which one would it be and why?
Louis Armstrong. Because his trumpet playing was unlike anything before or since and he brought so much joy to people.

Note: You will note that Louis comes up a few times. What a guy!

If you had to name one song from any genre that really speaks to you, which one would it be and why?
The first one sprung to mind was "Champagne and Wine" by Otis Redding. Beautifully sung... delicate and soulful. An homage to his wife with exquisite guitar playing from Steve Cropper.

Are you a Mulder or Scully? Do you believe aliens have visited planet earth and if so what do you think they think about mankind?
Dunno from Mulder or Scully but I am absolutely sure we've been visited by aliens, but then they got the hell out of here after seeing the damage that we've done to the planet and each other.

Note: Dunno Mulder or Scully? I found somebody who doesn't know!

What was the happiest day of your life and why?
Receiving our first gold album (as Bad Company) in Boston on the final night of our gruelling first American tour.

If "God" (whatever your idea is on that) were stood before you now, what one question would you ask him/her and why?
To God: Why racism? It's held back our entire civilisation.

Note: Dude, spot on, shouldn't even be an issue. Just stop it already!

As an expressive artist in the music industry, how does the state of the planet make you feel?
I'm teetering on the brink of hope and despair.

Do you think as a person of some influence that there is a duty on us to help influence humanity for the better?
Absolutely, we have a duty as musicians to help and heal the world. Music is the only true universal language.

Note: All together now… (humming some lovely sixties peace and harmony tune.)

What one cause would you say you feel most associated with and why? Whether it's equality, poverty, politics, the environment or other?
One cause for me — a dead heat between combating addiction and climate change.

If you were stood before the leaders of the world, what would you say to them?
Erase all world debt

Note: I completely agree. Where do I send my credit card bill please?

And finally, my last question is in fact one written by Freddie Mercury: If there's a God in the sky, looking down what can he think of what we've done to the world that He created?
"I can fix this, but you have to help me."

Ron Sexsmith

When he was only seventeen, Ron Sexsmith was being called "the one man jukebox". After a chance meeting with a movie composer he managed to get his first album out called Grand Opera Lane. It was so good he was offered a record deal and pretty soon he was appearing on TV and performing alongside people like Elvis Costello and bands like REM. He's released duets with the likes of Coldplay's, Chris Martin and even written books. And what more accolade can you have for your songwriting abilities than to have stars like Rod Stewart and Michael Bublé cover them? We met on Twitter and soon we were doing the old interview routine.

If you could be any other musician past or present, which one would it be and why?
Most of my musical heroes... I don't think I would want their life to be honest so I'm happy just being me (which is hard enough sometimes).

Note: I'd be Jimi Hendrix just for the drugs.

If you had to name one song from any genre that really speaks to you, which one would it be and why?
"The Kiss" by Judee Sill. I can't quite explain it but it just really moves me to tears.

Note: Why oh why would you listen to it then?

Are you a Mulder or Scully? Do you believe aliens have visited planet earth and if so what do you think they think about mankind?
I'm more Mulder, in fact I saw a UFO once and am still kind of blown away by it. It was right over the house across the street and was witnessed by a whole bunch of people in 2012.

Note: And like Mulder, you didn't take a photo then?

What was the happiest day of your life and why?
The day I got to perform at Massey Hall for the first time. It had been a lifelong dream of mine...

Note: My dream is to have certain elements of Dolly Parton for my pillows at night. Don't suppose that'll ever happen.

If "God" (whatever your idea is on that) were stood before you now, what one question would you ask him/her and why?
I guess I'd ask him if he/she thinks I'm a good person or not.

As an expressive artist in the music industry, how does the state of the planet make you feel?
It makes me feel anxious for the most part and helpless.

Note: Well dude, you've done your bit by getting into this book! Now remember to recycle and sponsor some homeless puppies.

Do you think as a person of some influence that there is a duty on us to help influence humanity for the better?
Perhaps... I certainly try to fill the world with hopeful songs and pretty melodies.

What one cause would you say you feel most associated with and why? Whether it's equality, poverty, politics, the environment or other?
I'd say equality. It seems so strange that in these times, there are still so many people who are not treated or paid equally.

If you were stood before the leaders of the world, what would you say to them?
Stop bickering and do something good for a change.

Note: Are you listening world leaders. Have you noticed how you ain't getting anybody loving you?

And finally, my last question is in fact one written by Freddie Mercury: If there's a God in the sky, looking down what can he think of what we've done to the world that He created?
I'm sure God is quite perplexed by our behaviour but then he did give us free will to fuck everything up.

© Neil Chapman

Simon Hinkler
The Mission

There aren't many instruments Simon Hinkler can't play. He's an accomplished and yet self-taught musician with the band, The Mission — a band formed from a few members of Sisters of Mercy back in 1985. After touring with The Cult they released their first single and album and found themselves in the charts. Hit after hit followed. Simon then left to pursue a solo career and released a couple of solo albums. Then in 2011 The Mission got back together and now their highest accolade is that Simon got to talk to me.

If you could be any other musician past or present, which one would it be and why?
Like a lot of rock musicians, I'm completely self-taught. I sometimes wish I was classically trained on the piano, so I suppose I'd want to be Chopin... wouldn't want his life though. Really, I never think of wanting to be someone else.

Note: Personally I've always fancied being Marilyn Monroe, but we won't go there.

If you had to name one song from any genre that really speaks to you, which one would it be and why?
That's difficult. I'll say "Such a Small Love" by Scott Walker. The arrangement is dynamic and takes you places. The song is sad and glorious at the same time; simultaneously expressing the power of emotion and yet how insignificant that emotion is in the greater scheme of things. Life is like that. The glorious bit is recognising it. Putting it in a song is no small achievement.

Are you a Mulder or Scully? Do you believe aliens have visited planet earth and if so what do you think they think about mankind?
There are certainly ancient unexplained things, about which people like to put two and two together and make five, calling it evidence. I wouldn't rule out the possibility but remain sceptical.

Note: Having been abducted at least twice now I have to disagree with you. Pass the LSD dude.

What was the happiest day of your life and why?
Oh I dunno. Maybe my 40th birthday. I had been living in the US for a few years and I came back to the UK for a visit. Unbeknownst to me, my wife had planned a surprise party, inviting people from all over, cousins, aunts and uncles, old school friends, old bandmates. A real "this is your life" event.

Note: Dear wife, if you ever try this one on me I will put all your jewellery in the dustbin.

If "God" (whatever your idea is on that) were stood before you now, what one question would you ask him/her and why?
I wrote a song called "Thank You Lord" containing the words "Was this your intention? Is it all a mistake? Or did you just get lazy on that seventh day?" I don't believe in God. If there was one it's clearly sadistic, uncaring, and not to be admired.

Note: Somebody tell Brian.

As an expressive artist in the music industry, how does the state of the planet make you feel?
Very disappointed. It's such a shame that humans have the potential for greatness, which unfortunately only some of us can see and recognise, and yet it's squandered to the brink of collapse. The greed for power, hoarding wealth and depriving the world of resources. These are not the acts of great people, or even good people. The fact that we still chop down rainforest, over-farm, over-fish, churn out plastics and burn fossil fuel — having known for decades it will bring about our own destruction, is testament to how cynical, deeply immoral and uncaring those in power are. Just educate the masses enough to keep the machines rolling and pay them just enough to make them believe they have freedom of choice... the choice to buy our crap. Keep 'em scared. Keep that religion going, thinking it's all god's will. Breed a sense of mistrust in each other and once in a while set 'em to war for some reason... doesn't matter what. Religion is always a good one.

Do you think as a person of some influence that there is a duty on us to help influence humanity for the better?
We all have a duty to be good people; "spread that positive energy," don't be an asshole. It's actually easy. People who are nasty, aggressive, confrontational, greedy, just don't get it. Yet you have to recognise it's not their fault; they weren't born that way. Within the circle of influence afforded me by the band I seek to include and be friendly to everyone. I think we all do, and there is certainly a sense of togetherness, family, surrounding the band and fans... more than most I reckon.

What one cause would you say you feel most associated with and why? Whether it's equality, poverty, politics, the environment or other?
They're all part of the same thing. Understanding where we stand, how it came to be this way, and why it's not getting any better. Educating the world to grasp the reality that we're all in this together as we spin around on this lump of rock; a speck in the universe. Sparing and sharing the resources, having fewer babies. Self-governing as a species. Finding harmony and balance. It will never happen.

If you were stood before the leaders of the world, what would you say to them?
Listen you lot, your job is to look after the best interests of the people. All the people. That means you have to find accord rather than fight for what's best for your little corner of the globe. If you've come to the table for an argument then go home and send someone better.

And finally, my last question is in fact one written by Freddie Mercury: If there's a God in the sky, looking down what can he think of what we've done to the world that He created?
Freddie was truly one of the greats. However I choose not to postulate on some imaginary god having thoughts about humans, cos that's just silly.

Note: I'm gonna tell the Pope what you said.

© Chad Coppess

Ron Keel
Keel, Steeler, Black Sabbath

Ron Keel has seen it all, done it all and is doing it all over again. Lead singer for the eighties rock band, Steeler and a short stint as singer for Black Sabbath. After Steeler, Ron started the band, Keel, although nobody knows where he got the name. They toured the world and sold millions of records with Gene Simmons of KISS producing two of their hit albums. He's also released country music albums and his songs have appeared in dozens of movies. He's fronted several bands, a radio show and written a book. How on earth he managed to find time to chat with me I don't know, but I'm thankful he did!

If you could be any other musician past or present, which one would it be and why?
Paul McCartney. He is the greatest rock musician of all time — he plays all the rock instruments like a virtuoso, his voice and songs have been the soundtrack of my generation, he is the ultimate model of persistence and longevity. The Beatles literally changed my life when I saw them on TV at the tender age of two... now I'm sixty and he's still viable and making great music! That first solo album where he played all the instruments himself... the Wings hits... Paul is the ultimate rock royalty.

Note: I suppose he has some talent yes. One day he'll make it I'm sure.

If you had to name one song from any genre that really speaks to you, which one would it be and why?
All music speaks to me. My job is to create songs that speak to you.

Are you a Mulder or Scully? Do you believe aliens have visited planet earth and if so what do you think they think about mankind?
I neither believe nor disbelieve in aliens. And I certainly don't believe most of what I see, hear or read. I do believe there is much more to the universe than I can perceive or understand, and I believe in infinite possibilities. I think that if we have been visited, there is a strong chance the visitors are from other dimensions, or from the future. Biological anthropologist Dr. Michael Masters puts forth a very convincing argument about that in his book "Identified Flying Objects."

What do I think they think? If they are researching us, I'm sure they see all aspects of humankind — stupid, ignorant, crazy, beautiful, amazing, worthless and everything in between.

What was the happiest day of your life and why?
Today is the happiest day of my life, until tomorrow. That's how I choose to live. I have had many dreams come true in life and music — a measure of success on my chosen path, beautiful children, a woman who truly loves me who is my best friend. All those memories and feelings are alive within me today, and I honour them by choosing to live today to the fullest.

If "God" (whatever your idea is on that) were stood before you now, what one question would you ask him/her and why?
If there is a "God," an all-powerful creative/destructive force that transcends the physical realm, then that force is no doubt standing before me right this very minute. I think most of us would have the same question… what happens when we die? Are all my family and friends still alive in some form, somewhere?

As an expressive artist in the music industry, how does the state of the planet make you feel?
The planet's just fine. It's the people on the planet that are screwed. Earth is billions of years old, and I believe many civilisations have risen and fallen during that time. Ours will fall too when the next mass-extinction event occurs. We're all on a one-day contract, and I just want to hold up my end of the deal by being a creative, loving person who hopefully makes a positive impact on others with my music and my presence.

Do you think as a person of some influence that there is a duty on us to help influence humanity for the better?
That's a great question and one I struggle with often. Musicians, artists, songwriters are influencers by nature — we express ourselves, and others react. I realised early on in my career that the messages in my music were having an effect on others, so I did make a conscious effort to put the accent on positive messages. I sing about strength, empowerment, perseverance, love, friendship, adventure. I don't preach politics or religion because I'm not sure my beliefs are correct. In my lifetime, I believed a lot of stuff that turned out to be bullshit. I voted for and supported politicians that ended up being criminals and mass murderers. The best I can do is encourage my audience to believe in themselves.

Note: Dear Ron, run for President.

What one cause would you say you feel most associated with and why? Whether it's equality, poverty, politics, the environment or other?
I suppose that would be our military veterans. I did not serve in the military because I was off chasing that rock 'n' roll dream, but I have experienced first-hand the amazing dedication and sacrifices made by those who do serve. I have had dear friends and mentors who paid that ultimate price, and as a touring musician performing on military bases around the world, I have developed a

special kinship and admiration for our veterans that transcends politics. So I do what I can to help repay them in some small way by being actively involved in a number of veteran's charities.

If you were stood before the leaders of the world, what would you say to them?
I would raise my middle finger in each of their faces and say, "fuck you."

And finally, my last question is in fact one written by Freddie Mercury: If there's a God in the sky, looking down what can he think of what we've done to the world that He created?
Like I said, I think the world is fine — it's the people that are screwed. I do believe in the inherent goodness of humankind, but true evil is everywhere and so many are embracing the darkness instead of fighting to see the light. If there is a God, he's probably thinking what a shitty job he did when he developed our genetic code.

John Picard
(Mister Zero)
The Kings

Otherwise known as Mister Zero, John Picard is the guitarist and songwriter for Canadian rock band, The Kings. You may remember them for their 1980s hit song, "The Beat Goes On". Since then they have toured extensively with people such as Bob Seger, Eric Clapton, Jeff Beck and The Beach Boys. They have released several albums, reaching platinum status.

If you could be any other musician past or present, which one would it be and why?
It would be easy to say any number of them, but they were all on their path and we are on ours. This life is what you make it and I realised early that I'm a team player and we got here by trying to do original music, we didn't know we could until we tried and worked at it and the sum was far greater than the parts. Anything we have was earned.

If you had to name one song from any genre that really speaks to you, which one would it be and why?
Again, so many to choose from but I like "Stardust" a lot. The musical sophistication aligns perfectly with the melancholy mood set by the lyric.

Are you a Mulder or Scully? Do you believe aliens have visited planet earth and if so what do you think they think about mankind?
I think that given the number of stars and planets in the universe, there probably is other life out there. Have they come here? Seems a long way to go without saying hi. What would they think about us? That we are hell-bent on destroying this incredible planet which is bad enough but the number of other species that we are killing in our greed and ignorance is insane.

What was the happiest day of your life and why?
I try and be not unhappy and enjoy the good moments as they come floating by.

If "God" (whatever your idea is on that) were stood before you now, what one question would you ask him/her and why?
What does that girl in high school look like now?

As an expressive artist in the music industry, how does the state of the planet make you feel?
Pretty bad when I think about it.

Do you think as a person of some influence that there is a duty on us to help influence humanity for the better?
Not really except by example. All you can help is yourself.

What one cause would you say you feel most associated with and why? Whether it's equality, poverty, politics, the environment or other?
Ridding the world of patriarchal religion.

If you were stood before the leaders of the world, what would you say to them?
You all know the truth but yet you choose sides like some high school debate club.

And finally, my last question is in fact one written by Freddie Mercury: If there's a God in the sky, looking down what can he think of what we've done to the world that He created?
To whom much is given, much will be required... we've been given a beautiful living world and we are killing it in the name of greed.

Emily Barker

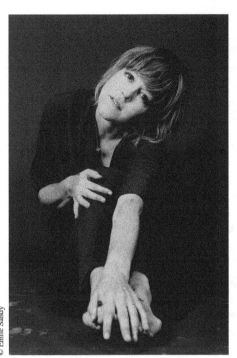

© Emile Sandy

Singer, songwriter musician and composer, Emily has a lot to shout about. She shot to fame when she composed the themes to the BBC dramas, Wallander and The Shadow Line. But there's much more to this wonderful Australian. She's also released several albums, composed film scores and answered my questions.

If you could be any other musician past or present, which one would it be and why?
I would choose to be Carole King for her deep understanding of music. On the surface her songs appear relatively straightforward but if you look under the hood, you'll find there's a complex world of music theory hiding in her use of hybrid chords, modulation and harmony. Perhaps the most genius thing about her writing is how seamlessly she uses this toolkit to write timeless, accessible, universal songs that cut to the heart of the human experience.

Note: Yeah, but can I tap my feet to them?

If you had to name one song from any genre that really speaks to you, which one would it be and why?
I would have to say Aretha Franklin's version of "Respect". I first heard this as a teenager and it blew me away. I would shut myself in my bedroom after school and try to sing along with Aretha. The power in which she sings her demand for respect from her partner without a doubt empowered and educated me as a young woman to ask for the same. Looking at it more broadly, I think respect is a foundation for equality.

Are you a Mulder or Scully? Do you believe aliens have visited planet earth and if so what do you think they think about mankind?
I've not seen *The X-Files* and I have no idea if aliens have visited earth.

Note: What is it with these musicians. Never seen The X-Files. You ain't lived.

What was the happiest day of your life and why?

Wow that's a tough question. I don't think I have a happiest day that wins over all others. I'm from Australia but live in the UK and was last home at the end of 2019 to the beginning of 2020 before the pandemic struck. All my family are in Western Australia and I'm feeling pretty homesick of late so today my answer for happiest day of my life would be a day I spent back in Western Australia that started with a coffee on the veranda with my parents and my husband, Lukas, listening to the morning birdsong, then walking my two nephews and niece (who live next door to my parents) to school. I was holding my niece's hand and she was chatting away to me like I was her best friend. My two nephews were walking up ahead with my husband talking excitedly over the top of one another. Lukas and I then went for a swim in the outdoor pool, took a walk along the Blackwood River, I did some song-writing in the afternoon, and then we picked the kids up from school. The evening involved a barbecue and sundowners on the veranda with my parents and the pinkest and brightest of sunsets and the caw of black cockatoos in the eucalyptus trees by the house.

Note: That's what I like, a simple answer to a simple question. Gonna run out of paper.

If "God" (whatever your idea is on that) were stood before you now, what one question would you ask him/her and why?

Can I please sit by Aretha?

As an expressive artist in the music industry, how does the state of the planet make you feel?

I feel incredibly concerned about the state of our planet and how much worse it is set to become. We're losing species at such speed, so many vital to the ecosystems we're dependent on as human beings. It is heart-breaking to be losing birds and other animals — the stars of our childhood stories — and to know our children will never know so many of these beautiful, brilliant creatures.

I wrote a whole album about climate crisis called *A Dark Murmuration of Words*. In it I reckon with guilt, anxiety, sadness, helplessness and loss. But I also wrote about hope and where to find it. For me that was discovering the story of Wangari Maathai who founded The Green Belt Movement in 1977 in Kenya. She started planting trees and organised protests to protect the forests from destruction. In the process she educated women and girls in forestry skills and the movement is still going today with over fifty million trees having been planted. I believe art and storytelling has a vital role to play in translating the science into emotion, in creating empathy.

Do you think as a person of some influence that there is a duty on us to help influence humanity for the better?

I believe that small actions can have huge, lasting impact and therefore regard everyone as being a person of influence. It is often our peers that influence us the most — we want them to regard us well, it's a biological survival skill — so we shape our views and behaviours to keep their favour. I think people who have a platform should use it responsibly but also that "influencing humanity for the better" could be as simple as making someone feel connected and understood through a song that resonates with their feelings. Who knows how this positive experience could go on to impact their life and their relationships? — it's hard to quantify.

What one cause would you say you feel most associated with and why? Whether it's equality, poverty, politics, the environment or other?
I would say environment: When we destroy our earth and its ecosystems, we destroy the very life sources we depend upon for survival. But I think that so many of our problems — such as poverty and inequality — are inseparable from environment and could be solved through climate justice. One of the best resources I've found on this is Kate Raworth's book, *Doughnut Economics*, which outlines how these issues intersect and provides clear solutions on how economic reform could serve to solve them.

If you were stood before the leaders of the world, what would you say to them?
Read *Doughnut Economics* by Kate Raworth.

And finally, my last question is in fact one written by Freddie Mercury: If there's a God in the sky, looking down what can he think of what we've done to the world that He created?
God just did a facepalm.

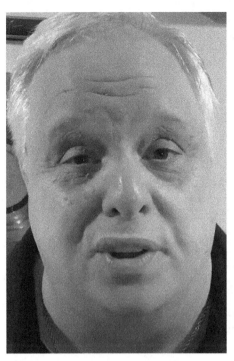

Frederick J. Balboni, Jr.
The Platters

I was going to write a bio, but the answers came with this, so why rebuild the Great Wall of China when you have your own rockery?

"These are responses of Frederick J. Balboni, Jr., International trademark holder, producer, and manager of the rock & roll, vocal, and Grammy Halls of Fame group, The Platters"."

So now you know. Frederick has rather a lot to do with that legendary band, The Platters. Sort of a mind behind the band. And after all, why should it always be the singers and drummers who get to speak up? Go for it Fred!

If you could be any other musician, past or present, which one would it be and why?

Neil Diamond is the quintessential communicator in the universal language of music. As a singer-songwriter, he carefully weaves his personal history, faith, and family in his melodies and lyrics, taking us on a sonic journey through our emotions that bring his creative works to life while inspiring ours.

If you had to name one song from any genre that really speaks to you, which one would it be and why?

The song is "I'm Getting My Act Together and Taking It on the Road", music by Nancy Ford, and Gretchen Cryer's lyrics as it speaks to the power of friendship and love that binds our spirits together.

Are you a Mulder or Scully? Do you believe aliens have visited planet earth, and if so, what do you think they think about mankind?

I'm Fox Mulder all the way! The truth is out there, and we will find it! I believe aliens have visited our planet. It would be limited to the power of knowledge to think otherwise. It isn't easy to hypothesise what they would say, but I'm sure they would almost immediately discern how social we are. Unfortunately, in the era of Covid-19, narcissism has infected a competitive, class-centred society at all levels.

Note: At last, somebody who has heard of The X-Files.

What was the happiest day of your life and why?
So far, the happiest day of my life was my "legal" marriage to my partner of twenty-eight years.

Note: Awe, bless.

If "God" (whatever your idea is on that) were stood before you now, what one question would you ask him/her and why?
I'd ask if the earth was an experiment in free will, and was my contribution meaningful? Your dreams are our goals.

As an expressive artist in the music industry, how does the state of the planet make you feel?
Sad, but hopeful.

Do you think as a person of some influence that there is a duty on us to help influence humanity for the better?
Yes. I design all of The Platters' live performances to touch all participants' souls and put people in tune with each other through happiness and inner peace. At least for a moment, I hope that people will come together as one, feel the creativity and diversity of each other through the universal language of music, and remember the experience.

Note: Amen Brother!

What one cause would you say you feel most associated with and why? Whether it's equality, poverty, politics, the environment or other?
The environment is our life-force. As humans, we have evolved as living beings of the planet, and it is our destiny to protect it and leave a legacy for lives that are yet to develop. It is our destiny to defend it, not destroy it.

If you were stood before the leaders of the world, what would you say to them?
Let's take the day, agree on a standard message of unity, write a world anthem together, and teach the world to sing it in perfect harmony.

Note: I'd like to build the world a home, And furnish it with love, Grow apple trees and honey bees, And snow white turtle doves... ("I'd Like To Teach The World To Sing" by The New Seekers).

And finally, my last question is in fact one written by Freddie Mercury: If there's a God in the sky, looking down what can he think of what we've done to the world that He created?
Lama sabachthani (why have you forsaken me)? But I'm sure the Creator of all living things is hopeful that the world can master free will and the world can come together as one.

Dolan Ellis
Official State Balladeer of Arizona

In 1966 the Governor of the State of Arizona appointed the first ever official State balladeer. That man was Dolan Ellis. In his official capacity he has written over 300 songs, performed across the United States and the world.

In fact, Dolan was a member of The New Christy Minstrels and released several albums, with many of them going gold and winning a Grammy in 1963 for Best Band. They were regulars on the Andy Williams TV Show.

I managed to get to interview Dolan with what are probably the most bizarre set of questions he's ever had to answer.

If you could be any other musician past or present, which one would it be and why?
Sammy Davis, Jr. is one of my heroes. He could do anything. He could sing, dance, act, do comedy, had heartfelt emotions, was a courageous performer, full of energy, and set a fine example for others to emulate.

If you had to name one song from any genre that really speaks to you, which one would it be and why?
My favourite song is, "My Way". To me, that song expresses the essence of "The American Dream", of our pilgrims, our mountain men, our pioneers, our cowboys, and the attitude that has catapulted us so high and so fast, as a nation.

Are you a Mulder or Scully? Do you believe aliens have visited planet earth and if so what do you think they think about mankind?
I think that there is a possibility that the Earth has been visited by aliens. It seems reasonable, to me, that if they were advanced enough to know how to get here, then they surely would have also been more advanced technologically and sociologically than we are. Therefore, I would assume that they would look upon us as a more primitive people, who are still in the process of learning how to live together and how to understand science.

What was the happiest day of your life and why?
Though I have had many extremely happy days, I do not have a favourite happy moment. I am extremely happy nearly every day, just to be alive on this beautiful and bountiful planet, and to have had so many wonderful blessings bestowed upon me throughout my life. When I die, I will die with a smile on my

face, because I will be thinking about the wonderful life that I have had, and the wonderful experience and mystery that lays just ahead.

If "God" (whatever your idea is on that) were stood before you now, what one question would you ask him/her and why?
I would ask God… "Why didn't he/she create us as creatures who are totally good? If he/she is indeed God, then he/she certainly could have done so, if desired.

As an expressive artist in the music industry, how does the state of the planet make you feel?
I am feeling increasingly sad. The world is such a wonderful and beautiful place. It boggles my mind to know that so many people have confused themselves, (or allowed others to confuse them),to the point that they are no longer able to be happy citizens of Earth. Most people believe that money and things are the key to happiness, and a certain amount of them is certainly important. However, all the money and things in the world will not bring you happiness, without loving and be loved, and having purpose for your life. These are the things that bring real happiness. You can be happy living in a cave.

Do you think as a person of some influence that there is a duty on us to help influence humanity for the better?
I believe that we in the entertainment world, absolutely have a duty and a personal responsibility to influence humanity for the better. However, not in a preaching and negative sort of way, and while on stage. The audience did not come to see us and spend their hard-earned money to see that. They came to be entertained and to have their spirits lifted. We should, instead, influence the world through our personal example… off stage.

What one cause would you say you feel most associated with and why? Whether it's equality, poverty, politics, the environment or other?
The Environment… If a person can learn to respect the environment, they will automatically learn to respect others. Respect is respect, and once the habit has been learned, it will flow naturally into all situations of life.

If you were stood before the leaders of the world, what would you say to them?
I would say to those world leaders, "You have all forgotten how to be selfless servants to the people of your country. None of you are statesmen, anymore. Today, our car salesmen and pawnshops owners have more integrity than our politicians. Shame on you!

And finally, my last question is in fact one written by Freddie Mercury: If there's a God in the sky, looking down what can he think of what we've done to the world that He created?
Well, if there is a god in the sky, (I don't think there is, per say), I don't think that he/she would be very surprised at our inadequacies as humans. After all, he/she is supposed to have created us. Right? It only seems reasonable to me, that any entity that is powerful enough to be a God, would certainly also have the power to create creatures that are perfect, if he/she wanted to. Therefore, he/she must have done it intentionally, with the full knowledge that there would be troubles ahead.

© Miguel Dorset

Ray Dorset
Mungo Jerry

During the early 70s, television viewers would have seen Mungo Jerry as a regular on Top of the Pops. In the first four years of the decade Mungo Jerry had eight hit singles, but the one single most associated with them was "In The Summertime". It was a global hit and went to number one in twenty-six countries, selling six million copies. To date it has now sold over thirty million and been covered by such greats as Bob Dylan and Elton John. It is officially the most played summer song of all time and has won Ray Dorset a Sony, MTV and Ivor Novello award.

But quite apart from all that Ray is a good friend and one of the nicest blokes you could ever meet. That's why he had no choice but to answer some of my lame questions.

If you could be any other musician past or present, which one would it be and why?
I don't want to be any other musician except for myself, past or present. I'm just me and that's it.

Note: We are too Ray!

If you had to name one song from any genre that really speaks to you, which one would it be and why?
I like songs from all kinds of genres. I like all kinds of stuff so I'm not going to say that one song is better than the other and any song particularly speaks to me. But obviously, from my career, and I've written what is the supposedly most known summer song in the whole world. Lyrically line by line you can pull out lots and lots of underlying sentiments within the phrases of the texts. So I guess I would choose "In The Summertime", so I don't think I need to pull at any other one, any other people's songs out there at all.

Are you a Mulder or Scully? Do you believe aliens have visited planet earth and if so what do you think they think about mankind?
I'm sure aliens have visited planet Earth, because I'm pretty sure I've seen aliens.

I came back from a gig, must have been in the mid-seventies, I was in Surrey, and in the early hours of the morning, I saw a cold kind of army of what looked like aliens crossing the road.

They were walking like two at a time behind each other. They had little kind of antennas on their head and their eyes were quite big and oval shaped and I thought I was actually seeing things. I didn't believe it, but I thought maybe it was a group of deer, because there's a lot of deer out that way.

The person that was with me saw them as well. So yes I do believe we have aliens probably among us and certainly I am convinced right up until this day that I have seen aliens on planet Earth, in Frencham in Surrey.

What do they think about mankind, well I haven't got a clue. But if I was an alien and came to planet Earth, round about this time, I'd say "what a strange place, why have we got so many earthlings, that have got a beautiful planet and they have decided to mess the whole place up, by overloading it with rubbish, plastic?" We've got climate change and global warming.

Nobody seems to pay attention to looking after the planet. Everyone seems to be more interested in what they can get out of it, make as much money as they possibly can to the detriment of their brothers and sisters.

For many years I've believed that the whole misuse of technology is messing up the whole world, and it has done for generations and generations.

You've got this problem with jealousy and pride and greed and honour and ego, and if we can get rid of all that and get rid of the ego you'll probably get people to be more easy going and less uptight about everything.

What was the happiest day of your life and why?
I don't think I've got to that day yet. I don't think I've got to the happiest day of my life and if you ask me why, what is the happiest day of my life? I'd say because I was happy.

Erm, lots of things have made me happy, I've been happy about many, many things.

I've been happy about the birth of my children, and the fact that I've got from one place to another without falling down and getting killed, or dropping out of the sky in an aeroplane, or getting drowned on a crazy voyage, I've been on many of those.

So I would say the happiest day of my life, I don't know yet, but yet to see at my old age, who knows what is going to be put in front of us.

If "God" (whatever your idea is on that) were stood before you now, what one question would you ask him/her and why?
I believe in the power of nature, the law of nature. I believe in the science of nature and if everybody was to think that God is nature and we obey the rules of nature that means we obey the rules of the science of nature and the law of nature and the law of God is the law of nature and you can't mess with it because nature will always come out on top.

It doesn't matter what you do. As soon as you make an imbalance in the universe that we live in and on the earth that we live in, there are going to be significant problems.

Do you think as a person of some influence that there is a duty on us to help influence humanity for the better?
The state of the planet is not good, everyday there are thousands of species of

plants and insects and life that are disappearing.

I'll tell you what's really sick, the American Indian used to use just about everything from a buffalo and then when the settlers went over to the States and decided they were going to clear the land of the native Americans and drive their food out so they couldn't exist so that the railroads could be built.

We see this as a big, big problem with wild animals becoming extinct and again it's another question of balance going completely out of the window.

So I would say, whoever you are, if you have a degree of empathy and sense about what's going on in the world at the moment, it's always been the same.

All of these so-called great nations they always come to implode. Really everybody, most people, rise to their own level of incompetence. You look at world leaders you look at prime ministers you look at kings and queens, they think they're invincible and they take it too far.

Nobody is immortal, we're here on this planet to preserve the human race, we're breeding and we're all insignificant and that's the bottom line.

What one cause would you say you feel most associated with and why? Whether it's equality, poverty, politics, the environment or other?

There is a duty on us, but whether people will pay attention and carry out their duty, who knows, it doesn't seem so, because everyone seems to be more concerned, well not everyone, there's a lot of people out there that are not only concerned with what they can put in their pocket.

Unfortunately society, media, has led us to believe that success is the accumulation of material wealth, but that's not true.

Being successful is if you are happy. Being happy with yourself, happy with the people you are around, happy with your family, relaxed, calm and content.

You don't have to have loads and loads of money, big cars, jewellery. This is something that you don't need.

You should be absolutely content to be who you are, and don't let anybody take that away from you.

Jeff Christie
Christie

The band, Christie, shot to fame in the early 1970s with their single "Yellow River". It was an amazing success and went to number one in twenty-six countries.

They followed up with more hits like, "San Bernadino" and "Iron Horse". Most of the bands' hits were written by the one and only, Jeff Christie and so we tracked him down!

If you could be any other musician past or present, which one would it be and why?
Burt Bacharach (Randy Newman, Jimmy Webb) supreme musician / songwriter/s and many more to mention but this is a good start.

Why: intelligence, wit and emotional depth, lurk in simple songs when that can be the hardest task as well as more complex ones, but always stacked with killer melody lines and great poetic and lyrical content.

If you had to name one song from any genre that really speaks to you, which one would it be and why?
Another impossible question but "Smoke Gets In Your Eyes". Why: it's just so melancholic and beautiful and can almost reduce me to tears whenever I hear The Platters sing it.

Are you a Mulder or Scully? Do you believe aliens have visited planet earth and if so what do you think they think about mankind?
I never watched the show so that's an easy cop out for me.

What was the happiest day of your life and why?
I once read that happiness is a habit that you need to cultivate, which makes sense if you think about it. There have been happy moments and unhappy moments throughout my life like everyone else, but I've learnt that essentially, I'm happy if I'm not unhappy and the older I get the less I'm interested in material things and so it's hard for me to pinpoint the happiest day and with so much suffering in the world I have to count myself fortunate in many ways and that

translates as happiness too, I think. Sorry if that doesn't chime but that's my take on happiness.

If "God" (whatever your idea is on that) stood before you now, what one question would you ask him/her and why?
To help me have more control over damaging emotions, roll with the punches; to rise above pettiness, fear, anger and self-absorption, without aspiring to acquire Bodhisattva status, but just to be the best person I can possibly be in the short space of time allocated to me. I know that's a big ask and invariably I fall short but that would be something if it could be realised. I can only be responsible for myself not the world which seems hellbent on self-destruction I can only try and change myself.

As an expressive artist in the music industry, how does the state of the planet make you feel?
Worried.

Do you think as a person of some influence that there is a duty on us to help influence humanity for the better?
Yes!

What one cause would you say you feel most associated with and why? Whether it's equality, poverty, politics, the environment or other?
Peace in the world because anything is possible if that could be a reality. If humans would stop killing each other then who knows what we might achieve. Jaw, jaw better than war, war. (Winston Spencer Churchill). There is a dearth of great leaders who could be Masters of the Universe.

If you stood before the leaders of the world, what would you say to them?
God gave Noah the rainbow sign, no more water, fire next time.

Conclusion

appy now? Now you finally know that the vast majority of music stars actually do believe that aliens have visited planet Earth. I must say that one completely blew me away.

Overall, this project may have been damned hard work, but it was also incredible fun. When else could I get to sit around talking to Francis Rossi! I don't think I could do it again without sedatives, but it was fun.

One thing that does come across strongly is concern. There are a lot of very talented, intelligent musicians in this book who are very concerned about society and planet Earth. These people very often have an intuitive feeling and reaction to things they see. I know, some of them just like wearing pretty clothes and having their photos in the magazines, but that aside, the wonderful people who came forward to speak in this book did at least make that effort. They made it because they see and feel the pain and want to do something about it. The same reason I started this bloody project.

Seriously though, there are issues we need to deal with. Don't despair because all of humanity is stupid. It's not our fault. It's evolution making fun of us. What we need to do is wake up a little and shake the person at the side of us into making a difference. If everybody reading this book did that we'd have at least 15 people living life slightly differently.

First thing to do is stop hate. Hate causes us to be bigoted, racist, sexist and more. Stopping hate will bring us closer together to concentrate on issues that really matter, such as the environment. Hate is a big issue and it comes from fear.

From the news media to politicians. From social media to the movies. From the pulpit to the playground. Hatred is engineered, sold and spread. It is used as a tool to control and manipulate the masses. It has been this way for a very long time.

It is in fact a natural part of being human and grows from that basic universal and instinctual inner element of fear. This fear is natural. All animals have it. It helps us and them to spot threats to our lives and way of life. But this fear is being used by very clever leaders in government, media, religion and business. These four elements are in fact all connected at many levels.

This fear causes hatred and that hatred is used to garner votes, sales and members. The threats created by those in power manipulate our thoughts and beliefs and cause us to hate other countries, races and everything else you can imagine. We take sides because we are conditioned to do so.

There is a route out of this hatred and it is as old as man. It is time to unlearn hatred. Hate causes us to despair. It takes over our minds. It grows and causes nothing but more hate. Eventually it causes war and millions die. If you hate, ask why? Why do you hate blacks or whites? Why do you hate the Russians? Do you know these people? They have friends, family, likes and loves, just like you. Some of them hate you too and for the same reason. They have been conditioned from birth.

Politicians, hungry for power, stand before us and demonise the opposition. They spew forth vile hatred on their social media sites and gather around them followers. Religious leaders tell us there is but one God — theirs. Business tell us to fear numerous things and sell us the cure. They are all doing the same thing. Causing division.

These tactics have been around for a very long time. Today we find them on mobile phones, but in ages past it appeared on hieroglyphs, architecture and books. Learning to fight off these negative influences involves more than just arguing with them. This just causes conflict.

The best route out of hatred and fear is knowledge. Our ancestors had a word for it, Gnosis, which actually means knowledge of the most esoteric kind. Fables such as the holy grail, Solomon's Temple and more, are in fact treasure chests of knowledge that reveal inner natural truths about mankind. It does not need an external deity, shaman, priest or president. It just is. The goal of this Gnosis is to discover this true 'inner reality' which also gives us an insight into the very universe.

To escape hatred and fear we must recognise that all those external things in the world, such as politics, religion, media and business, are nothing but distractions. Feeding them feeds negativity, or what our ancestors called sin. Our job to save ourselves and the planet, is to starve the negative aspects of our existence and feed the inner self in balance. Understand that the hatred spewing forth from others has been placed there by an imbalance in society. Our job is to not return that hatred, but to balance it with love.

In geology there is a rock known as a xenolith. It is a rock that has been engulfed by the mighty power of volcanic magma. And yet, it remains totally unchanged. It has stayed true to itself. We must be like the xenolith in this mad world of ours and remain unchanged by the bias and hatred spewing forth from the minds of divided humanity. We must unlearn the hatred that has morphed our true reality and discover ourselves again.

Never in the history of man has there been a perfect time and so we need not seek out a sunken Atlantis. Never in the future of mankind will there be a perfect civilisation and so we better not sit and wait for *Star Trek* to fix things for us. No one religion is righteous for all fall short of the glory they call God. No State has created the ideal place to live. No family is flawless, no friend wholly committed. We are the best thing we have. We have to live with ourselves while others can run away from us or lock us in a room. We will be in that room with our self and so that is where we must find the truth and that is where we must discover balance and harmony. Listening to the world of man will simply confuse our minds yet further. Listening to nature, which has perfect balance and indeed is powered by the force of balance, is the right place to go for help. We must return to the garden.

This is an economic world. Whether you live in the so-called democratic West or the Communist East. It is structured around money and anything that gets in the way of the machine is more often than not moved or eradicated. There is no room for anything to oppose this. Each one of us is in the system whether we like it or not and we believe there is often precious little we can do about it. If we truly wish to make a change to the way we live and help the environment, animals and us then we have to start by understanding what put us here in the first place. How did all this begin? And who was the originator of the system?

In the beginning mankind was nomadic. For a period so long that it staggers the mind we travelled along coastlines, around lakes and traversed river systems. We simply could not travel across land because most of it was covered in trees and vegetation. We did so purely to hunt and collect foodstuffs and then returned to our boats. This is the way and form mankind evolved his mind over vast periods of time. In tune with nature. We were in-tune with our needs and natures larder. We followed herds as they migrated; we knew which plants were safe to eat and we only took what we needed because we simply could not carry an overabundance of produce. All the anthropological evidence reveals that mankind was more peaceful and even lived longer lives than his later descendants who would settle down.

Populations grew and nomadic cultures began to partly settle down. These settlements were probably originally staging posts for extended stays during winter or other such times and eventually the rot set it. Remaining in one location for extended periods brought with it all-manner of problems. Firstly it brought the need to cultivate the land and to store provisions because the animal larder would carry on moving and natural vegetation would carry on and follow the seasons. Secondly it brought disease because of human and animal waste and all kinds of other filth. And thirdly it brought strife in ways that the nomadic smaller groups would not have foreseen. These settlements would be attracting more and more people into one single location — forcing people together for longer and longer periods of time, in cramped and rapidly unnatural environments.

Mankind was growing apart from nature and had to learn a whole set of new skills, from building to being more socially oriented. Structures of wood and structures of society brought with them hierarchy and alpha dominance in a different way to the previous nomadic lifestyle. Groups were now bigger and so conflicts between those who would be in dominance would have been more frequent. But it was too late, the old ways were rapidly being forgotten. It is amazing how quickly the skills of the past generation can disappear.

For example, today there are people who do not even know how to cook because their lifestyle has simply never called for the skill. My kids don't even know how to use a VHS machine. You never know when you might need to pop in a video tape! We are constantly battling the balance between the income stream and the spending stream and we find very little room for such trivial matters as cooking, let alone time for our children. But cooking is only one of the many skills that we are losing due to mass production of ready-made meals and lifestyle habits.

Eventually our newfound settlements had to find ways to deal with their new social problems and the mind of man has a unique tool for the purpose — imagination. Man developed from within his own imagination, new social structures of tribal leadership and those who had maintained or learned new skills important for the group would become dominant. These were not always the strongest and best fighters or hunters, but more often than not those who knew how to heal and gel the community. We call these people medicine men, shaman and latterly priests. As the Old Testament so eruditely informs us, it was the priesthood who would guide the people and even crown kings. The Royal family of England is still to this day crowned by the Church as a direct result of this same ancient power structure — uniting religion and State.

With this new advent of power came many new ways of manipulating the growing masses who were herded into the new imaginative religious structure and given rules in the form of dogma, doctrine and tradition. Now power was from the gods and nobody could argue with such imagined power. The knowledge of navigation, of the stars, of the seasons and of course of the reality of the mind of man became powerful tools in the armoury of the Church. To know the seasons enabled the priest to appear magical and in-touch with God. To know how to read the stars for navigation enabled the tribe to trade and invade. To know the mind of man allowed the priesthood to manipulate and control. All of this was truly a powerful knowledge. This knowledge was passed down within the brotherhoods in symbolism, latterly in texts and certainly in tradition.

Tradition is not simply something we imagine our grandparents had. Our English term tradition comes from *Traditio*, a Latin word meaning the 'delivery of doctrine' and 'surrender', but more pertinent to us it means 'something handed down.' Tradition is the continuance of something profound.

In the very first usage of the word we find that it was in fact used *for the passing on of doctrine and religious dogma* — a sacred act itself and something which became symbolic. The word 'sacred' itself comes from Old Latin *saceres* meaning to bind, restrict, enclose and protect. And this is where much of the truth lies — in symbolism and sacredness, for both are binding and surrendering to something being passed down.

There is no truth that the taking of the bread and wine at the Eucharist ritual is actually the body and blood of Jesus Christ. No, the act is symbolic and solemnly reminds the religious initiate of the fact that he is part of a greater Christian brotherhood; that he is accepting Christ and that His body was broken and blood spilt for us and that he is a *continuation of a long line*. Whatever one's opinion on that religious act, the fact remains that it is a very powerful tool for reminding the masses of their place in the world via an act that is emotionally strong. This is a manipulating tradition, kept alive to keep the sheep in the fold.

As we can now see, tradition can be a very strong device when allied to emotion and psychologists have discovered that allegorical tales are very often absorbed better than any literal telling.

We have to understand our ancestors were able to do this and we have to start by realising that they were humans just like us. They had fears, hopes and struggled to survive and to comprehend their very place in the universe. In the depth of understanding our ancestors discovered that they needed to find a way of passing on the knowledge they had uncovered and they formed tales. Our historical friends were not simple folk as we are led to believe. They had the same brain size as ourselves and in fact in many ways they were better attuned to the thing we now divisively call *nature*.

You see, in our 'modern' materialistic state we forget that we are human beings that have come from and live in the natural universe. We forget, because we create things from within our own imaginations and surround ourselves with them, and hence we today find ourselves in an imaginary world of 'things.' It is this ability of the mind to *create a concept* that has spawned stories and tales, myths and fables to explain to each new generation the knowledge of the last. And so what is the key we need to understand these concepts? It is imagination in tune with intuition *or our connection to nature*.

These incredible and intuitive 'traditions' emerged from early man and his understanding of the world around him and how he survived. Settlements became trading posts for vast quantities of goods and demarcation of roles emerged with blacksmiths, farmers, potters and all-manner of other roles. Trading went on like this for millennia, with the priesthood often controlling the process and growing in power themselves as their own communities prospered. They would take a percentage of the produce and offer it to the gods in-order to maintain the weather and good fortune of the tribe.

The greatest of gods — the sun — would be worshipped and aided in its journey to reappear the following day. It was the giver of life and the destroyer. It mirrored the duality in the mind of man himself and so we were formed in his likeness. We were solar beings, formed and given life by the power of the golden orb and nothing became more important than ensuring its daily and yearly cycles. The priests of this great power were the alpha males, the medicine men or shaman of earlier times. It was they who gave authority to the king or pharaoh who himself must be the son of the sun on earth. He was the marketing tool of the priesthood and history is awash with the violent downfalls of the solar king when he stepped out of line and upset the priesthood.

Control of the trading markets, both of the land upon which it was carried out and the navigation required to operate it, grew so powerful over time that the priesthood would do almost anything to maintain control. This is why much religious literature is awash with rules and regulations for trade and commerce.

The system of trading eventually needed organising differently because of lies. It all began because of deceit and it remains pretty much the same today. At the market a thing called a promise emerged whereby a man trading a goat for a pig would promise to bring his goat the following market day only to fail in his promise. The priesthood or leader who controlled the process realised that some new system was needed to come into play and so created money — from the word *monere*, meaning "to warn."

This new money was very cleverly based upon the gods themselves adding incredible weight and fear to the promise. Gold was manifestly the solar divinity — the sun. And silver was the lunar deity — a mirror of the sun. Handing over a symbolic representation of the gods was a powerful promise and the gods would know if you reneged on your promise. The Church itself backed the promise and so became the bank. Power was well and truly in the hands of the few and the rest of us simply had no choice but to conform. This situation is almost unchanged and today. These days our money is traded in the new market place of the Internet — itself a place of many kinds of worship.

Our lives are still, and more so than ever, run by money and we have no choice but to live in the world of commerce. Everyday we hand over our images of the solar deities, which are no longer even real gold but instead are promises of gold. There are more promises of gold in the world than there is gold and so the system, created because of lies and deceit, is itself a total lie. But it is the system we live in and individually we must make our own decisions on how to do so. But there is more deception than we know and it is to these deceptions we must now turn.

From the moment we wake up to the moment we fall asleep we are subjects of a massive machine. We are plugged in like a light that is only alive and lit by the machine and because of this we no longer know how to shine for ourselves. But many do not realise that the machine in fact feeds from us — using our energy to capture and grow the machine that in turn captures more and more people hourly. We are all in one way or another slaves to the machine.

We have seen how money enslaved us because of the lie and deceit of man and how power was built and maintained by the few over the many. Today it is the driving force of society. Every single one of us must sell something to get money. Whether we sell our skills, services, products or even our very soul, we all must constantly sell to earn. And because everybody is selling to everybody else we also buy and buy. In our overpopulated world, full of people who no longer know the skills of basic survival we must buy the basic products such as food and even water. But man has used his unique imagination to make better and more

MINDS BEHIND THE MUSIC

imaginative food and water — or so we believe.

In fact we dress up the ordinary and use our own in-built psychology to convince others that this added value is worth the extra money. We place a clever label on a bottle of water, add mystique and then charge a ridiculous amount of money for what is basically a free product of the earth that we can no longer have access to as individuals because of the society we have created. We do the same for all-manner of goods.

In addition to this we also create products or services that we do not need and again add value or perception that we want to buy into.

In the end the whole marketing process reveals how easy it can be with this special knowledge to take from another. Create a dream and then sell it and nobody realises that they are in fact buying into exactly that — a dream from within the mind of another. It is not reality, if indeed we can decide on what reality truly is any more. It is not needed, it is just desired because of our bastardised social norm and position. We pay more for water in a fancy bottle than the worth of both the bottle and the water and all because it may have a classy sounding name. This water is shipped thousands of miles to get to your door, when all along there is water almost everywhere on this planet. We pay a fortune for a ready prepared plastic bag full of salad produce that "meets with our modern lifestyles", whilst all along we fill our gardens with plastic lights, barbecues and pretty plastic flowers. In parallel with this, people starve in the Third World. What is reality? Ask a starving child and see if it the same as your own perception – if you truly need a personal benchmark.

Our reality, is not true reality. It is not reality and it is not needed, it is all self-perpetuating a massive lie and we all in our daily lives help to continue the cycle. We all make dreams and sell them to others and we then end up believing them ourselves and before anybody realises it we are all living in a dream world that simply does not exist.

Billions of children around the world are being fed non-realities by computer games. They live out their precious lives in a world that is not real, whilst Mom and Dad spend their every waking moment battling and selling to pay for the products of the delusional world. This causes yet more division within each mind but also within the family unit and because all of this is an illusion not one of them is truly fulfilled and so the family eventually breaks down and division in the form of divorce often occurs. The child is only being prepared for one thing — a life of exactly the same as his parents — a treadmill of buy and sell and lack of self-knowledge.

Instead of learning the simple basic skills of life and love, children today are taught how to manipulate the illusionary world of computer screens, moving imaginary characters around, killing and maiming the enemy, which is normally some politically propagandised evil role-model. Most people do not realise the incredible amounts of money made from the multi-million-dollar worlds of illusion, but they also don't realise the propaganda content is immense. In fact there are many games strategically funded by governments and other agenda driven authorities and organisations that are specifically written to suck in the minds of the youth into particular ways of thinking. This creates masses of later controllable young adults for the financial war machine and good voters who are now loyal to the cause. We are all pawns in a game that has gone out of control, because it is a life spent in an illusionary world with nobody specifically controlling it anymore.

Now we have a world of technology that is overtaking us and we have to somehow try to keep our heads wrapped around the lightning speed with which it moves. There are even extensions to the computer game dream world, as with mobile phones we can in fact take this world of illusion with us anywhere we go.

There is no escaping this phenomena because the human tribal instinct to be as good or better than everybody else and to be accepted in our society, forces us to participate. In addition, these are new ways for the marketing man to catch us — because they now 'buy' advertising space in the illusionary world of the computer game. So even the marketing man is being sold an illusion — a billboard in the land of illusion. Advertising billboards in a fake downtown city carries the same old messages and we subconsciously buy into the perception encoded and created. We are lying to ourselves in a world of lies and we only have ourselves to blame. We kill ourselves to afford to buy a product we don't need at an inflated price because of advertising costs of billboards in a land that doesn't exist. Stand back and think about how stupid this all is and then think about the eyes of a starving child. How does it make you feel?

And so technology, like everything else we humans create, is truly an extension of ourselves and it yet again is a world of falseness, covering up the real mess we are in. The truth is that the technology we created with all good intentions is now driving us and we have become extensions of the machine itself.

These leaps in technology are part and parcel of the human evolutionary cycle from the flint spear to the space shuttle. We cannot stop them, but we ought to be aware of their effects upon the human mind. Before we realised it, technology had transformed the office beyond all recognition with word processing, design and of course the Internet and email. Everybody had to speed up and now the truly successful alpha people multi-task — using more than one technology at a time just to keep up and to stay alpha dominant and of course, to earn more of that illusionary money.

The system is now beyond human-nature — we have created a monster, a Frankenstein, and we have lost ourselves. The lesson to learn is that just like the Frankenstein monster, it is a mirror of ourselves and it is destroying the very essence of what we are. It is also separating us further and further from nature itself.

All of this is why even now in the 21st century we remain stupid humans who constantly battle with each other, because we are forcing ourselves away further and further from the truth of what we really are. We have created a world of imagination in which we can live out a dream life and to pay for it we live in hell.

The truth is that we can help our own madness and that we do not require drugs or priests to do so. All we need is *strength, will* and *knowledge*. We can take these three words and use them to better ourselves by seeking balance in our lives. We are all positive and negative and we constantly cycle between them. The true understanding will only be found in the point between these cycles — in a neutral state and it is in this state that people find greater understanding, artistic expression and calm.

How do we do this? It is simple and yet seemingly a million miles away from where we are. Every element of your past needs to be understood to be in the past. It is not with you now unless you make it so. The future too need not be worried about, for worry causes conflict and chaos and tips the balance. Both the past and the future are poles and if we live in either then we are again dividing our mind. To live now is an anagram of own and it is time that we owned our own lives and stopped shuffling responsibility for ourselves, beliefs, actions etc on other times — let alone people, states and religions.

This balancing of the extremes and finding the place between is multi-levelled and works on all things in our lives. If we all applied this balance then we would all be happier and more content — but we would have to apply it to every level of our lives. This, like gravity, would affect those people around us and cause a more balanced society. So too if we are chaotic and unbalanced then we would cause more division in others. Influence is itself a good benchmark — how are we influencing others? This book is an attempt to influence society at large through the unique influence musicians have. The questions were created with this in mind. Had I asked loaded political or racial questions then I would have ended with chaos.

We can all have influence. We can cause all-kinds of cycles around us, from influencing a cycle in our children with simple things like swearing, to influencing them with love, balanced with discipline. All of this is true for society at large too.

Francis Bacon, the 16th century writer and once Lord Chancellor of England, said that no matter how good your intentions may be, if you have not the right knowledge, then you will be like a dry fountain — useless. We must show willing to improve but begin in small ways and improve ourselves first before attempting to infect others.

You see, we are really all to blame for the state of affairs. For the environment; for feeding anti-depressant drugs to children; for our own psychosis. Each one of us knowingly uses other people to feed our own self-propelled delusional state. For instance we all know beyond all doubt that music stars are ordinary human beings and we also know that a lot of them are not happy, regardless of their fame and wealth.

Drink, drugs and debt are more often than not the only outcome. Suicide rates increase; children are brought up in the most insane delusional and illusionary world outside of the Vatican and the cycle repeats. Out of every star who supposedly makes it big time there are not hundreds, not thousands, but millions of people who struggle to pay their rent whilst serving coffee. But these millions delude themselves with the dream of the few and in this they lose themselves.

In today's world there are millions of battles fought daily between marketing men and advertisers, producers and directors, radio hosts and designers, all scrambling around finding the latest and most advanced method of producing an "experience" for the people, to grab their attention, keep their interest and form desires leading to actions. Alas the actions required are now more often than not to spend our money or move us to vote one way or another. They are manipulations of a brain that is not thinking for itself and therefore will do as it is told. This is why images, sound and feel are all created for us by the corporate giants — so that we don't have chance to think for ourselves and therefore follow like lemmings, however subtly this may be.

Escape is so easy and yet so difficult. It is easy to say and yet harder to do. The first dilemma is how do we even become aware that we are in fact caught in a trap? There are a great many who know all about the trap, and yet are happy within it. This is no different to the film The Matrix, whereby Neo has to decide whether to take the pill that will free him from this dream world state once and for all.

People are simply happy not to have to work the brain, especially when everything is done for them. Others, like Neo, see that the reality of freedom is much more liberating for the mind. Most, if not all, revolutions of mankind's history have been caused by one man or a few men finding freedom and then passing it on to others. They suddenly see, as if in a flash of light, that they have been oppressed by their leaders. Often in the light of our modern minds these historical oppressions seem obvious to us now, but at the time it was not so, because the people were living in the cage and not outside of it.

Once the rabbit is out of the cage the freedom sighted spreads like wildfire and all the rabbits start gnawing. I am hoping that people reading this book discover their own opinions and understand that what mankind is doing to the planet is wrong. I am hoping that this energises them and that they too become an influence on others. Spread the word enthusiastically. We must change. Now.

Today billions of humans exist on this planet of ours and it is growing by the day. We are storing up and creating a human bomb that will one day explode inwardly or outwardly as a result of the oppressive nature of our media and capitalist lead system. This is no different to why Russia exploded with the red revolution or why the French rose up against the oppressive Royalty.

It seems that no matter which period of modern history we wish to look at, the same forms of oppression and dumbing down have been utilised to great extent, whether by government, religion or Royalty. But what can we do to escape this living Matrix? The first thing to know, is thy self. This self is trapped in the unconscious world, forced downwards by the conscious world of mankind.

Our brain has a function that closes down unnecessary perceptions. We may be subconsciously aware of these things, but only to send messages to the unconscious world and often for defence. For instance we may always be listening out for threats. But the unconscious world is aware of all this, works with it, is driven itself by the forces of nature. The conscious world cannot cope and closes down perceptions. This is why dumbing down humanity works so well, because we all have so much to think about and do.

There are just too many things for us all to concentrate on and so we entrap ourselves in the less sensory world, alleviating our minds of the pressure. But this is a false answer to the conundrum, because by allowing our minds to close off even more we in fact are able to deal with less and less, until eventually we are no better than caged rabbits. The conscious mind needs expansion by feeding it good food that teaches it to cope with the expansion and allows it to be one with the unconscious world — in tune with nature and the force of nature.

We need to break out of the cage and run around in the wild like a fluffy tailed bunny rabbit in world of freedom — for believe me, there are plenty of carrots for the picking.

Once we have understood this we can begin to find ourselves under the conscious realm. We need to sit calmly and open our perceptions to the person we are and not who we are told to be or try to be. I am not the many people I revere and adore, I am me and I am part of the natural force. I do not need another man to imagine my world for me or draw pictures in place of the written world. I have my own imagination and powerful thoughts that can discover the links to archetypes within my unconscious realm. Give me the real and full story, don't patronise me; give me something useful and fulfilling, not how to become a supermodel or racing car driver. Let us be part of nature once again and stop fighting it with our silly ways. You never know, we may in fact find that we enjoy the freedom.

But one thing is sure, just thinking a little about the world upon which we exist needs us to start caring for it and not destroying it. Let's be healers, both in society and in nature.

Phil G

Special Thanks

I simply have to name and thank those wonderful people who formed part of the army that helped me put this book together. You are all wonderful!

Stevie Horton of Iconic Music and Media
Sally Long for helping with Francis Rossi
Michelle Liebetrau of ML International Talent
Scott Sexton of 2911 Media
Jordan Berliant of Revelation Management
Iona Elliott of Artist International Management
Helen Miller of East Central One
Joyce Wilde for helping with her husband, Marty
Nicole White, she knows why
Casey Jones for helping with her Dad, Kenny
Jennifer Schwalenberg for helping with Don Dokken
Cara DeCarlo-Wirscham for helping with James Atkin
Linda Peterson for helping with Ted Nugent
Pedan Beckett for helping with Peter Beckett
Robby Lochner for helping with Jack White
Mark Appleton for helping with Blaze Bayley
Jill Stean for helping with Dee C Lee
Lara Fessler for helping with Brad Walsh
Lindsey Key for helping with Jeff Wayne

CPSIA information can be obtained
at www.ICGtesting.com
Printed in the USA
LVHW010602301121
704738LV00022BA/314

9 781912 782871